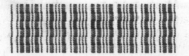

Edgar Snow's
Journey South of the Clouds

Edgar Snow's

Journey
South of
the Clouds

Edited with commentary by
Robert M. Farnsworth

University of Missouri Press

Columbia and London

Copyright © 1991 by
The Curators of the University of Missouri
University of Missouri Press, Columbia, Missouri 65201
Printed and bound in the United States of America
All rights reserved
5   4   3   2   1   95   94   93   92   91

Library of Congress Cataloging-in-Publication Data
Snow, Edgar, 1905–1972.
    Edgar Snow's journey south of the clouds / edited with
commentary by Robert M. Farnsworth.
       p.   cm.
    Includes index.
    ISBN 0–8262–0777–4 (alk. paper)
    1. East Asia—Description and travel. 2. Asia,
Southeastern—Description and travel. 3. South Asia—
Description and travel. I. Farnsworth, Robert M. II. Title.
DS508.2.S56   1991
915.404'358—dc20   91–6790
                                 CIP

∞™ This paper meets the requirements of the American
National Standard for Permanence of Paper for Printed
Library Materials, Z39.48, 1984.

Designer: Rhonda Gibson
Typesetter: Connell-Zeko Type & Graphics
Printer: Thomson-Shore, Inc.
Binder: Thomson-Shore, Inc.
Typeface: Garamond No. 3

Frontispiece: Snow on board the SS *Radnor,* on the trip from
New York to Hawaii.

Mr. Snow's life was testimony to the sincere friendship between the Chinese and American peoples. Back in the period of the Chinese people's national-democratic revolution, he had already entered into friendship with China's revolutionary forces. Breaking through the numerous obstacles of that time, he enthusiastically introduced to the American and other peoples the Chinese revolutionary struggles and the 25 thousand li Long March of the Chinese Workers' and Peasants' Red Army, which were undertaken under the leadership of Chairman Mao Tsetung. After the liberation of our country, he came again on several visits and reported the progress of the people's revolutionary course of New China led by Chairman Mao. His writings were widely appreciated both in China and abroad. Even during his serious illness, he never ceased turning his mind to working for better understanding between the Chinese and American peoples. The Chinese people will not forget such an old friend of theirs. Mr. Snow has left us, but we believe that the friendship between the Chinese and American peoples, for which he worked all his life, will certainly grow daily.

(From Premier Chou En-lai's
message of condolence, February 16, 1972.)

Contents

III. Indo-China and Yunnanfu (Kunming)

Acknowledgments

In November 1988, I was writing a book on Edgar Snow's thirteen years in China (1928–1941) and needed to summarize the events that occurred between late September 1930 and early August 1931. Snow had left China to resume his originally intended trip around the world, and during those ten months he wrote many travel articles. I turned to those articles with great frequency and had such difficulty restricting my use of quotations that I finally was forced to consider the possibility that Snow's experiences, and their importance to his career, warranted a book of their own.

I wrote Lois Snow and proposed that her husband's travel articles be reprinted as a book to which I hoped to add a commentary relating them to his life and work as a whole. She agreed with my proposal, and I want to express my deep appreciation for her support.

I owe many other debts of gratitude. Mary Clark Dimond had the vision to establish the Edgar Snow Memorial Fund in Kansas City and to begin the special collection of Edgar Snow papers upon which my work has so heavily depended. In 1979, Mary Clark Dimond invited me to join the Executive Board of the Fund. Regrettably, she passed away in 1984. Her husband, Dr. E. Grey Dimond, who worked closely with her on this project, succeeded her as President of the Fund. Both have dedicated themselves to informing the public of Edgar Snow's significant achievements and to supporting the friendship and understanding between the American and Chinese peoples that was so central to Snow's life. To them my personal and professional thanks.

Dr. Henry A. Mitchell, an extremely able and committed university administrator, was to be coauthor of the book on Snow's China years. We had tried for some time to work out a satisfactory mode for sharing the peculiar demands of writing a book. While we were never able to arrive at such an arrangement, he shared with me much of his invaluable research and gave me strong support and cogent advice on my own research and writing. Dr. Mitchell withdrew as coauthor of the original book before I thought of this work, but my debt to him is great and my gratitude proportionate.

Marilyn Burlingame, archivist for the Edgar Snow Collection, has far surpassed her professional responsibilities in answering my endless and often befuddled requests. In the early stage of the collection, the extensive papers were so diffuse that my memory and notes often failed me when I tried to retrace my steps. Her professional patience and diligence saved me time and time again.

The staff at the Hoover Library in Palo Alto, California, were also very professional and helpful on my two visits there to review the Nym Wales papers.

I owe a special debt to Robert Willson, who served as chairman of my department throughout my work on this book, for his support and encouragement of this professor of American Literature who wandered from his professional domain into the exotic world of American reporting in East Asia. I am grateful to Carol Rust and Associate Dean Burton Dunbar for their roles in producing a typescript from hard-to-read copies of original newspaper and magazine articles. Max Skidmore, Dean of the College of Arts and Science; Eleanor Brantley Schwartz, Vice-Chancellor for Academic Affairs; and George Russell, Chancellor of the University of Missouri–Kansas City all encouraged and supported my work far beyond their professional obligations.

To my colleagues on the Faculty Research Council who awarded me travel grants for my research, I can only say this work could not have been done without your support. I thank you.

During my academic career I have been appointed a Fulbright lecturer in American Literature to India in 1966–1967, to Turkey in 1973–1974, and to the People's Republic of China in 1984–1985. These opportunities to live and teach in Asia helped me in countless, undefinable ways to understand what Edgar Snow experienced and wrote during his journey "South of the Clouds." My deepest appreciation to those who have made and continue to make the Fulbright exchange of scholars possible.

Editorial Decisions

During the early part of Snow's career in China, the Wade-Giles system was the most commonly accepted method of representing Chinese names and expressions in English. Although it has since been supplanted by Pinyin, the articles in this collection are meant to give a strong sense of the particular period in history that Snow describes. Thus it seemed appropriate to retain the Wade-Giles system, adding editorial explanations in brackets where they might be useful. Inconsistencies in spelling or punctuation that Snow used for emphasis have been retained. However, obvious typographical errors have been corrected, and punctuation has been standardized, where necessary, in the interest of clarity.

In the *New York Sun,* the *China Weekly Review,* and the *New York Herald-Tribune Magazine,* articles were subdivided in sections with headings added by the editors. This practice developed because newspapers are designed for rapid reading. Without breaks an extended column, or series of columns, of short lines appears formidably long. It seemed appropriate for book publication to eliminate these editorially created breaks and headings and reprint the articles in what was, most likely, their original form. In stories for which there were two published texts, I was also thus spared having to choose one editor's headings over another's.

I have reproduced nine photographs from the Edgar Snow Collection. Eight of these were taken on this journey. The ninth is a photo of Snow taken on board the SS *Radnor,* presumably somewhere in the late stage of his journey from New York to Hawaii. All seven of the photos in which he is not the subject were taken by Edgar Snow. Also taken from the Edgar Snow Collection are Snow's letters and diaries as well as copies of several of the articles cited in this book.

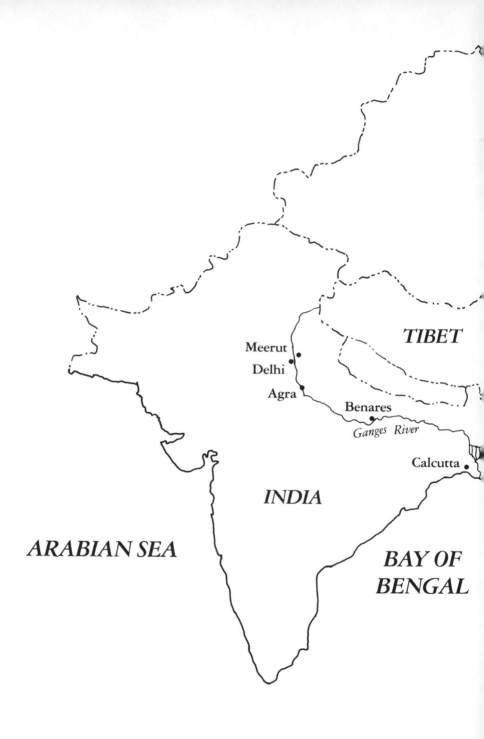

TIBET

Meerut
Delhi
Agra
Benares
Ganges River

Calcutta

INDIA

ARABIAN SEA

BAY OF
BENGAL

Edgar Snow's
Journey South of the Clouds

Introduction

Edgar Snow played an extraordinary role in U.S.–China relations for thirty-five years, from the publication of *Red Star over China* in 1937 until his death in 1972, within a week of Richard Nixon's historic visit to China. When Snow trekked into northwest China in 1936 to meet Mao Tse-tung and the Red armies at the end of their Long March, the world, and even most of China, knew very little about them. They were caricatured in the public press as "bandits." *Red Star over China* rapidly changed that perception and proved historically prophetic, probably even beyond its author's expectations.

The Communist leaders whom Snow made known to the world came to power in China in 1949 and ruled China for decades, some continuing in positions of power even today. For the rest of his life Edgar Snow enjoyed a special professional relation with China's leaders. During the Cold War that special relation often seemed more curse than privilege, but in 1960 Snow was one of the first Western journalists invited to break China's isolation from the West. He returned for extended visits in 1964 and 1970, each time significantly elaborating the story of the emerging modern nation begun in *Red Star.* Snow's observations on a changing China were recorded and recognized throughout the world in the books that followed *Red Star: Battle for Asia, The Other Side of the River,* and *The Long Revolution.* Snow also published numerous articles in the *Saturday Evening Post* and other leading magazines and newspapers worldwide.

The story of how Snow came to experience and write about such a pivotal period of China's history (1928–1941) is detailed in his 1958 autobiography, *Journey to the Beginning.* This work also relates his experiences as a foreign correspondent during World War II and his much less happy experience during the Cold War that followed. *Journey to the Beginning* makes clear Snow did not intend, particularly during his early years, to commit himself to China as deeply or for as long a period as he eventually did. China was to have been only one of many stops on an around-the-world journey begun in 1928 from New York. Two years after landing in Shanghai he was still promising his family he would soon resume the world journey that would eventually bring him home. After the unexpected death of his mother in 1930 he finally started out again.

For ten months he traveled leisurely through Southeast Asia intending to go on to the Middle East, Europe, and home. But deepening economic depression in the United States, changes in the family he left behind, and some recognition that China had taken a strong, inexplicable hold on his emotional and imaginative life caused him to return to Shanghai rather than New York. Most explicitly he returned to write a book, *South of the Clouds,* about his adventures traveling by caravan from Yunnanfu into Burma. That book was never completed. Within a few weeks of Snow's return to Shanghai the Japanese invaded Manchuria. His story of that invasion, *Far Eastern Front,* preempted his caravan tale, and his professional commitment to historical journalism from then on became significantly more rewarding and demanding than his interest in romantic travel writing.

I have borrowed Snow's intended title for this collection of his articles written during the ten months he traveled through Southeast Asia. These articles reveal a somewhat unpolished but already effective and engaging travel writer. Snow knew that tolerating the petty frustrations of travel off the beaten path was the inevitable price of finding the significant detail so satisfying to the intelligently curious imagination. He worked earnestly at the craft of writing, laboring with considerable success to hide the signs of that labor so that his audience would read his writing with a quick sense of pleasure. Those skills eventually helped him develop into a world-famous historical journalist.

When Edgar Snow first arrived in Shanghai in early July 1928, he was youthfully eager to win fame as a writer. He had no way of knowing how his personal ambitions would combine with historical events to bring him international recognition. He had left New York City five months before as a deckhand on the SS *Radnor.* He planned to work his way around the world, but hoped that writing up his adventures would pay for at least part of his journey. Waiting for him in Shanghai was the exciting news of his first success. Charles Hanson Towne, who had befriended and encouraged him before he left New York, had accepted his mildly humorous rhapsody about the tourist pleasures of Hawaii for *Harper's Bazaar,* and had paid him a very handsome fee of $300.[1]

1. "In Hula Land," *Harper's Bazaar* (September, 1928): 98–99, 136, 138, 142. John Maxwell Hamilton writes that Towne paid $500 for Snow's "In Hula-Land," *Edgar Snow* (Bloomington: Indiana University Press, 1989), 19. Hamilton apparently misread Snow's handwriting. On June 26, 1928, in a letter expressing his gratitude for the acceptance of his article, Snow advises Towne: "Please deposit my $300.00, after deducting your commission, with the First National Bank of New Jersey" (Charles Hanson Towne Papers, Manuscript Division, New York Public Library).

After three days in Shanghai and just eight days before his twenty-third birthday, Snow wrote elatedly to his parents, "The Gods are infinitely gracious." He was uncertain whether he would stay in Shanghai for three weeks or "possibly that many months. If I can get a job on a boat sailing south to the Philippines or India I may leave at once. Otherwise I shall try to get a job and stay here till fall."[2] China was then only one of many remote and exotic places that stirred his curiosity and sense of adventure. He knew little of its history and even less of the press of events that was turning China toward a fate with extraordinary international implications.

Just a year before Snow arrived, Shanghai had been the scene of one of the more brutally tumultuous events of modern Chinese history. Chiang Kai-shek had nearly obliterated the leftist wing of the Kuomintang in a massacre he had arranged with the Western leaders of the International Settlement and a brotherhood organization known as the Green Gang. J. B. Powell, owner and editor of the *China Weekly Review*, whom Snow called on almost immediately after his arrival, was still trying to convince his client American business community that the Kuomintang was no longer radically leftist. Powell had stuck his neck out in support of the Kuomintang, now dominated by Chiang, while the taipans of the International Settlement had little doubt that it continued to be run by bolsheviks. To Powell, Chiang Kai-shek's bloody move against the left vindicated his faith, but Powell was still trying to mend fences with his advertisers.

Edgar Snow had left his hometown of Kansas City four years earlier, to follow his older brother Howard to New York to establish a career in advertising. He started work at the Medley Scovil Advertising Company in September 1924. Except for an academic year at the University of Missouri School of Journalism, he worked at the ad company until February 1928, when he slipped quietly out of New York to travel around the world. In those early years his interest in journalism seemed to stem primarily from a desire to further his career in advertising. Of his two journalism courses at Missouri, one was in advertising. He had previously enrolled in two evening advertising courses at Columbia University in New York, but completed only one. Just before leaving New York, he had sold a significantly expanded advertising project to Kelly Graham, president of First National Bank of Jersey City. Almost simultaneously Snow had learned that Scovil was not

2. Letter to parents, July 9, 1928.

giving him an expected raise because he had a congenital problem arriving at work on time. His resentment of Scovil's pettiness along with a growing unease about spending a lifetime in advertising triggered his decision to satisfy his youthful hunger for faraway places and to try his talents as a writer on the open market. Richard Halliburton was then stirring the imagination of a generation of youthful Americans. His tales of derring-do in exotic places were told and retold in lectures and newspaper accounts as well as collected in *The Royal Road to Romance* and *The Glorious Adventure*.

Snow had taken a course at Missouri from Dean Walter Williams, who energetically promoted his school's ties with East Asia. Williams provided Snow with a letter of introduction to Powell, a Missouri graduate, just as Powell had had a letter from Williams to Thomas Franklin Fairfax Millard, another Missouri graduate and the previous owner-editor of the *China Weekly Review*, eleven years earlier. Thus, months after leaving New York, on the other side of the world, Snow walked right into a job as assistant advertising manager of the *China Weekly Review*. As the first school of journalism in the nation, Missouri had taken a big early lead over other schools in establishing its graduates in key positions in East Asia. Snow quickly became the youngest member of what other journalists sometimes referred to as "the Missouri Mafia" in China.

Snow wrote his mother the good news almost immediately, at the same time reassuring her that he intended to continue on his journey:

> I have just been taken on the staff of the *China Weekly Review*, at Shanghai $400 per month, a princely salary on which one can become simply filthy with luxury out here on the fringes of the world. From this you may conclude that I intend to fertilize in China for the next ten thousand years— which decidedly ain't so. I shall remain here till the fall and the cessation of the torrid heat of the tropics, at which time I shall leave the heathen and go forth to conquer such fantastic names as Malaysia, Burma, Siam, India, Afghanistan, Persia, Arabia—oh, I've given you all the places before. At the latest I expect to be back in New York by next May.[3]

He had sent similar unfulfilled promises home from New York.

By late September, Snow could write to his brother Howard with pride of the one hundred advertisers who brought in a total revenue of $15,000 for the "New China" issue of the *Review* planned to commem-

3. Letter to mother, July 26, 1928.

orate the tenth anniversary of the Chinese National Revolution. He added, "I am regularly contributing to the *Review* now, as well as working on the advertising. This week I had three articles in. . . . Last week I contributed my first editorial."[4]

Powell and Thomas Franklin Fairfax Millard, who was still working in Shanghai, became Snow's mentors. Shanghai was the recognized base for the strongest international commercial and political interests in China. The *Review* was a respected critical commentator on American interests in China. Thus, by joining the small staff of the *Review*, Snow had innocently assumed a remarkable vantage point. From there he initially viewed China's modern national revolution and its struggle to resist aggressive encroachment from its more industrialized and militarized neighbor, Japan. American interests were already deeply involved, and thirteen years later the bombing of Pearl Harbor would brutally incite a reluctant America to go to war against fascism in two widely separate areas of the world.

Snow was an apt and eager student, though his dream of traveling throughout the world would never die. Within a few months of his arrival a small but telling international incident occurred in Shantung, a Chinese coastal province which had, under the terms of the Versailles Peace Treaty, shifted from German to Japanese political control, to the great indignation of the Chinese. At an international conference in Washington, D.C., in 1922, in which J. B. Powell had played a significant role, it had been agreed that Japan would withdraw its troops from Shantung, and China would control the railways within its own boundaries. But the Japanese were still in Shantung in May 1928, when Chiang Kai-shek led his armies there on the Northern Expedition to unify China. A clash occurred that degenerated into mutual atrocities. The Japanese quickly brought in a superior force and occupied the provincial capital, Tsinan, declaring it a neutral territory. An uneasy truce followed, but indications persisted that Japan had impounded much of the rolling stock of the Chinese railways that passed through Tsinan and that it regularly interrupted the flow of traffic. Thus there was broad surprise when the Japanese legation in Peiping issued an uncompromising denial that Japan was in any way interfering with Chinese railway traffic.

Sun Fo, son of Sun Yat-sen and then minister of railways, immediately saw the opportunity for a public test of the Japanese statement.

4. Letter to Howard, September 28, 1928.

He arranged for a special railway car to travel from Pukow to Tsinan. He invited J. B. Powell to ride. Powell could not leave Shanghai at the time and sent Snow, by then five months in China, in his place. Snow joined two other Western observers: A. J. Hearne, the British chief engineer of the southern division of the Tsinpu Railway, and Alfred Batson of the *North China Daily News*. Their train was repeatedly delayed by Chinese railway officials acting on Japanese orders. The party finally walked the final three miles into Tsinan, passing the repair depot where impounded railway cars were clearly visible. When Hearne, as a railway official, challenged the Japanese in charge, the latter made it emphatically clear that military strength would prevail over civilian railway credentials.

Snow wrote his first significant, and scathing, report exposing the hypocrisy of the bland official public statements of the Japanese.[5] But his meeting with Alfred Batson also renewed his dream for Halliburton-like footloose travel and adventure. He wrote to Howard that this "ex-Canadian army officer, ex-Nicaraguan revolutionary, ex-seaman, ex-cross country walker, ex-actor, ex-oh, a score of different high sounding things" was a personal advisor to Sandino in Nicaragua for sixteen months. Forced to flee when the marines moved in, Batson retreated with only $1.88 in his pocket. He was "royally entertained by presidents and generals, captured by bandits, fed upon bananas and tortillas, attacked by giant cobras, seduced by glowing senoritas, pursued by the Mexican army and, finally, escorted with a guard of honor, across the Rio Grande." His experiences were to be published in spring under the title *Beating Back through Central America*. Snow did, however, express one reservation about Batson: "He cannot forget that he went to Harvard."[6] Two years later, when Snow arrived in Rangoon fresh from his own caravan trip from Yunnanfu to Burma, he would receive a letter from Batson announcing yet another book of romantic travel experiences. That probably reinforced Snow's own ambitions to write about his adventures.

Snow's Tsinan article served Sun Fo's purpose admirably. It probably was a factor in Sun Fo's arranging for Snow to travel the extent of China's railways to report on the scenic and historic wonders still available to tourists. That trip would furnish him with both a valuable

5. "Why the Rolling Stock Isn't Rolling out of Tsinanfu," *China Weekly Review* (January 12, 1929): 274–75.
6. Letter to Howard, January 17, 1929.

firsthand grounding in China's geography and attractive possibilities for independent travel stories. While he was waiting for his trip to receive official clearance, Powell offered him the post of associate editor of the *Review* at an increased salary. Snow wrote his family that he hated

> to refuse J.B. for he has been incredibly kind to me. But if I permit myself to become harnessed in this job . . . I know the grim future that is ahead of me. . . . So you see, I've *got* to get out of here. Or very soon I shall find myself bound to a promise that I shall despise. I think that I shall leave here, regardless of any plans or hopes unrealized, by May 1st. I cannot endure the thought of being away from home any longer than such a date of departure will mean.[7]

From April through early June, Snow traveled the railways of China gathering material for his four-part tourist series. He ended his official trip in Mukden. There he met the heir-apparent warlord of Manchuria, Chang Hsueh-liang, the Young Marshall, and his adviser, W. H. Donald, a former Australian newsman now playing an active role in the political affairs he used to report. The Japanese allegedly had killed Chang's father, Chang Tso-lin, the Old Marshall, by blowing up his railway car a year earlier. The Young Marshall would later focus world attention on China by holding Chiang Kai-shek hostage in Xian. In December 1936, just as Snow was beginning *Red Star over China* and informing the world through news dispatches of the Red forces' strength in the Northwest, the Young Marshall would force Chiang to agree to terms for a United Front between the Kuomintang and the Communists.

Snow clearly saw more than tourist attractions on his railway journey. Besides interviewing the politically significant Young Marshall, he almost certainly was briefed by Donald on the potential international conflict inherent in competing political and commercial interests in Manchuria. While in Mukden he wrote a prescient warning of the ominous possibilities, "Which Way Manchuria?" for the *Review*.[8] The Japanese invasion of Manchuria two years later would become the subject of Snow's first published book, *Far Eastern Front*.

Even as his political and historical education in the East proceeded,

7. Letter to parents and sister, February 20, 1929.
8. "Which Way Manchuria?" *China Weekly Review* (July 20, 1929): 333–40.

he wrote to his mother from Mukden trying to explain why his return home had been so long delayed:

> In another 47 days I shall be 24 years old. (This is not a reminder to send me a greeting card with forget-me-nots and roses, inscribed with the conventional mother-to-son-on-his-birthday slush.) A little less than a year ago I was fretting in Honolulu, worrying about when I could get the next boat that would take me home in 60 days. Never, in my remotest dreams, did I imagine that this month would find me in this hinterland of civilization, miles away from my friends, and a three day journey to even the nearest of my Far Eastern acquaintance. And yet men speak of planning their lives. Well, I suppose we do, to a certain extent. But certainly I have not willed to stay away from home so long. There is some larger influence behind it all, someone else who pulls the strings. Of this I cannot but think, as I plan today (as I planned six months ago) to take my leave of China, and all things, Sinoese, in the very near future.[9]

In *Journey to the Beginning* Snow tells of another by-product of his tourist assignment that unexpectedly became a key turning point in his life. There was famine in nearby Inner Mongolia. The railway ministry's representative, assigned to accompany Snow, refused to regard famine as a tourist attraction. But, taking advantage of his charge to travel the extent of China's railroads, Snow overrode his protests. The awful human spectacle of waste and exploitation that Snow saw at Kalgan and Saratsi formed a sharp contrast to his own childhood; he wrote, "how vastly greater my opportunities as the child of a rich, open, frontier civilization, where nature laid its bounty before man, asking only that he work to enjoy it, as compared to the problems of survival in old China, where the struggle had to go on in a society encrusted with thousands of years of traditional exploitation of man by man on the harshest predatory level." This nightmare experience of human suffering would surface repeatedly in Snow's writing. For the rest of his life he remembered it as a terrible initiation that began to answer "Why did China begin to mean something to me?"[10]

About the time of Snow's visit to the famine area the Harbin police raided the Soviet Consulate, triggering tensions between China and Russia over Manchuria. J. B. Powell wired Snow that he should return immediately to Shanghai to take charge of the *Review* as the new assistant editor. Powell apparently gave Snow no choice regarding pro-

9. Letter to mother, June 2, 1929.
10. *Journey to the Beginning* (New York: Random House, 1958), 11.

motion this time. The *Chicago Tribune* had ordered Powell to Manchuria, so Snow would also serve as South China correspondent for the *Tribune* while Powell was away. It was a heady temporary opportunity, and Snow accepted Powell's order.

Being an editor in charge of a magazine and holding press credentials from the *Chicago Tribune* was a satisfyingly maturing experience for a young man of barely twenty-four. Snow gave Millard credit for ready help and advice while Powell was away and suggested that Millard's "anti-colonial, pro-equality-of-nations, pro-republican, pro-self-determination—and pro-American" point of view shaped many University of Missouri products, including himself.[11] He proudly explained to his parents that he worked from ten in the morning until ten or eleven at night with leisurely time for "tiffin" (a colonial British term for lunch) and dinner. He wrote articles and editorials himself and bought, rejected, or encouraged articles by others. He had "two or three interviews a week with high government officials, such as Chiang Kai-shek, C. T. Wang, T. V. Soong and others. As a representative of the Trib I have no difficulty seeing them."[12]

Yet to his sister he confided his dream of another larger, freer world:

> I sit in an office, Mil, that is literally filled with books. Fiction, biography, travel, adventure, mostly stories about China or the other lands of the Orient. It is painful to record that I have read precious few of them, but the very atmosphere seems redolent with things I love and I fancy some of it seeps down from the shelves and is the thing that keeps me satisfied with this drivel I have to turn out. In a corner is an ancient leather armchair and a broken reading lamp beside it. And here I sit many a night, long after others have taken the din of office hours with them and gone home, smoking unnumbered cigarettes, and turning the pages of books I should like to read if I had time. I will just get started in something I like, when the cables start coming in and I will have to give it [up] and immerse myself in the storm of the news.[13]

It must have been on such an evening that Snow began to dream of the Halliburton-like adventure that is the centerpiece of this book, to pour over the large-scale relief map that Maj. H. R. Davies had drawn up of Yunnan and to imagine the railway trip from Hanoi to Yunnanfu (Kunming) and the subsequent caravan trip across forbidding

11. Ibid., 30–31.
12. Letter to family, September 6, 1929.
13. Letter to Mildred, September 14, 1929.

mountain ranges, along the route of Marco Polo down into romantic Burma (see "Entering the Notorious Yunnan Province in South China and Planning a Caravan Trek across This Mysterious Bandit Ridden Region," below).

In early November, however, Snow received news that broke harshly into his dreams of adventure. His mother was ill, and the doctors suspected cancer. He wired home immediately, "How's mother?" But by that time letters were already on the way reassuring him that his mother's operation was minor and tests indicated no cancer. After learning the good news he wrote his mother:

> Until this closeness of personal tragedy, I do not think I quite realized how all-important you and father and Mil and Howard are to me. It is for you I work; for you that I strive to make a new line or two that may not die. I do wish to avoid being melodramatic, but this is true; I do not know how else to express it. I am not in love; there is no woman to spur me to perhaps futile successes. I work first for self-realization, but without you there would be no necessity, no urge for this. Approval from others—I have a few real friends—is always pleasing; but praise from you is life-giving nourishment. By "you" I mean all of you—dad, sis and Howard.[14]

Ten days later he wrote his mother again. By then he was growing impatient with Powell's prolonged absence:

> Yes, J. B. is still in Manchuria. Why he persists in staying there, when he has interests so important in Shanghai, is beyond the understanding of all of us. Unless I knew his presbyterian habits so well, I should say that he has acquired a Russian concubine (which is very inexpensive in Harbin), whom he is loathe to leave. Anyway I have written him my position, and he surely knows that his extended stay has, if I may be pardoned for saying so, "shot my plans to hell."[15]

Powell returned to Shanghai at the end of November, and Snow immediately resigned from the *Review.* David Lawrence and Drew Pearson were organizing a new foreign service news agency called Consolidated Press. Snow was asked to be a correspondent. It was just what he wanted: It gave him an adequate salary, a ready outlet for his writing while permitting him to publish his lengthier work in magazines, and freedom to travel to find his own stories. He hoped to resume his round-the-world trip soon, but since he wanted to return by way of

14. Letter to mother, November 12, 1929.
15. Letter to mother, November 22, 1929.

Russia, and Moscow in winter was not an attractive prospect, he advised his family he probably would not leave Shanghai until late in spring.

Shortly after Powell's return another crisis took Powell to Nanking, and he persuaded Snow to temporarily resume his editorial duties. By January, Snow was again free, and late in February he told Horace Epes, vice-president of Consolidated Press, of his hopes to travel home through Europe via Russia. Epes readily accepted his plan. Meanwhile, in addition to his dispatches to Conso Press, Snow continued to write lengthier pieces for a variety of publications.

But late in March, Snow was stunned by the tragic and completely unexpected news of his mother's death. He had not known of her most recent illness or her reentry into the hospital. A moving exchange of letters with his father records Snow's insistence on knowing the circumstances. His father himself had much difficulty getting clear, credible information about the cause of his wife's death. She had become feverish and incoherent. There were fears that she was losing her mind. There had been embarrassment over the bill, and it might have caused Snow's mother to fall in the hospital. The autopsy was not made available to the father, and his account of his troubles with the Catholic hospital and of the confused tensions with his wife's family over religious loyalties left the young Snow feeling frustrated and guilty about his distance from the family scene. Snow's memory of the religious conflict between his skeptical father and devout mother was deeply and persistently sealed.

His father sadly advised him to put it all behind him. There was nothing he could have done even if he had been there.[16] Ironically the autopsy and medical records make clear that his father's worst suspicions were groundless. Anna Snow's fever was due to physical disease, not mental disorder. Her death was caused by significant infection in the abdomen and urinary tract following an operation; the fall was not a factor in her death.[17] But those conclusions were not made known to father or son. Afterward, Snow wrote of his mother's death only in brief and distant terms, but both of the women he later married have spoken of how deeply he felt it.

Snow had lost faith in his mother's Catholicism in his adolescence, yet his father's skepticism provided him with cold comfort at this

16. Letter from father, May 12, 1930.
17. Medical records of Anna Snow, St. Mary's Hospital.

tragic loss. In his last days in Shanghai he reviewed *Infidels and Heretics,* an anthology for agnostics edited by Clarence Darrow and Wallace Rice, for the *China Weekly Review.* He complained of many omissions in the collection, but particularly that the editors meant "to confine their treasury to Western writers." Then he cited a passage of Hafiz that he found notable for its rich cynicism. His choice gives some insight into how he defended himself against emotional pain:

> Then from the fragile table seize a tass,
> And drain the wine of life before the glass
> Shall crumbling all, with table and with you,
> And with your god into oblivion pass. . .[18]

In May, Snow took a two-week vacation in Japan. In his letters home he indicated that he went to the American embassy in Tokyo for help in obtaining visas to cross Russia. But he spent one week at Atami, a resort whose beach reminded him in its beauty and configuration of Kani-Hanalei in Hawaii. Atami, however, had the added attraction of *geisha* and *oshima* (sleeping partners) strolling on the beach walk. He played games and learned the lyrics to some Japanese jazz from a young woman named Nasam. He spent a second week at the Uwanaton Hotel in Enoshima. He records his pleasure at having a little Hana-san play for him on her sanisen while he ate "Japanese chow." He learned, from a Japanese friend, to pretend a little deafness to draw these women closer.[19] When Snow finally left Shanghai in September he noted in his diary his disappointment that a woman named Chiyako was not there to see him off. Several entries, particularly during the first few months after his departure, note his tender reminiscences of Chiyako and remind him to write to her. Chiyako is not clearly identified, but she seems to have been Japanese and an intimate friend for some time prior to his departure.[20] His mother's

18. *China Weekly Review* (August 9, 1930): 386.
19. Snow, transcript of diary 2: 15–18.
20. In *Journey,* 35–37, Snow tells a rather hard to believe story of a friend, Larry, taking a naive young Edgar to visit a well-appointed geisha house under the pretense of introducing him to two young Japanese "modern girl" banker's daughters. The memory of this visit is supposedly triggered by a conversation about *modan garu* on the Japanese ship from Shanghai to Formosa. Snow does not clearly date its happening, although he implies it took place when he arrived in Yokohama from Honolulu. It probably never literally happened as described. It is more likely a deliberate, romantic tale designed to memorialize publicly, but discreetly, his visit to Atami after his mother's death and his subsequent relation in Shanghai with Chiyako or, as

death apparently encouraged him to "drain the wine of life" before the glass crumbled.

By early June he knew that Russia had refused his visa. He suspected it was because of his close association with Powell, who had written sharply critical articles after a recent short visit to Russia. He changed his plans and wrote to Conso Press for approval to go home through Southeast Asia. Epes again quickly approved.

Two of the several articles Snow wrote during that spring and summer have special meaning to his career. "The Americans in Shanghai" appeared in the August issue of *American Mercury.* Both H. L. Mencken and his magazine were well known in Shanghai, and the *China Weekly Review* announced Snow's soon-to-be-published article with obvious misgivings: "Evidently Mr. Snow, by his acceptance in *The Mercury* will do for China what Olan D. Russell has been doing for Japan. *The Mercury* dedicates itself to debunking American scenes. This has become tiresome after six years; so nowadays *The Mercury* which has lost its former sting, is considered puerile by the critical group, but it is still read by young intellectual upstarts and college freshies giddy over the new freedom." The *Mercury* among other named magazines enjoys "taking religion for a ride."[21]

A scrapbook Snow kept of his early publications suggests that the *Mercury* was popular with more than "young intellectual upstarts and college freshies giddy over the new freedom." Snow's article was excerpted and reprinted in the *Kansas City Times,* the *Lincoln* (Nebraska) *Star,* the *Sioux City* (Iowa) *Tribune,* the *Omaha* (Nebraska) *World Herald,* the *Enid* (Oklahoma) *Eagle,* and the *Mexico* (Missouri) *Ledger.* In his article Snow regrets that the single strongest concern shared by Americans and Chinese in Shanghai is with money. He points out that the property requirements of the voting franchise permit a small group of wealthy Britishers to "rule the [International] Settlement as one of the narrowest oligarchies in the world today. . . . Yet Washington naively accepts dual responsibility with London for what is done, while virtuously assuring the plain people that America has and wants no concessions in China." He claims that it was widely known

---

he sometimes spelled her name, Chiyeko. The two banker's daughters are named Seiko and Chiyeko. Snow's elaborate efforts to disguise and yet tell the world about his romantic experiences in *Journey to the Beginning* are more clearly traceable in the story he developed of the Burmese nurse, Batalá (see introduction, section V). The story of the geisha house is probably a foretaste of such romantic fiction.

21. *China Weekly Review* (August 9, 1930): 386.

that Stirling Fessenden, the "American Mayor" of the settlement, was in the pocket of the British. Prostitution and missionaries come in for scathing comments and anecdotes. He concludes with the charge that Americans, whether businessmen or missionaries, "little bother themselves about what is happening in the hearts and minds of the multitude around them." They live in "a hermetically sealed glass case."[22]

The *Shanghai Evening Post & Mercury* responded eagerly to Snow's article with an editorial that Snow did not paste into his scrapbook. Apparently aware of Snow's near exit from Shanghai, the editors ask: "How many of these traveling, bustling, prurient journalists have we had with us for a season, peering at us from the outside rim, and from the particular section of that rim that suits their tastes, (or the tastes of the magazine to which they hope to sell their stuff) broadcasting with authority to the world?" The editors then attack this "golden youth, all glamorous with wickedness," for his lack of proportion in failing to report the more decent and virtuous aspects of American life in Shanghai:

> We quite understand that you and Henry [Mencken] would not think much of the Community Church that these uninteresting Americans keep up; or the two American units of volunteers, and many other things too wholesome to be quaint which your investigations on Soochow Road kept you too busy to find. But busy as you are, did you never meet an interesting missionary. . . ? Well, well, Edgar, it's so hot and sticky—and the decent people are concealed, you say. And besides they're dull. Maybe Mr. Mencken wouldn't even buy a story about them.[23]

The very next day Snow replied to the editorial. He begins by dryly suggesting that he was surprised the paper was so liberal: "In other days I might have looked for a rope and a swing high in the trees from a gang led by such men as you." Instead he feels he has been treated as an adolescent to a pants-down whipping. Following up this image, he defiantly moons the editors with elaborate euphemism: "I am sanguine enough to believe that your verbal posterior attack will not wholly incapacitate that part of me for your especial reference when in the future your virtuous indignation is again aroused."

Since he had been in Shanghai long enough to see "the birth of the American NEWS, and its metamorphosis first into the POST, more

22. "The Americans in Shanghai," *American Mercury* (August, 1930): 437–45.
23. *Shanghai Evening Post & Mercury,* August 16, 1930.

recently into the Anglo-American POST & MERCURY," he suggests that the charge of adolescence is more properly attributable to this two-year-old paper than to a twenty-five-year-old journalist. But there is a more earnest note of sincerity when he protests, "As for finding Americans in Shanghai dull, or the city itself uninteresting, I made no such statement. On the contrary, a more engaging and instructive community would be hard to find, and I shall soon bid my temporary farewell with reluctance."[24] It is not clear whether the word *temporary* was simply a politic gesture or in fact he harbored some thought, even before he left, of his eventual return to Shanghai. To most readers Snow seemed to be burning his bridges behind him.

The second article of special interest was not published until after Snow had left Shanghai. While it did not attract nearly as much comment, in light of his later achievement it is perhaps even more significant. On July 27, 1930, the Communist forces that had regrouped in the mountains of Kiangsi following the 1927 Shanghai debacle attacked and occupied Changsha. It was the first major city to come under Communist control since the brief, but abortive, capture of Shanghai in 1927.

Snow had begun gathering information for an article on the Communists prior to the taking of Changsha. He sent the manuscript along with a letter to the editors of *Current History,* "Some months ago I cultivated the friendship of a few local members of the C.P., with the hope of cutting through the secrecy with which it is necessarily surrounded. This acquaintanceship, together with a study of the Red activities over recent months, has helped me to form certain concepts which I believe you may find of interest."[25]

While Snow had become increasingly disillusioned with Chiang Kai-shek's leadership of the Kuomintang, and hence eager to find some more promising alternative, his description of the Kiangsi Communists was not particularly flattering or hopeful:

> During the last 12 months the Reds have captured, looted, and pillaged over 350 cities and towns in the provinces mentioned above. In Fukien province 14 hsien or county districts have been ravaged; in Kwangtung 16 hsien; in Chekiang 12 hsien; in Anhwei 18 hsien; in Hunan 28 hsien; in Kwangsi, Hupeh and Honan, lawlessness has prevailed over such wide

24. Letter to editor, August 17, 1930, *Shanghai Evening Post & Mercury* (undated issue).

25. Letter to editors, August 17, 1930, *Current History* (unpublished).

areas that it is impossible to estimate the extent of the damage actively directed by Communists.

Worst of the sufferers has been Kiangsi province, where out of a total of 83 hsien, 45 have been taken by the Reds. An itemized report issued not long ago from the Kiangsi capital listed the estimated losses in districts occupied by Communists as approximately $215,000,000 including a total of 37,000 houses burned. Incidentally, 82,000 Chinese, mostly merchants and "long gown" men and women, have been murdered.[26]

After giving all the information he had gathered about the Communist forces in Kiangsi, Snow ends his article with speculation about the implications of the strength of the Communist movement in China. The editor at *Current History* chose to cut these editorial comments. But it is precisely these speculations that tell us most about Snow's mind as he was about to leave China, presumably for good, and to travel through nations of Southeast Asia under colonial rule.

He saw Chiang Kai-shek engaged in a fruitless struggle with the northern warlords, Yen Hsi-shan and Feng Yu-hsiang. With Chiang unable to buy them out or militarily defeat them, he saw the most probable result: "the creation of deeper hatreds and estrangements among members of the only group capable of establishing a stable, democratic government, and the physical and financial exhaustion of both north and south." He was even more concerned with the attitude of the "imperialistic" powers, "among which the Chinese now include the United States." If the Communists began to challenge Kuomintang power in the cities, Western governments would feel the pressure to intervene. At Changsha, "after Americans and other foreigners were evacuated, the U.S.S. *Palos* returned and engaged the Reds, tallying over 30 casualties against them. British and Japanese gunboats participated in similar affrays." If the Communists won sufficient strength to attack Hankow, naval retaliation by the foreign powers was even more likely and probably would be much heavier. The issues at stake would then become momentous:

26. In "The Strength of Communism in China," *Current History* (January 1931): 521–26, Snow's numbers were changed significantly: "*350* cities and towns" in the first sentence became "*250* cities and towns." The *45* of 83 hsien in Kiangsi province captured by the communists was changed to *55*. The *82,000* murdered Chinese in the last sentence became *32,000*. Snow wrote, "In Kwangsi, Hupeh and Honan, lawlessness has prevailed over such wide areas that it is impossible to estimate the extent of the damage actively directed by Communists." *Current History* edited, "In Honan, Hupeh, Kiangsu, and Suchuan [*sic*], outlaws and marauders were everywhere, but their activities were not communistic, although in some instances village soviets were established." (See also typescript, "Communist Strength in China," 4–5.)

For should China go Red, the repercussion[s] among other Asian peoples might be disastrous for world peace. Indo-China, where the French are having their difficulties with revolutionaries, India, where British rule is gravely imperilled, the Philippines, where nationalism is struggling out of infancy, the Dutch Indies, Korea—all through the East the structure of colonial capitalism would be severely rocked by a thorough-going People's Revolution in China.

Russia is in the background now, but would she remain there in the face of an "imperialistic invasion," directed against her Chinese proteges? It is debatable. Certainly she might be expected to worry the Nanking government, after the Manchurian pattern of "unofficial war," if she perceived that the Chinese Reds were being robbed of triumph through foreign interference.

Thus, a great war of Asia, and a mighty world conflagration such as the more fervid Russian leaders have constantly sought to ignite, lies ever embryonic in the Chinese revolutionary arena. It is a spectacle that can be averted. But merely laughing it off as a bugaboo will not dispell the ominous thrust of the threat.[27]

The seeds of *Red Star over China* and *Battle for Asia* are in these speculative remarks. Snow would travel great distances over remote paths and down hidden streets before these conceptual seeds would develop into such sturdy books. Communism was already an important factor in the revolutions of Asian nationalism then in ferment. What was its nature, and how significant would its role become? These questions challenged the ambitious journalist of world affairs. The map of Snow's future was obscure, but he was more than ready to travel, preferring to avoid the direct path and meandering where whim and curiosity would lead him.

On September 17 Snow sent Horace Epes an itinerary that had him leaving Shanghai for Formosa on September 24. From Formosa he was to travel to Canton, Macao and Hong Kong, with the longest stay in Canton. He planned to leave Hong Kong for Indo-China on October 17 and be in Yunnanfu by late October, then travel by caravan into Burma, arriving in Rangoon late in December. In early January he was to sail for India and by late January he hoped to be in Peshawar and Quetta. He added, "I will furnish you another itinerary when I reach India, to cover my trip through Persia and Arabia."[28]

When he left Shanghai in 1930 he must have had mixed motives for making his first stop Formosa. It was not then prominent, as his men-

27. Typescript, "Communist Strength in China," 16–18.
28. Letter to Horace Epes, September 17, 1930.

tion of the few Westerners on the island indicates. But it did have a long history of colonial control. After the Dutch were driven out by a local rebellion the Chinese assumed a loose suzerainty over the island for two hundred years. Following the Chinese-Japanese war in 1895 the Japanese claimed the island. Thus Formosa offered a significant example of what future Japanese domination of China and other Asian countries might mean. But Snow's visit to the aboriginal Taiyal country suggests that he was interested in Formosa's remoteness from history as well as what it might reveal about the current forces shaping the fate of Asia. The lure of romantic travel continued to balance his interest in history in the making.

Canton was the home of the modern Chinese revolution about which he had been learning so much for the last two years. Snow had traveled the railways along the central coastal regions of China, through much of the north, and even considerably inland into the northwest. But Canton was the city where the Kuomintang had first taken power. It stood as a test of the promise of Kuomintang rule. It was from Canton that the Northern Expedition to unite China in effective modern revolution began. Thus as he was leaving China he also was filling in an important gap in his personal experience of the modern Chinese revolution. Macao and Hong Kong were colonial entrepots on the edge of the Chinese mainland that for now were only incidental to his travels.

Indo-China had once been a part of the far-flung Chinese kingdom. Now under French colonial rule and beginning to stir with nationalist rebellion, it was principally an entry to Snow's grand adventure, the caravan trip from Kunming into Burma. While only mildly curious about the peculiarly French nature of colonialism, Snow was fascinated by the rich pluralistic history of the many peoples of the region comprising northern Indo-China, southwest China, and northern Burma. Here time was truly disjointed; a traveler might step back centuries by crossing a mountain or even a street.

Snow arrived in Yunnanfu early in December 1930, six weeks behind schedule, and difficulties arranging reasonably safe travel by caravan delayed his leaving until late in January 1931. The pause gave him time to reconsider his feelings about returning home. He had been surprised, just before leaving Shanghai, to receive news of his brother's marriage. He had just enough warning to purchase a wedding gift and have a friend send it for him. In Yunnanfu he wrote to Mildred: "Since you and Howard are both tied up in marriage and domesticity, I see no reason for my urgent return now. Possibly I may linger in Europe a while. All the reports I get of depression and business difficulties in America do not encourage me to hasten thither. What a gap has been left in things for me, now that Howard has started a new life."[29]

His caravan trip from Yunnanfu into Burma was a partial fulfillment of the dream for which Snow had left his advertising job in New York almost three years earlier. He thought of it as the potential centerpiece, if not the whole subject, of a romantic travel book. The lure of that market was enhanced not only by Richard Halliburton's phenomenal success, but also by the writing success of his traveling companion on the first leg of his caravan, Dr. Joseph Rock. Snow and Rock had many disagreements, some extensive, about the terms of their travel arrangements, but they nevertheless maintained a curious professional respect for each other. Snow certainly envied the substantial advance and contract Rock could command for a book as well as the high prices he received for writing for *National Geographic.* It probably encouraged Snow's diligent diary entries in anticipation of writing his own book.

The caravan journey itself was exciting and demanding. Once separated from Rock and on his own Snow sounded the appropriate Halliburton note in his diary by listing "the simple, primal thrills that no city dweller, no one who clings to the pavements can ever feel," "riding into the morning mist an hour ahead of the sun, driving yourself, on foot, over hills that tax the utmost strength of your limbs, and arriving toward sundown in a new valley, knowing not what room will hold your cot at night, and hoping only for a quiet, well-earned sleep."[30]

He did not compose articles from his notes until after he arrived in Burma. However, the first day in Bhamo, at the end of his journey, he met a beautiful young Burmese woman. She influenced what he subsequently wrote about his caravan trip and his stay in Burma, both in the articles he sent on to Conso Press and later in his autobiography, *Journey to the Beginning.* His romance in Bhamo was followed by a second in Rangoon. The two relationships are fused into one in his published accounts. The details of those relationships are given in my introduction to the final section.

He slightly altered the facts of his experiences in Formosa to make a better story. In his account of his Burmese experiences he protects his own and others' privacy while expressing something of the romance of

---

29. Letter to Mildred, January 22, 1930 [*sic*].
30. Snow, transcript of diary 6: 2–3.

his experience. The fictions that appear in the articles in this collection do not seem a serious offence against his reader's right to know the literal truth. They primarily concern Snow's personal life, not matters of substantial historical concern. They are well-crafted vignettes that do in fact reveal some insights into his personal experiences as long as the reader does not expect literal factuality. The reading audience Richard Halliburton had developed probably understood this.

The fictions that are revealed by comparing these articles to Snow's diary do lead to more complicated questions about Snow's representation of these same experiences in his autobiography, written in a very troubled period many years later. However, to explore all the implications, both biographical and professional, of these later fictions goes outside the boundaries of this book.[31] Nevertheless, the evidence revealed here strongly suggests that what Snow wrote in his autobiography of his 1930–1931 experiences in Indo-China, Burma, and India overstated his contacts with and focus on the national revolutionary movements in those countries.

The caravan trip in its own right, however, proved a most satisfying and testing adventure for Snow. He reversed the route of Marco Polo, who centuries before had brought the dream of the East to the West, and the excitement and wonder of his accounts frequently echo Whitman's "Passage to India":

> The first travelers famous yet, Marco Polo, Batouta the Moor,
> Doubts to be solv'd, the map incognita, blanks to be fill'd,
> The foot of man unstay'd, the hands never at rest,
> Thyself O soul that will not brook a challenge.

Burma was principally a romantic interlude during which he mined his diary notes and recovered from the physical ordeal of his journey. Inevitably his romantic liaisons raised the troubling question of what direction his life—both personal and professional—was taking. In Rangoon he received a happy letter from his new sister-in-law. His response was humorously playful, but it repeated what he had already written his sister from Yunnanfu about how Howard's marriage affected his own plans:

> The news that Howard had actually got married startled me, shocked me. . . . Always I had thought that when I got back to New York it would

31. See also Hamilton, *Edgar Snow,* 208–11.

be for a life with Howard. We would know girls, of course, after the careless way: but nothing disturbing for longer than necessary experience, nothing that would outlast its own first rapture. . . . And then abruptly you broke in on the scene and it seemed to me that the whole future had to be reconstructed.[32]

In India, Snow found national revolution on a scale as vast and complexly challenging to his historical imagination as he had in China. Lord Irwin had negotiated a pact with Gandhi, following the latter's famous "Salt March" to the sea and subsequent imprisonment. This pact had been ratified by the National Congress party, but many on both sides held serious reservations about its terms and political wisdom. Snow dutifully called on editors, political leaders, and intellectuals in Calcutta, Simla, and Bombay. Yet having recently struggled so hard to extricate himself from the compulsive concerns and needs of the modern Chinese revolution, he had little stomach for all the study and preparation necessary to engage himself deeply in the Indian national movement. He was frequently preoccupied with his personal decisions. He reached Simla far behind the schedule he had outlined for Horace Epes from Shanghai. On May 28 he sent a letter to Conso Press proposing an amended schedule for traveling through Persia and Arabia on his way to Europe and New York. But the very next day he wrote to his sister:

> I am disheartened and tired. . . . The essence of the matter is that I am homesick. But my dilemma is that I can't quite decide whether it is nostalgia for China or for America. I am strongly inclined to believe it is China. This does not mean that I have lost affection for home and old friends and family. It means that I am afraid. I don't like the thought of going back to find familiar things that are no longer familiar.

In this same letter he writes of his memories of his mother: "The other day I ate ice cream and I thought of her. She loved it. . . . She had the simplicity of a child in her capacity for enjoying trifles. A movie was an event and even going to church or taking a walk. She seemed to invest these things with glamour. Her sweetness in moments when you had done something kind for her—my God I'm afraid I'm crying." And in another part of the letter: "How often I think of her. I try to convince myself that she is dead and I realize that this will not be possible till I actually go to look for her where I last saw her. Then,

32. Letter to Dorothy, March 20, 1931.

when she is not there, perhaps I shall believe it. This is foolish and superstitious. Yet whenever I think of home I cannot imagine it without mother presiding."[33]

Late in June, Snow received a cable from Horace Epes canceling Conso's support for travel through Persia and Arabia. Snow was to be kept on the payroll through July, when he was expected to be back in New York. Epes wrote a letter dated June 23, the same day he sent the cable, explaining: "While we have been well pleased with the results of your travels and *The Sun* is awaiting with interest the stories still to come, it seemed better to eliminate Persia and Arabia because the trip already has extended far beyond the original plan." Conso had budgeted $1,500 for his trip. His monthly salary through June would bring their expenses to $2,700. When Snow arrived in New York, Conso would take up "the question of some additional allowance for extraordinary expenses."[34] The news from Conso decided him, but to return to Shanghai, not to New York.

Once again Snow kept the bad news to himself, not telling friends or family. The economic depression that was ominously spreading across the United States may have been in part responsible for Conso's decision, although Epes's explicit explanation seems reasonable enough on its own. Snow was kept on Conso's payroll long after he returned to Shanghai, but at a monthly stipend reduced from the $300 intended to cover traveling expenses. Later, in published work, Snow would cite the Depression as the determining factor in his return to Shanghai, implicitly minimizing or dismissing the role that changes in his family played.

Snow sailed for Shanghai from Ceylon on July 12. China was for now his choice as home. Once back, however, Snow was even more anguished to learn that editors at Conso Press had for a time thought about asking him "to join their regular European staff and go into Russia." Conso had subsequently made other satisfactory arrangements to cover Russia. Snow wrote to Epes:

> That agitated me no end and, rather rashly I suppose, I at once cabled you to consider me if your arrangement was not permanent. It seemed to me ironic that, principally because the prospect at home was so unpromising, I had turned back from Bombay. Apparently the Russians have forgotten whatever grievance they had against me, too. Since my return here it

33. Letter to Mildred, May 29, 1931.
34. Letter from Horace Epes, June 23, 1931.

has been intimated that now my request for a visa would be granted with no difficulty.[35]

Within days after his ship docked an energetic, beautiful, and deliberately modern young American woman, Helen Foster, who had been avidly reading his stories in the American press, would arrive in Shanghai fresh from the States. She would come looking for him the day her ship landed, and sixteen months later they would marry. After leisurely honeymoon travel, which repeated many of the stops Snow made on the journey detailed here, they would make their new home in the quiet old "northern capital" of Peking. However, then it was officially designated Peiping, "northern city" in Chinese, because Nanking, "southern capital," wanted no competition for its title. Peiping was different from Shanghai. In Peiping, the foreign presence, while still substantial, was more subdued, more respectful, more interested in living within a dominantly Chinese milieu. It represented a China where the ancient past was strongly and visibly present. There Snow lived in the first deliberately chosen home of his own.

Snow wrote Epes that he had developed a 106-degree temperature on the steamer coming into Shanghai. Although travel-weary, he was eager to try his hand at drawing his writing together into a book. He particularly hoped to use the articles concerning Yunnan and his caravan trip into Burma that appear in this collection. He intended to title it *South of the Clouds*. But only a few weeks after his return to Shanghai, the Japanese invaded Manchuria. Many Western journalists in China, including Snow, feared it was the beginning of another world war. They were right. Instead of *South of the Clouds,* Snow's first book, published in 1934, became *Far Eastern Front*—a dire warning of the imminent world conflict. Japanese aggression in Manchuria exposed the woeful inadequacy of international treaties and of the League of Nations as guardians of international order.

Major historic events unfolding in China naturally took precedence over Snow's more romantic travel experiences. Yet his longing for adventure and his desire personally to explore remote areas of the world would long continue to be part of his best writing. *Red Star over China* is not only a startlingly informative book about the nature and extent of the Red forces then gathering in northwest China. It is also

35. Letter from Horace Epes, September 11, 1931; Letter to Horace Epes, October 25, 1931.

the thrilling eyewitness account of a resourceful man venturing into dangerous, forbidden territory. And the stirring report of the Red armies' Long March was inevitably enhanced by Snow's own adventures in the rugged mountains of Yunnan, through which the Red forces would pass almost four years after his caravan trip.

His meandering travel through the nations of Southeast Asia provided a valuable firsthand introduction into the continent's colonial problems even as his trip along the railways of China had previously given him a profitable introduction to the country's peoples and geography. Snow never completed *South of the Clouds.* But many years later he would write his autobiography, *Journey to the Beginning.* In 1958, caught in the abrupt change to Cold War politics following World War II, Snow was famous but politically out of favor. In his autobiography he would dwell on many of the events of his journey with tender nostalgia. His memories had become a significant part of his life.

I. Formosa

Introduction to Section I

Formosa was Edgar Snow's first stop as he resumed his around-the-world trip. In 1930 the scant news coverage of the island provided little reason to anticipate its coming role in the Chinese Civil War and thus in world affairs after 1949. Although Formosa had briefly known Dutch and Portuguese rule, and even a brief period of independence, the culture of China had been the dominant influence on the island for centuries until the Japanese assumed control in 1895. For Snow, still only twenty-five, Formosa held a double attraction. Its remoteness promised adventure, but he was also curious to see the island as a test of what "the little Mikado-worshipers from the north" could do when they assumed "the white man's burden."

Snow's introduction to Japan two years before had been memorable. He had been a stowaway aboard the *Shinyo Maru* bound for Yokohama from Honolulu. He quickly sold the story of his adventure to more than one newspaper, although it was not published in Japan until after he left.[1] At the end of his trip he evaded customs officials by pretending to join the ranks of professional reporters who had boarded the *Shinyo Maru* to cover the landing of a passenger far more notable than he, the future Princess of Japan. That successful ruse apparently led him, once in Japan, to unwisely note *reporter* as his profession when registering at a hotel. Subsequently, when detectives questioned him, he made a second mistake by telling them the name of the ship on which he had arrived. He quickly realized that he would be in danger if they checked the ship's registry. The detectives' interrogation made him vividly, personally aware of Japanese sensitivity to the views of Western reporters, although at the time he probably was unaware that this sensitivity flowed from Japanese ambitions to replace Western nations in leading Asia into the modern industrial age. Snow ended his initial, harried visit to Japan abruptly, sailing on to Shanghai.

In Shanghai, working for the *China Weekly Review,* he was tutored in the current politics and recent history of east Asia by J. B. Powell and Thomas Franklin Fairfax Millard. Their deep-seated anti-imperialism was directed at least as strongly against latter-day Japanese aggression

1. See *Japan Advertiser,* July 10, 1928; *New York Herald Tribune,* October 21, 1928; *Kansas City Journal Post,* November 11, 1928.

as against older European colonialism. Americans living in China were also particularly sensitive, fairly or not, to Japanese ambitions to carve out a dominant role for Japan in Asia comparable to the American role in North and South America. Snow's sardonic description of the Japanization of the Formosan people in his first two columns written for "The World Today" in the *New York Sun* made welcome reprints for the *China Weekly Review.*

The *Review* also published two other pieces that were critical of Japanese-ruled Formosa. These were originally written for Consolidated Press, but did not appear in the United States. The first concerned Japan's thirty-three-year-old "enlightened experiment": licensing the use of opium on Formosa. Although the program had received much favorable publicity, Snow questioned the flimsy statistical claims of its success. In 1930 even the Japanese administration recognized the need for significant changes, indicating that the program was not all that it seemed. Licensing was so liberal that it tolerated, if not encouraged, addiction. Snow found no evidence of treatment programs to reduce drug use. Most tellingly, the chief of the Foreign Affairs Division, Mr. Kishimura, stonewalled him from seeing firsthand how the program operated and denied him any significant information. He noted in his diary that the information in his article in fact came from the American consul, Mr. Reed.[2]

The second article, which ran only in the *Review,* concerned Japanese efforts to safeguard Formosan morals through prohibition of public dancing. When an official of the Department of Social Affairs was challenged with the fact that social dancing was not banned in Japan, he drew a distinction between the peoples of Japan and Formosa that revealed the bias characteristic of an imperial power. "In order to enjoy dancing without demoralizing results, there most be a general state of culture and refinement among the populace. If a civilization is strong enough, as ours is in Japan, the evil effects dancing may produce on the unsophisticated can be resisted. . . . Formosans have not advanced sufficiently to regard this amusement with balanced judgment." Snow closed his article by observing pointedly that both Chi-

2. "Formosa, the Island of Monopolies," *China Weekly Review* (October 25, 1930): 277–78; Snow, transcript of diary 1A: 36, 47. Before leaving Shanghai, Snow wrote an article on opium, "Celestial Poppy Smoke," that was published in March 1931, in *Asia.* His interest in the subject while he was on Formosa was a follow-up to his previous research.

nese singsong girls and Japanese geisha continued to operate without restrictions—probably because they paid "a fat license" fee.[3]

The vague assumptions with which Snow boarded the *Chosa Maru,* bound for Formosa, would later emerge as firmly stated views in the conclusion of *Far Eastern Front.* He noted that there were then in Asia two political driving forces "destined to be historically great," forces requiring "a workable ideology, with strong evangelical leaders and a vast amount of faith from followers ready to die for their beliefs. These two forces are Japan, and Soviet Russia as an Asiatic Power. Both are vital, dynamic, and inherently aggressive. Both menace the Western imperialist system (behind which, in the West, lies no similar faith) as it functions in the Orient."[4]

Japanese and Russian dynamism, the decline of European imperialism, the ambivalence of American policy—ostensibly anti-imperialistic while protecting American commercial interests, which often meant in effect siding with imperial interests—and the national aspirations for independence of Asian, and particularly the Chinese, peoples would become Snow's major preoccupations for the thirteen years he worked as a journalist in Asia. Snow would return to the United States in 1941. Pearl Harbor would subsequently precipitate a new phase in his career as the *Saturday Evening Post*'s first foreign correspondent, but it would also validate his worst fears and his previous, frequent warnings to American readers.

His first published book, *Far Eastern Front* (1934), covered the Japanese invasion of Manchuria and the breakdown of international treaties and the League of Nations as instruments for maintaining international peace. *Red Star over China* (1937) predicted the dynamic potential of Communist forces in the national aspirations of the Chinese people. *Battle for Asia* (1941) recognized Japan's open warfare against China, following the invasion of Peking in 1937, as further evidence of Japan's ambition to wrest domination of Asia from Western powers and interests. *Battle for Asia* also questioned American policy in Asia. Snow's argument was catastrophically reinforced by the bombing of Pearl Harbor within months of the book's publication.

Snow was curious about Russia and its Marxist experiment that was

3. "Protecting the Morals of the Formosans," *China Weekly Review* (November 22, 1930): 429.
4. *Far Eastern Front* (London: Jarrolds, 1934), 304.

rippling out to affect revolutionary nationalist movements throughout Asia. As he left Shanghai his hopes of traveling through Russia had been thwarted by the refusal of his request for the necessary visas, but he certainly meant to monitor the influence of Marxism on the nationalist movements he might observe as he traveled through Southeast Asia. He already had firsthand experience of Japanese ambitions.

While Snow would long list Lake Jitsugetsutan, Lake of the Moon and the Sun, in his diaries as one of the most impressive natural wonders he had ever visited, his trip to Kaban and the former head-hunting Taiyal aboriginals proved a deflating disappointment as romantic adventure. But a week after he left, the Taiyals' fierce uprising against the Japanese added a welcome, if belated, sense of excitement to the experience.

Besides giving a reader insight into the origin of Snow's later, major historical themes, these columns also provide an early glimpse at how Snow developed his own anecdotal version of the personal journalism that was then popular. At the close of the first article on his visit to Formosa he cartooned a waitress, whose pidgin-English makes her an easy mark, and a single male Japanese customer of crude nationalist and sexist arrogance. In his diary Snow described encountering two separate Japanese businessmen in the Keelung chaya, from both of which he drew the composite figure of his article. The waitress is also a composite of two waitresses, but Snow met their source figures later in Tainan, and they were from "Singapoah" rather than Shanghai, as represented in the article.

He chose not to tell his readers the colorful story of his actual encounter with these two waitresses. In Tainan he visited the shrine dedicated to Koxinga and later met a Japanese professor, B. O. Gohara, on the road. They had dinner together and enjoyed teasing Kobi-san and Kitchiko-san, the two waitresses, into telling their stories in colorful pidgin-English. After ample drinking at dinner, Gohara took him to another teahouse to introduce him to a geisha friend. Although heavy with drink, Gohara still saw to it that Snow made his 9:30 P.M. train. Waiting at the train to give him a rousing send-off were the two waitresses, the chief of police, and his guide during the day.[5] The waitress at the Keelung chaya in his article is a memento of his good time made to serve in a quite different narrative setting.

This is the first of several narrative vignettes in Snow's columns that

5. Snow, transcript of diary 1A: 30–34.

were quilted together out of disparate personal experiences. While not literally factual, the fictions often express feelings and insights aroused in Snow by his travel experiences. His own role in these anecdotes is not made grand or heroic. He characteristically describes himself modestly or neutrally, although he does at times omit details that might cast doubt on his apparent innocence. These are early experiments in the first-person journalism that was to become a hallmark of his most successful books.

Chronology 1930

September 26	Leaves Shanghai, 12:15 P.M.
September 28	Arrives Foochow, late P.M.; Spends night at YMCA
September 29	Leaves Foochow, late A.M.
September 30	Arrives Keelung, 6:30 A.M.; Takes night train to Nisui
October 1	Arrives 4:29 A.M.; Leaves for Gwaishetei at 6:48 A.M.; Takes "Kiddie-Car" train to Gajo; Spends night at inn near Lake Jitsugetsutan
October 2	Arrives Tainan, 4:30 P.M. on train from Gajo; Leaves Tainan, 9:30 P.M.
October 3	Arrives Taihoku, 6:45 A.M.
October 5	Leaves Keelung, 8:45 P.M.
October 6	Amoy boat stop
October 7	Swatow boat stop

The Japan-ization of Formosa

What should be at worst a 32 hours' trip from Shanghai to this gateway city of Japan's southernmost colony is made into a tedious journey of four days via the only transport line the Nipponese permit to operate between the two ports. Leaving Shanghai on a Friday, our vessel did not touch Keelung till Tuesday morning. A day of this was spent in Foochow, on the China coast, but for the rest it was bumpy ocean travel in the *Chosa Maru,* little more than a ferry, a matter of 2,300 gross tons of steamship.

The manner in which they have monopolized the passenger traffic (to the latter's great inconvenience) is indicative of the spirit in which Formosa has been Japanized by the Imperial Dai Nihon. One notes this at once, upon entering the hill-embraced bay of Keelung, for there is about it the same appearance that characterizes so many ports of Japan—largely the incongruity of cheap Western architectural line awkwardly outlined against a gentle emerald horizon that finds true harmony only in the slow grace of Chinese roofs.

There are other signs that one has reached Japan. Half an hour out from the pier, brass-buttoned customs' officials board our ship and courteously request my passport—and half an hour later are still examining it. Scurrying little figures dash above and below decks, searching for something or somebody or other. Japanese men, dressed in European clothes, who have been my fellow passengers, suddenly begin their mutual sayonaras. Exchanging formal grins, they press their thighs and bow—from habit and the hips. Out of the third class quarters now emerge the wives of Japanese business men who have been travelling first class.

Even before we dock it seems to me that I can sniff in the air those odors that are peculiar to ports of Nippon: of vegetables simmering in shoya sauce, of glowing charcoal, of orange pink soap, and heavy Japanese perfume. Above all, the penetrating smell of that ubiquitous disinfectant that foreigners never forget. It is as though all Japan was scouring last year's bathtubs.

This much has happened in less than half a century, for before 1895 Formosa was part of China. Tradition, population, propinquity— these marked the island as Chinese. True, other nations, in the past, had claimed it. Many had desired it. A few, other than China, had even possessed it. But when the farce known as the Sino-Japanese War occurred toward the close of last century, there was no country that could legally dispute Japan's possession of it. Thus, as a result of a few absurd battles, ostensibly staged to maintain the "independence" of Korea, Japan acquired from China an important link in the chain of her island empire.

Formosa, which includes the Pescadores and many smaller islands, is a night east from Foochow, while it is two days from Moji, the nearest port of Japan proper. The channel which separates it from the mainland of China is about 100 miles wide, and spotted with innumerable small islets, volcanic in contour. Facing the Pacific on the east, and the Philippines and Hongkong on the south and southwest, the main island is approximately 240 miles from north to south and 90 miles at its widest part, but its shape in general resembles an elm leaf. Altogether, it is only a trifle under 14,000 square miles, larger than Holland, but smaller than Switzerland.

To most Americans, used to the broad vistas of our own plains, such an inconspicuous spot on the earth's surface may seem worthy of little attention. Yet to the European land-grabbers of three previous centuries the abundant wealth of this magnificent, mountainous island country beckoned with promise of quick fortune and opportunity for enterprise. It was the cause of many minor wars—between European nations and between oriental potentates. At one time every country in the West that had a battleship on the China coast secretly coveted it— yes, even the non-aggressive United States.

As at so many other Eastern lands, the Portuguese reached here first. To foreigners, this sub-tropical country still bears the name they gave it—*"Ihla Formosa,"* or "Beautiful Island." But not one in a thousand of its present inhabitants has ever heard this name. To them, Japanese and natives alike, it is known as *"Taiwan,"* a Chinese word that has been in use for centuries and means "Terraced Hills."

Shortly after the Portuguese adventurers of the sixteenth century had "discovered" the principal island, Dutch traders arrived and, after killing a few hundred of the head-hunting savages who opposed them, settled in the south and established forts at Tainan and Anping. In 1603 they had got their foothold in the Pescadores and two decades later they announced that they had taken possession of all Formosa, in the name of their king.

The fact that the Chinese had intermittently "controlled" Formosa since the early Sui Dynasty, about the seventh century A.D., did not deter the ambitious Dutchmen. They built a model city on their rocky point at Tainan and for 38 years actually furnished practically the only government of the island—despite the protests of the declining Ming rulers of China.

Much of the folk myth and legend of the natives of Taiwan centers round the time-great figure of the pirate chief, Koxinga, a Chinese adventurer who finally evicted the Dutch from Taiwan, and temporarily established a kingdom of his own. He clashed with the Spanish also, who had occupied a port in north Formosa. By 1662 he had "driven the foreigners into the sea"—a feat which his brothers on the mainland tried to emulate, without success, during the Boxer Rebellion, in 1900.

Koxinga was one of the most picturesque characters of the nineteenth century, and an adequate appreciation of his greatness has yet to be written in English. A courageous and able leader, his memory has stayed with his countrymen till this day. Shrines for him are numerous in Taiwan and throughout south China. He is especially venerated as the only Chinese who ever won a war against a European nation.

To the natives the Japanese have given the spirit of Prince Kitashirakawa to be worshipped as the patron deity of their island. Nominally most of them do homage to him in some of the elaborate shrines that have been erected at scenic spots throughout Formosa. But it is the record of Koxinga that they hold noble; and it is to his personal shrine in Tainan that they make their pilgrimages.

The sons of Tang Sing-kong (Koxinga) proved unequal to the task their father had marked out for them in his kingdom. The gallant pirate's dynasty crashed in 1682 when the Tartars who had conquered China reached out beyond the channel and took possession of Taiwan. From then on, except for periods of brief foreign occupancy, such of the country as had evolved from barbarism and headroasting was under the loose domination of the Manchu Son of Heaven at Peking.

The British, the French, the Spanish, one after another made "punitive expeditions" into Formosa in reprisal for the alleged brutal murders by the savages, of their sailors who had been shipwrecked off the island's rocky coast. Admirals, and some consular officials, of these nations, strongly recommended to their home governments that Taiwan be officially occupied. But formal proceedings were in each case deferred. Meanwhile, in the north, the Japanese grew up, built a navy, looked for conquest, and decided upon this mountainous extension of their archipelago to the south of them. Thus ended dreams of European imperialists for another "foothold" in Asia.

So Formosa, although for the most part still a primeval state when the Japanese arrived to "civilize" it, had already known what, for want of a better word, may be called "government," under Tartars, Mongols, Chinese, Dutch, Manchus, Spanish and British, besides supporting the independent dynasty of the romantic Messrs. Koxinga.

Rich in coal (for which the foreign fleet commanders were particularly avid), rich in mineral deposits, laden with fine untouched forests of pine and camphor wood, endowed with a soil more fertile than any found in China or Japan, blessed with a varied and salubrious climate, the "Ihla Formosa" was a lucky bag for *Kami*—that legendary watchman of the Mikado's realm. For a decade so busy removing the surface wealth of the land that they had little time for construction or improvement, the Japanese in recent years have done much to make up for the earlier exploitations. Their official guide book now boasts that the colony is "astonishingly modern," and the phrase is well chosen. Since there was no necessity here to wait for an earthquake to remove outmoded structures and machines—there being none to speak of—everything built is twentieth century, and bespeaks of "capital P progress."

In this connection the Japanese burst with pride over their harbor in the city of Keelung. On improvement work they have spent over 30,000,000 yen until today, the spacious navigating facilities are the equal of any port of similar size in the world. Along the shores run numerous docks, capable of nesting ships up to 10,000 tons, while for the larger vessels mooring buoys have been placed in the outer harbor. Cargo sheds, breakwaters, godowns, canals, bridges, steam hoists, dredges, modern cranes—all the paraphernalia that thrusts out at the incoming traveller are here seen in glistening display.

It is rather a curious discovery, when one has finally struggled past the customs examiners—odd fellows, not at all impressed by one's manner of alien importance—to find so many Sino-profiled individuals running about the spacious, macadamized streets. Somehow they seem as out of place here as the million burden bearers in Europeanized Shanghai. But it is a reminder that, after all, the bulk of the island's population is still Chinese, despite the Japanese Government's vigorous efforts to emigrate its surplus millions to this oriental "land of opportunity."

The population of Keelung is said to be 60,000. Of these about 45,000 are Chinese—or, if you like, Formosans—the rest being imported colonizers and business men from the homeland, Nippon.

Throughout Formosa the population shows an even larger percentage of Chinese, the figures being roughly 4,000,000 of the latter as against some 200,000 Japanese and about 120,000 surviving members of aboriginal tribes. Although the government has exerted itself to suppress the use of birth control methods among its own subjects in Taiwan, it is asserted that the Chinese continue to be more fecund. Further increased by constant immigration from the mainland, their number steadily grows more rapidly than that of their colonial rulers.

Were it not for the Chinese, one would ponder the absurd width of the streets in Keelung. Even they do not seem to justify these extraordinary thoroughfares—and it is a wide street that does not seem crowded with a dozen Chinese abroad. These spacious avenues measure 150, some of them 200 feet across. Perhaps this extravagant use of pavement is explained by the fact that there are few sidewalks, an item which the burghers apparently thought unnecessary.

Seemingly unaware of the humor of their position, squat little slant-eyed policemen stand at intersections to direct the traffic that makes its appearance, moving at a leisurely pace, and in sparsity so pronounced that one wonders if it would really matter whether it used one side of the street or the other. But, Keelung is the chief port of the island. It must have its traffic policemen. It needs also have its *geisha,* whom I observed pigeon-toeing it up the center of the street. And fortunately—for I had no breakfast—it need have its *chaya.*

Into one of these establishments I strolled, the only white foreigner in Keelung (there are but 53 on the whole island), and ordered a meal in Japanese vulgate which I cultivated in Shanghai. To my amazement, I was answered in English. Well, sort of English.

"Scramberred yeggs? Cah-hee? Buttu tostu?" queried a little maid enrobed in a purple and gold kimono. She giggled, amused at my surprise, and secretly as delighted as any Nipponese professor to display her knowledge of "Ingirishu."

When I asked her about it, she explained:

"Ano, ne, mae watakushi wa Shanghai shigoto arimasu," enjoying the sensation of talking to a foreigner in pidgin-Japanese, after having suffered so often in pidgin-English herself. "My wuk Shanghai suki-yaki place before. My know prenty American pipple. My arrasame sink you berong American man. *So-deska?*"

I confessed her divining powers were correct. Before she shuffled off on her cork-soled *zori* to confer with the cook regarding my breakfast, she made a brief bow, and remarked, so quickly, so ludicrously that I was still laughing when the eggs arrived:

"My savvez! My berong prenty speak Ingirish! My okay! Have got Shanghai Ingirish baby-san have got husband too!"

While I was masticating the Scramberred Yeggs, a middle-aged gentleman, clothed in spotless black serge, entered the chaya and seated himself beside me, after nearly touching the floor with his close-cropped head while executing an elaborate bow. My worst suspicions were confirmed. He announced that he was the porter from the Taihoku Hotel, and that he was at my service. I had successfully eluded all porters after escaping from the ship, but this one, I knew at once, would be relentless. I gave in without a murmur.

He excused himself, and left. Five minutes later he returned with a railway ticket to Taihoku, capital of Formosa. Whether I liked it or not, I was on my way. These hotel porters, particularly the English-speaking ones, have a manner of handling travellers in Japan, or in Japanese possessions. Eventually everyone succumbs, and I have known foreigners to become so dependent upon them that, unless one puts in his appearance at a station platform, they are practically helpless. I permitted this fellow to dispose of my luggage, knowing perfectly well that, now he had control of me, I should probably never lose sight of him till I sailed out of Keelung for other ports—leaving behind with him five yen that might have been more happily used elsewhere.

While I waited here for the train to arrive, a Japanese gentleman, dressed in a European woolen suit, arrived in a perspiring state. He called upon all the *jochu-san* at once, and they came running, clicking their *geta* across the cement floor—for this was a modern chaya; none of your old-fashioned *tatami* mats here. Ordering all of the Tokio-made electric fans to be concentrated on him, he requested a bottle of beer.

After a few moments, both the beer and the fan having failed to bring down his temperature, this man removed his coat, folded it neatly, and sat on it. This not sufficing, he next took off his shirt, and revealed some vermillion underwear, longsleeved. He soon had off his trousers, which he also folded neatly and sat upon. Only when he was stripped to his one-piece underwear did the man seem to approach comfort. He called for another bottle of *Asahi biiru,* and appeared to notice me for the first time. But he didn't put on his trousers. He simply sat on them, staring out at the street, and absorbing beer and electrically agitated air.

I decided that Keelung, despite its 30 million yen harbor, was not so terrifically sophisticated after all. Perhaps there ought to be only a small "p" in the progress mentioned above.

For verily, even on the hottest and dustiest days in Tokio, one does not see many gentlemen running about in their drawers nowadays. It's really not being done any more.

But my train had come. There was the porter, bowing, making urgent suggestions. Reluctantly, I left for the capital. And so I shall always be curious to know whether that Japanese put on his trousers before he departed from the tea house, or whether, in the formerly approved Tokio fashion, he carried them home under his arm.

Some Results of 35 Years of Japanese Rule in Formosa

It is said that if you scratch a Russian you will find a Tartar. No such engaging test is necessary to tell that most Formosans are Chinese—but the case may be different another generation from now. The servants of the Mikado are overlooking no means of Japanizing the population with all possible haste. Thirty-five years of effort begin to show results.

Through schools, churches, temples, newspapers, *geisha, sake,* and the far-reaching effects of social and business contacts the less than 200,000 Japanese in Formosa have worked a remarkable influence over the 4,000,000 Chinese "subjects."

But in the official language, and in the common speech of all Nipponese here, there are no "Chinese" inhabitants. There are only Formosans, or *Honto-Jin*—"Island Men." It is something studied and humorous, this persistence with which the Japanese avoid calling the "conquered" race by their true name, Chinese. It is almost as if they wished the latter to forget all about their relationship with that straggling mainland to the west. It is almost as if they feared the 4,000,000 might some day suddenly remember their commutuality with China, might declare their independence—or at least express a desire for a few genuine "republican" wars.

However, there are few visible signs of approaching revolution in Formosa. One obvious explanation is that there are no Chinese warlords here. No warlords, no revolution. And there hasn't been a really capable Chinese military man on the island since the picturesque pirate chief, Koxinga, carved himself a brief dynasty during the seventeenth century.

The Japanese took Formosa from China in 1895, and they have been careful to see that no disappointed and restless emigrée satraps from the continent settled here. Retiring Chinese generals are permitted to go to Japan, to such resorts as Beppu, Unzen and Karizawa. It is believed that at these spots they can safely release any remaining steam, while frolicking with their concubines in the very excellent hot baths. There are hot baths in Formosa also. But for some reason the Japanese do not consider them so salubrious for disgruntled warlords as those in Japan proper.

Other precautions are taken to keep the Honto-Jin from absorbing any of the spirit of Chinese nationalism. No Kuomintang has branches here, at least not openly. No *San Min Chu I* [Sun Yat-sen's Three Principles] is read in the schools, nor are there any parks or boulevards called Chung Shan, in memory of the now apotheosized Sun Yat-sen, leader of invariably defeated Chinese revolutionists for 40 years.

But there are other gods for the Chinese to worship; the Japanese have seen to that. Scattered throughout the island are shrines and temples erected to names sacred in Shinto, the Japanese state religion. There are dozens of Buddhist monasteries, maintaining the peculiar Japanese form of faith. There are expensive and stoutly built houses of worship dedicated to Kami, that highlord of the prosperity of Dai Nihon. And then there is that National Shrine, erected to the patron saint of the island, Prince Kitashirakawa, who had the good fortune to pass to his seat in the Hall of the Great during the Japanese military expedition to subjugate Formosa, toward the close of the last century.

It may be that "these shrines are the object of enthusiastic worship on the part of the islanders," as the official guide book to Formosa states, but the writer failed to note the presence of more than three or four Chinese within the vicinity of any of them. However, their own Confucian and Taoist temples seemed no better patronized. Possibly the Formosans are not a very religious people.

But they are anxious for education, and it is here that Japanizing has made greatest progress. The Japanese have developed an excellent educational system; at least, from the standpoint of number, the schools seem adequate. "Discrimination in educational opportunities between the Japanese and the natives has been completely eliminated," reads the Government year book, "so that this period may well be called an epoch-making era in the history of civilization."

There is now nothing to stop any Chinese child on the island from getting a secondary education—provided he is willing to forget that he is Chinese. For all except a few primary schools are conducted in the Japanese language, and according to the Japanese pattern. The Educational Law of Formosa "provides that the educational system as enforced in Japan proper shall be pursued."

For a total population of about 4,250,000, including 84,000 aborigines of Malayan descent, there are 132 elementary schools, 720 public schools, 20 middle schools, 4 technical schools, three normal schools, and special schools of commerce, agriculture, forestry and medicine. At last estimate the percentage of Japanese children attending school was 97.63, while that of the Formosans (Chinese) was 32.34.

Due to what seems to have been a protest against the deracializing influence of Japanese schools on Chinese children, the authorities have lately founded a "University of Formosa," where Japanese is not the exclusive language. "English" is also used. But there are no courses in Chinese—here, or in any school on the island. Honto-Jin who wish their children to have a Chinese education are permitted—but not encouraged—to send them to China.

In order to be admitted to the middle schools it is necessary that students "speak Japanese as the language of daily life." The number who qualify is astonishing. It is estimated that there are about 9,000 Chinese children going through the Japanizing process in Formosan schools each year.

To a traveler just arrived from China, there is something incongruous about a group of Chinese children emerging from a Japanese school in a quiet, orderly manner, carrying their standard knapsacks and waterbottles like little soldiers, the girls in their blue and white uniforms, black stockings and shoes, and wide sunbonnets, the boys with their military caps and brassbuttoned coats, all of them looking like so many rising suns cut from Nippon flags. It is hard to realize these solemnfaced, disciplined youngsters are of the same blood as those across the channel who, more like American kids—recognize in the daily dismissal from school a signal for the release of suppressed energy, marked principally by a series of shrieks, yells and a general exchange of friendly thumps and bumps.

This liquidation of Chinese traditions among the Formosans does not stop with the schools. It is grafted on the citizens in every turn of life. Native policemen are dressed in Japanese uniforms, even to the little silver sword of authority. Ricksha men pull Tokio-made conveyances, and wear the same dress, including that mushroom sun-hat, as Japanese in the same calling. Chinese businessmen are encouraged to wear Japanese kimonos and the high duties placed on Chinese imports make it cheaper to use Japanese furniture, cooking utensils, household goods.

In rural districts one sees hundreds of Chinese living in Japanese tatami-spread huts. Even houses with Chinese exteriors are finished *à la Japonaise* inside. Scrolls of Chinese gods are giving way to the conventional Japanese *kakemono* for interior decoration. Those few Chinese temples that have been built since the Japanese conquest have been cheated in their roofing and more nearly resemble Nikko than Peking.

One is impressed with the manners of the people which everywhere appear to be modelled after the Japanese instead of the once Celestial Kingdom. On the streets Chinese exchange low bows, grin and—actually draw in their breath through their teeth in the irritating Japanese fashion! Perhaps one's imagination races, but it often seems that many of the Chinese here lack that spontaneity, that quick response to wit and humor, that is characteristic of the laughter-loving continental, but so antipodal to the Japanese.

It is certainly true that many of the present generation of Formosans cannot speak Chinese. This applies particularly to those who have "been abroad"—to Japan—for a college education, where the Japanization has been completed, often to the extent of the returned student bringing home a Japanese bride along with his sheepskin.

If doubts remain as to the puissance of education, religion, and intermarriage as methods of changing the most homogeneous race on earth into stolid, Japanese-minded subjects, the writer urges a strikingly convincing visit to—Formosan graveyards! There you will find the most immemorial, and hence most sacred, of Chinese customs violated. Coffins recently laid to rest have been actually buried, as they are in Japan, and not placed above ground, as in China. Over many a plot of waving green grass stands nothing but a simple headstone to indicate that under this sod lies the dust of what was once Johnny Chang!

Yes, the Japanese have done their job thoroughly.

A Thrilling Ride on the "Kiddie-Car, Limited"

in Central Formosa and a Visit
to the Lake of the Moon and the Sun

Men before me have remarked that to get anywhere worthwhile in Japan you have to climb a mountain—perhaps several mountains. The observation may be applied with even more verity in Formosa. It is certainly true of Jitsugetsutan, "Lake of the Moon and the Sun." For this still mirror of crystal water lies high, cradled in the laps of a dozen green-clustered peaks, some of whose far summits are lost in diadems of fluffy, slow-moving clouds, more than a mile above the tropic lowlands.

But the Japanese have a way of subduing mountain ranges with their snorting steam engines. Much of what was once a long week's upward climb from the west coast of Formosa to this frontier of civilization may now be traversed by rail.

The start for Jitsu—but perhaps I should substitute its European name for this difficult, though flowery, Japanese one. To foreigners on the island the lake is known as Candidius, after the intrepid, soul-saving Dutchman Georgius Candidius, who first reached here in 1627. Like most places and cities of historic interest in Formosa it has still a third cognomen, in Chinese. By them it is called Leung Hu, or "Dragon Lake," for, according to the mythology of the natives, it was believed to be the abode of one of those remarkable chaps who snort fire and go about shaking the earth.

Lake Candidius is located 170 miles south of Taihoku, the capital of Formosa. South of it, only a few miles, is the imaginary line of Cancer, which separates the rest of the world from a belt more or less completely dominated by white-helmeted Englishmen who take their tea and whisky strong and carry the burden of empire on their shoulders. Formosa, due to an oversight in the hurried colony-making days of the last century, is not, however, one of their dominions. Here the little Mikado-worshippers from the north have taken up the white man's burden and put it on yellow backs for once.

Inconsiderate of tourists, the Trans-Island express dumped me in the unilluminated town of Nisui at four in the morning, and I was met, still in more or less semi-buttoned condition, by one of those inevitable hotel porters. This time I welcomed him; there would have been insulted husbands in the village had I gone around in the dim light knocking on doors and asking wasn't this a hotel. As it was I comfortably finished off the night in a paper-walled *yado-ya,* and when the almond-eyed *jochu* woke me at 7 she had a *bento,* tied in pink paper twine, ready to hand me for the noon meal.

From Nisui, the start to Candidius is made over a branch railway, privately owned, and in season used for transporting sugar cane to the main line. It takes in "paying guests," however, during dull months, and has available second- and third-class accommodations. I took a seat in the single second-class compartment. There were no other snobs in the neighborhood, apparently, for the rest of the train went third class.

We moved away from Nisui, with the engine hitched onto the passenger cars tail foremost; it was a single track line, and boasted no turntable at the terminals. Out in fields the climb started at once through a valley, which sloped, gently at first, up to a seemingly endless succession of sharp peaks, hazy blue in the distance, under dazzling tropic sunshine.

After two hours the "Sugar Express" has climbed as many inclines as it can. I change at Gwaishetei for the scenic man-power "kiddie-car" line that reaches into the hills for another ten miles. Unique and thrilling, these toy railways are one of the things people never forget about Formosa.

Each car of this midget train is accompanied by two Formosa coolies—some of them once wild men, tamed by the Japanese, who now exploit them in the tasks of their bright civilization. The cars are built to accommodate two persons. First class entitles one to a rattan seat with a canopy. Second class, and one is allowed only a rattan seat, with the hot heavens beaming down on one's pate. The Chinese ride second class—and bring along their umbrellas.

At an official signal from the Japanese station master's whistle, the coolies, stripped to a loin cloth, start the ascent, with a yell.

I have never grown used to seeing men misused as animals, but I have come to accept it as a fact in the Orient. Sentimentality is wasted, while the present system prevails. If, in the absence of mechanical transport, one wants to be carried, it can rarely be arranged by horses; the labor of men is cheaper than horses in the East. Pushing a tram-car is light work compared to employments in which I have observed men engaged in China.

Besides, these fellows are comforted with the thought that for every mile they shove, they will ride a mile in return. Coming back over this track I even envied the coolies. I would like to take that trip once a day myself. While the upward journey requires three hours, the down train makes the ten miles in thirty minutes.

That doesn't sound very stirring perhaps, twenty miles an hour. But on a little four-wheeled cart not much larger than a boy's toybox scooter, shooting down a pair of rails less than two feet apart, taking banked turns without a decrease in speed, racing across wire-supported bridges where a somersault would land one in a torrential mountain stream a hundred feet below, and sweeping from one magnificent valley onto a bit of roadbed hung onto the edge of a precipitous cliff—under such circumstances, twenty miles an hour is no snail's pace!

Small as it is, this push-car railway has tunnels of its own. They are considerably cleaner than those penetrated by the coal-burning lines. I am not sure foreigners concerned would not agree that it would be a great improvement if the Japanese transformed all their mountain railways into man-powered affairs, simply to eliminate the extraordinary punishment one takes in soot and filth and ruined clothes, under the present arrangement.

The Japanese have a passion for tunnels. The more tunnels, the more wonderful the railway, the more glorious the engineer. They think nothing of building a thousand-foot tunnel under a hill thirty or forty feet high. Certain as simple arithmetic is the fact that if you put your head out the window of a Japanese train you will quickly withdraw it and remark, "I thought so; another tunnel ahead."

The push-car has other advantages. If you get trainsick you can get out and walk, or, rather, run, for the coolies move at a trot even up the stiffest grades. If you want to stop and take a picture of a particularly entrancing panorama you can induce the head man to halt the caravan, for a silver gratuity. It is true that you may be held up for a few minutes by a stubborn carabao who refuses to recognize the rights of a Kiddie-Car Limited. You may run over a farmer's prize rooster—as we did—and be subjected to a sudden bombardment of choice epithets in Formosan. But eventually, if you are patient, you will reach your destination—even as I finally arrived at Gojo.

Experience has taught me that the first thing to do when one attains a strange city, where people speak a strange language, is to find some place to sit down. Now Gojo is surely strange, but, with its population of twenty-three, including the station master's eight children, hardly a city. Nevertheless, when I sat down on one of the stools in the single tea house which this railway metropolis boasted, the solution to my problems appeared. He was a Japanese engineer, and one who was about to start for Jitsugetsutan. In a few words he agreed to show me the trail to Jitsu—or, as I said, Candidius.

The trail follows a swift mountain stream that rises sharply 2,400 feet behind Gojo. It is a steady, leg-breaking climb and I find it arduous work to meekly hang on the heels of this thick-muscled Japanese who appears to have been doing little but humiliate mountains all his life.

After the first mile, I shed shirt and singlet; though only a few slants of the sun break through the high nave of this jungle forest, the air is unmoving, and, in the valleys, torrid. In zig-zag pattern we wind up the face of the peak, through canyons of great leaf-heavy camphor trees, banyan and southern pine, interspersed with immense ferns that rise to tropic heights of twenty or thirty feet. Golden yellow butterflies—"cho-cho-san," the Japanese call them—sink upon thick moss that carpets the steep trail. Other insects, of vivid hues, dart across the narrow aisles: a brilliant dragon fly, with wings of gauzy turquoise, and a velvety ebon head, is especially admirable.

At length, having crossed the mountain and begun the descent, we come out upon a knoll. Down there, beyond the tree tops, lies Candidius, girdled by a regal chain of soaring crags that stretch out into what might be infinity. Along the western shore a few Japanese houses and a cluster of native huts. Out on the placid lake waters little dots of color and movement are identified for me by my companion as fishermen, casting their primitive nets.

Where the trail turns into a road I thank the engineer and attend his instruction on how to reach the only inn in the village—where he has promised to have dinner with me tonight. Arriving at the Japanese yado-ya, perched aloof and perilously near the edge of a cliff that lifts sheer out of the lake, I discover I am the only guest. To one who has not grown effete of the East and bored with Japanese inns it is a novel situation.

For instance: At the gate I am met by a smiling jochusan, dressed as if she had just stepped out of Tokio, and as though this were not a lone hostel in a secluded hill station. Her kimono is a flame, her wide coiffure as perfectly enameled as any belle of the Ginza might prize.

Japanese men may wear sensible shorts and hiking clothes in these hard hills, but not the women; not even the servant girls. Perhaps they are wise, though. Perhaps they realize that in anything but kimonos few Japanese women can manage to be much but ludicrous little ladies whose legs are not in alignment.

At the inn a further reception awaits me. The whole staff lines up on the one-step veranda, bowing, uttering an inviting *"Irrashai!"*

A maid removes my shoes, I slip into straw sandals, and in answer to questions from the obasan and all the chattering nesan I remark that I am, indeed, tired, that the lake is lovely and inspiring, but how about a hot bath, à la Nippon, as an introduction! All this goes on in my own peculiar management of Japanese, and that has no regard for grammar or construction, but is somehow understood even by these country-folk, who are always a little more dense than the urbanites.

Up in my room laid with tatami mats, I undress and slip into a *yukata,* one of those light kimonos which every hotel furnishes its patrons, along with innumerable slippers and bars of perfumed soap. A nesan brings tea and some fragile sweet cakes that are more like sugar on paper than anything edible. She announces that the young master's bath is ready.

Being the one male guest in the one inn in a village imparts to the most humble of men a certain feeling of distinction. I confess I regard the procession to the bath as something approaching the royal purple, for as I swagger along the corridors I am followed by the bantosan, or clerk, the mistress of the hotel, and her mother, the aged obasan, without whom no yadoya maintains its serenity. Moreover, behind them trail the three nesan, for young servant girls are always interested to see how a *"keto-jin,"* or "hairy foreigner" looks in a bathtub.

But they are all genuinely concerned that I enjoy my stew in the near-scorching waters of the long wooden *o-furo.* As a matter of fact, they are on the verge of following me into the bathroom, but I make strenuous protests. Reluctantly, they are convinced I would prefer to wait till later to exchange news of the world for their local gossip. All, that is, save the bath maid. To her bumpkin mind it is wholly inconceivable how a man can massage his own back. When I politely object to her presence she sits stolidly on the scrubbing stool and waits for me to recover my sanity. It is a matter of endurance; not wishing to appear a prude I finally submit. The operation is brief, painless, but thorough. To be quite truthful it is the first time I have felt that my back has received adequate ablutions for months.

When the flesh is pink I emerge from the tub, go upstairs and sit on the floor of the low, half-inclosed veranda that looks out upon the distances of this ten mile lake. The sun has dropped beyond the lowest of mountains and the sharp thrusting peaks in the east are losing the last gold tinge of day.

Night descends swiftly in this equatorial region. It is already dark when the soft-slippered nesan is suddenly beside me, sitting on her feet, making obeisance so that her forehead nearly touches the floor. She has come, she says, to inform me that there will be sake for dinner, and sukiyaki, as I have requested.

Have you ever tasted sukiyaki? Beef and chicken, cut in thin cubes, and tender cabbage, young onions, mushrooms, bamboo shoots and many odd herbs, all broiled in shoya and sugar over a slow charcoal fire. There are few better preludes to contented sleep.

Besides, over a corner of the lake a white moon creeps up. Down in the courtyard, I hear the nesan greet Kumisan, the engineer, who has come to dine with me, and wine with me. Inevitably I think of Rupert Brooke, and of how he once said:

> Tenderly, day that I have loved, I close your eyes,
> And smooth your quiet brow, and fold your thin dead hands. . . .
> Day that I loved, day that I loved, the Night is here!

A Visit to the Formosan Aborigines

Before I started into the wilderness of mountains that incloses Kaban I made private as well as official inquiries regarding the eating habits of this particular tribe of aborigines. It was only after I had satisfied myself that the Japanese quite thoroughly had turned the appetites of the once wild men to rice and vegetables—instead of their former diet of human heads—that I undertook the journey.

Possibly it is a peculiarity of mine, but always it has seemed to me that a man who deliberately exposes his cranium to unnecessary abuse is either a fool or a saint. There are perhaps exceptions—but neither am I a Roosevelt, a Carl Akeley, nor a Mrs. Martin Johnson. I admit that the lucid paragraphs which might be written in appreciation of the delicious soup obtained from my head would be most instructive. Nevertheless, it is a story which I have no desire to have published—not even in the interests of science and the Consolidated Press.

Many were the heads sacrificed, however, before the Japanese brought under their control the majority of those notorious barbarians, the Formosan skull collectors. Japanese officialdom does not release the figures of total casualties among its own expeditionary forces, but it is said that during the early days of this century hundreds of lives were lost. One battle with the Taiyals, in comparatively recent years, was reported by foreign residents on the island to have resulted in 272 deaths among the Japanese and their assistants.

Before 1895, when the Japanese annexed Formosa (Taiwan) to their empire as an indemnity from China after her defeat by the legions of New Japan, head-hunting was a commonly practiced pastime among the 150,000 wild tribesmen of the mountain regions. Chinese living along the frontier—and in those days the frontier was anything beyond the western plain—were frequently carried off by the playful aborigines, who removed the heads and thoughtfully returned the bodies to the surviving members of the families.

Several foreign missionaries gave up their lives here in the seventeenth and eighteenth centuries—Dutch, Spanish, and English. A number of foreign sailors, shipwrecked off the island's rocky coast during the clipper-ship era, were never heard from again. It was believed that they were captured by the savages, who brutally murdered them. Innumerable Japanese pirates, as well as honest fishermen, fell victims to the head-hunters.

It seems that a head to these men was a kind of equivalent to the *toga virilus*. Until he had begun his collection, a young man of marriageable age could not select a bride. In every barbarian hut there was a skull shelf, upon which the male inmates placed their carefully catalogued trophies.

One of these was shown to me in Kaban by a grinning "tamed" man, whose father probably would have been unable to resist the temptation to add my head to his assortment. But the Kabanese are mild enough today. Even when I remained in their camp, long after dark, and listened to their music and songs, I had no feeling of uneasiness. I am told that there have been no murders marked up against this tribe for many years.

The Kabanese early came into contact with the Chinese, and by them were more or less civilized—at any rate Sinicized. They now wear clothes, similar to those worn by the Formosan Chinese; they speak fluent native dialect as well as their own curious tongue, and a smattering of Japanese. Permitted to dwell in this settlement, not far from a Japanese village, they have cultivated fields of rice and millet, vegetable gardens and banana trees, oranges, pomelos, and clusters of cocoanut palms, sufficient for their use. A few of the children even attend the hill station school conducted for them by the Japanese.

Like all subject races in the Japanese Empire—the Giliaks, the Ainus, the Koreans, the Orokhos—the Formosan aborigines are the physical superiors of their conquerors. Some of them are quite handsome: shoulders broad and muscular, legs straight and bodies tall, the majority close to six feet. The women are slatternly, however, except for a few rare and bright exceptions, when a young girl is suddenly remindful of the infrequent beauty of American Indian women.

There are other items which suggest similarities between these savages and certain of the Central and North American Indians. If we accept the theory that some of the American aborigines are of Malayan descent—and not all sprung from Mongol ancestry, as many ethnologists claim—there may well have been a racial connection with the earliest Formosans, milleniums ago.

Several of the Formosan tribes produced excellent tapestry, beadwork and leather ornamentations, which resemble articles turned out by American Indians. Some of their designs are especially reminiscent of the Navajos, Pueblos, Shawnees, and other western American "Redskins" who attained fine artistry in blanket and rug work. They had birch canoes, too, decorated with herb and bark pigments such as were used by the original Americans; like the latter also they had gaily plumed head-dresses, of the vivid plumage of wild birds.

The Ami, a tribe found on the east coast, manufactured a very durable cloth, made of wood shreds and not dissimilar from the ta-pa for which the Maoris, Tongan, and other South Sea islanders are famous. For their virgins the Ami wove grass skirts and on festival days the maidens performed a dance somewhat like the much misunderstood religious Hula of the race of Kamehameha, in Hawaii.

But little of the past of these primitive people has been recorded. The Japanese have made no serious study of them. They have been too busy pushing them deeper and deeper into the forests primeval, rich in valuable camphor wood, coal and other natural resources.

Over the Vanishing Aborigine the Japanese have shed few tears. Although the case of these first Formosans is much the same story as that of the American Indian, the Hawaiian, the early tribes of South America, their gradual demise here seems to have caused none of that type of sentiment which laments the race-annihilating tactics of imperialism. It is doubtful if the Japanese would stand for such "nonsense." Their idea is to make respectable Mikado-loving, Shinto-worshipping, Japanese-speaking subjects out of them. Where this is not possible they "liquidate" them. This is accomplished either by driving them further up the windy slopes of their tallest mountains, or, more simply, by supplying them with ample quantities of quasi-wood-alcohol with which the barbarians obligingly commit slow suicide.

A foreign missionary with whom I talked assured me that many of the so-called "trading posts" established in frontier regions by the Japanese are in reality little more than dispensaries of that ancient and not too subtle weapon of the West—"fire-water." The Japanese have learned quickly from us.

Like most simple people, the savages here have an insatiable appetite for intoxicants—a thirst which their administrators have done little to discourage. Indeed, in the official Government volume, called "Progressive Formosa," there appears this naive statement about the village of Kaban:

"Strange visitors are always warmly received by these people, especially when they are given presents, say, in the form of sake (Japanese rice brandy). On such occasions the whole village people come out and charming young women begin singing with the accompaniment of rice-pounding with their pestles."

Although there was an abundant supply of sake available at the nearby Japanese town, I neglected to purchase any before coming to Kaban—a fact which may account for my failure to discern the "charming young women" among those villagers who gathered at the communal center and put on their little show for me. Undoubtedly, it is an aid to the enjoyment of certain Oriental exhibitions if both the performers and the audience have liberally imbibed of native liquor.

It was sundown when I reached the settlement, a cluster of grass-roofed huts leaning against the side of a towering pinnacle that broods over lake waters held high in the bosom of a range of mile-tall peaks. The male inhabitants were returning, in their hollow log canoes, from the day's lazy effort at angling. A few of the more ambitious, who have gone into fishing on a larger scale, now drew into the shore with their big cumbersome rafts.

The latter are interesting. About thirty feet in length there is a round-roofed grass hut built aft, where the fisherman keeps his family and such worldly goods as he possesses. Three-fourths of the log raft is given over to the booms from which depends the great net. This is square, about twenty feet on a side, and is supported by four bamboo poles which extend from the main mast. The fisherman poles himself out to a likely spot in the lake and there drops his net. Every fifteen or twenty minutes he lifts it, hoping that a stray fish may have wandered into his little area. It is a slow and exasperating procedure, but it requires a minimum of work on the part of the operator. No doubt it was this last virtue which recommended it to the Chinese who invented the method, centuries ago.

Here in Kaban as elsewhere there are signs of the Chinese influence. These "tame" barbarians closely resemble some of the tribes of south China and it is probable that there has been intermarriage with the earlier settlers from the mainland. But neither their peculiar "orchestra," nor their singing, shows a trace of Sinicism. Both are unique—not merely to the island, but to this tribe alone.

My companion, a Chinese of a family that has lived in Formosa for many generations, introduced me to the headman of Kaban, and arranged for the entertainment. There was an exchange of silver, after which the chief emitted a yell that reached the walls of our mountain canyon and came back in an echo almost as ear-splitting as the original. What a shame to waste such lungs in a faraway tropic paradise, I thought. The fellow would be a certain success as a radio announcer.

His bellow brought the female talent to the lake-front. From the two dozen huts there straggled toothless grandmas, smoking foot-long Chinese pipes, mothers, who sullenly tied gaudy bits of cloth around their breasts, at sight of the foreigner, and five or six young women, dressed in Chinese coats and trousers. There was a number of children, more intelligent looking than their parents, and upon them fell the duty of carrying the novel musical "instruments."

These are long pestles, of varying lengths and weights. The ends are carved mallets, and between them is the narrowly tapered handle, from three to six feet long.

"How do they make the music?" I asked my Chinese friend. "Pound the mallets on each other's skulls?"

But my remark was overlooked, my ignorance forgiven. The chief led us to a little clearing in the center of which was a flat rock, about two feet square.

"Underneath," spoke my companion, "that rock is hollow. When the people of Kaban pound their rice and millet, they put it here, and beat it with these pestles. That was how they discovered this music of theirs."

Around the rock are now grouped a dozen women, ranging from those who have lost their molars to infants who can barely lift their pestles. At a signal from one of them, the orchestra begins.

Curiously, it has a sweet melodious fugue. A kind of tinkle at first, with little heaviness about it. The notes blend harmoniously, and as the time quickens they attain a definite allegro. Obligattos are accomplished by varying the number of beats of the large pestles to the small. It is suggestive of the kind of ensemble that might be obtained from a music box, a hand-organ and a guitar—were it possible to bring the latter into compatible moods.

Dusk softens the contours of the village huts, and the music breathes sweetly in the finer clarity of night air. It reaches suddenly into one, plucks something remote and unvoiced, something of pagan tenderness and the yearnings of youth. Somewhere, deep down, it touches a chord of wonderment and the swift dreams common to all races, all men.

But, abruptly, the pestles stop, the players rest. An old lady expectorates loudly, after which she lights her pipe. The little flame of the match illumines the circle of women whose grandfathers roamed these hills as free men and lords of their forests, unworried by Japanese who wished to curtail their singular desire for heads. But, ah, if they could awake from their troubled graves and recovering their own lost heads, observe what an effeminate world it has become! Here, in the midst of their descendants, sits a lone white man, with neither a gun nor knife to prevent a savage adding his pate to the family shelf.

The old lady knocks out her pipe, and the women gather together again and sing. It is a tribal song, some saga of their heroes—their ancestors. Out over the lake their voices drift and the sound is good. Unlike any Oriental music: too plangent for that. In me their singing recalls Hawaii, and a line from that island's heritage of song creeps back to me:

Ohu Ohu Oahu, I ka ilima . . .

You've heard it in English now, "The Song of the Islands."

For long the singing continues. The song varies, drops from crescendo heights of magnificent tone strength to the repetition of a triad of notes in muted softness, falls lower still to a conventional pattern of monotonous chanting, but rises swiftly, toward the end, and finishes in a rush of dazzling staccato, like blurred wings, intense and exciting. . . .

That's all there is, there isn't any more—because I forgot, as I said, to bring along any sake.

"But—only the women sing?" I ask the Chinese-Formosan.

"Yes, only the women. The music was composed in harvest seasons, long ago, when they ground grain. The men did none of the work. So.— —"

"They never found their voices?"

"Something like that. Anyway, they never take part in these performances. They do a dance though. At New Moon the elders put on their best leather coats and feather caps, and do a slow dance."

The *Sin Fan* (aborigines) worshipped the sun, the moon and ancestors. To those who have come under their cultural influence the Japanese have furnished additional deities, by way of Buddha, Shinto and the spirit of Prince Kitashirakawa, who, having had the misfortune to expire while the Japanese army was subjugating his pater's new southern colony, 35 years ago, has been made patron saint of Formosa. Officially, the Japanese declare that all but a few hundred of the aborigines now recognize the efficacy of Nippon gods: i.e., are "under control."

My investigations are not sufficiently complete for me to state how seriously one may take that phrase, "under control." According to the last figures of census, there are 84,177 barbarians surviving in the island today, and of these only the Taiyals, fiercest and most relentless of the tribes, still have a remnant that refuses to live under Japanese "protection." The number was estimated for me by the Chief of the Foreign Affairs Department, in Taihoku, at less than 500. They are on the east coast, which has never been completely explored; they still live, much as in early times, by fishing and hunting—occasionally heads.

The *aiyu-sen,* that a decade ago was 500 miles long, has now been drawn into a length shorter by 300 miles. Some years ago the Japanese were much criticized for their use of the aiyu-sen—an electrified barbed-wire fence erected to inclose the wildest of the tribesmen and discourage their attacks on border districts. Missionaries especially denounced it, after a number of the Sin Fan had electrocuted themselves. They called it "modern barbarism"—but the Japanese grinned, and reminded them that it was quite all right if such methods were used in fighting barbarians.

In compensation for the loss of their lands, the Japanese point out that they have brought "culture" to the savages, have built schools for them, hospitals, and a few modern villages. Wherever ambition lifts its head, it is said to be encouraged: there are numbers of graduate doctors, dentists and lawyers among the present generation of the "barbarians." The Government has built outposts high in the mountains, where the ex-head-hunters may come down and delight themselves with all the nicknacks purchasable at a Japanese general store—including unlimited quantities of the edifying sake.

How the subject mountain men feel about the present arrangement it is impossible to say. Those who think at all probably consider the bargain has not been entirely unequivocal. But it is doubtful if the majority are any more enthusiastic rooters for Dai Nihon than are the Igorots for Uncle Sam, or the Hindus for John Bull.

From Keelung to Hongkong—
Some Ship-Mates!

Aboard the S.S. Canton Maru, en route to Hongkong—this Japanese steamer, with a tonnage of about 5,000, runs from Keelung, in north Formosa, to Hongkong, via the China treaty ports of Amoy and Swatow.

A colony of the Japanese Empire, Formosa is reserved almost exclusively for Japanese shipping. No foreign ship may carry passengers to and from the island without the payment of excessive docking and anchorage charges. Japanese lines, principally the Osaka Shosen Kaisha and the Nippon Yusen Kaisha, both heavily subsidized by the Emperor, have a virtual monopoly on Formosan freight and passenger traffic.

The Canton Maru is an O.S.K. ship and moves leisurely down the China coast, unworried by competition from a better, swifter service operating from Formosa. There is none. If you wish to go to China you must wait for a Sunday and take passage on the weekly O.S.K. ship— or rot in Formosa.

Shunning the latter, which is the fate of certain foreign tea-tasters doomed to Taihoku, I have accepted the "available transportation." That happens to be second-class travelling in a ten-by-eight cabin stuffed with either sex, who share a common delight in sleeping with the windows closed.

You see there are only a dozen first-class cabins on board, and since I did not apply for passage till two days before sailing time, I was told the last berth had been engaged a week in advance. Nothing left but second-class. Ordinarily, this would not be disturbing news to any but the high-opera taipans, for second-class on most Japanese and foreign ships plying the Pacific gives practically the same eating and sleeping comforts as first-class. The main difference is that there is less leg room and the cutlery doesn't give one that "rich, expansive American feeling."

Much China traffic has piled up in Keelung over a full week. The holds of our vessel are crammed with cargo. More of it, for which there is no room below, spills out upon the open deck. Steerage is filled to capacity with almost two hundred Chinese. And second-class cabins have been booked full also, I am informed.

But it is only when we are out of sight of the shaggy, silver-rimmed hills that border the Formosa coast that I go below and learn the extent of deceit practiced by that be-goggled Japanese employee of the O.S.K. who remarked, when selling me my ticket, "Ano ne; siss ca-been verra nice. Arrasame first-class ca-been."

"No. 5," my ticket reads, so I hail a boy and have him trail after me with my meager luggage. I push back the curtains of No. 5, and look in. There must be a mistake. Some sort of meeting is going on inside. Perhaps Far Eastern W.C.T.U. But no, those are men lying there in their underwear, over in one corner of this cabin—more accurately, "cabinet."

"When is the pow-wow going to break up?" I ask the boy. "When are all these people going back to their own berths?"

The boy grins maliciously. "This is their cabin," he says. "They are not going any place."

I am unconvinced, so I count the heads. Six of them. I count the berths. Six, also. They are built in double tiers, on three sides of the room. And under the single port there is a "sofa," a sort of lounging seat, an "emergency berth." All this leaves a little square of about three feet of deck space between the bunks. And that is already piled high with baggage, so there is no place for mine.

After a brief hesitation, I push my way into the crowd. The two Chinese ladies smile. The Japanese girl giggles. And the three Japanese men look up agreeably. A "*keto-jin,*" a "hairy-foreigner," travelling second-class? This is really more than their money's worth. One of the Chinese ladies looks at me and queries, "*Ing-kuo-jen?*"

"No," I reply. "Not English. The specimen is American, from that land where all people drive their own motor cars and own ice-making machines." But none of them understands English, so I supplement, lamely, in Chinese:

"*Pu tui Ing-kuo-jen. Woh Mei-kuo-jen.*"

This announcement is followed by an exchange of comment among my fellow passengers. A Japanese gentleman, who speaks Mandarin, puts a kimono on over his underwear and tries to engage me in conversation. One of the Chinese ladies says that this is the first time she ever heard of an American travelling second-class. The other one, more mundane, tells her friend that she once was put in a cabin with some American missionaries. She asks me if I am a missionary, and when I deny the charge, everybody seems to feel better at once.

The Strait that lies between China and Formosa is one of the roughest stretches of water along Pacific shores. And the Chinese ladies are not good sailors. We are not half an hour out from Keelung before they climb into their berths. They do not change to pajamas, but simply remove a couple of layers of outer coats and trousers.

One of them has a full stalk of Japanese bananas in a wicker basket that takes up half the floor space, and she keeps eating these and carefully shooting the skins out the port hole. But presently her appetite wanes. The sickness she anticipated by going to bed has come over her and with each lurch of the ship she emits a slight gurgle.

But she is not invidious. She apologizes, turns her face to the bulkhead, and doubtless regrets having eaten so many bananas. The other Chinese lady is in a similar predicament.

To the Japanese girl, who has been sympathetically observing the Chinese ladies, I suggest that what one really needs to prevent seasickness is some fresh air. Wouldn't she like to go up on deck with me? She would.

We sit down in wicker deck chairs and I discover that she is more interesting than I had assumed. She is rather pretty in her blue kimono, flowered with chrysanthemums, and she possesses that utter femininity which is the secret of all that is fragile and charming in Japanese women. But she seems young to be travelling alone. Alone? Why, no, uncle is on board, although of course he has a first-class cabin.

And she is not, she admits, as young as I may think. Nineteen? Twenty-four, she corrects. Well, the Westerner who can come closer than five years to the age of Orientals is merely lucky. But I usually miss the mark widest in judging the years of men.

Yamanada-san (for that is her name) is going to Canton to be a nurse in a Japanese hospital. She has been in a Tokio hospital for three years. And now she will have a better position, with more pay, in Canton. But it is only after I have talked with her for half an hour, in my terribly halting Japanese, that I learn the real reason why she is leaving Tokio.

In one of her rooms at the Tokio sanitorium, there was a student from the Imperial University. He fell in love with Yamanada-san, and when he recovered from his illness and left the hospital, he asked her to marry him. It was highly agreeable to her, but the young man's parents objected. They had already chosen his bride for him when he was twelve years old. The family's honor must be preserved; the engagement could not be broken. And now Yamanada-san is going to Canton, to get far away from Tokio, and broken dreams of love, and old memories that would not be put down.

As we talk, two young men, dressed in Japanese kimonos, walk past. I greet them, for they are fellows I spoke to when I first came aboard. They already know Yamanada-san, so they sit down with us. One of them speaks English, and is a college graduate. The other is a doctor and is going to the same hospital in Canton that has employed Yamanada-san. But neither of them is Japanese, although they have been educated in Japan. They are Japanized Formosans—"Honto-Jin," descendants of pioneer Chinese immigrant families who settled two centuries ago on the island now owned by the Mikado.

When I ask them why they are going to China, they laugh self-consciously and exchange some quick words in Japanese. Then the English-speaking one says:

"We are sent to Canton by our parents. They want us to learn to become Chinese again. We have been in Japan so long our parents say we are not their sons, but Japanese boys."

Thinking of Yamanada-san's experience, I ask them if they are engaged to marry Japanese girls. They both smile as if they had a great many mutual sentiments. One of them admits that he formerly had a sweetheart in Osaka whom he wished to marry. But she was a geisha and his father threatened to disown him if he took her for a bride; besides it was his father's demand that he marry a Chinese girl.

The doctor, who is just beginning his practice, has had similar difficulties over a Japanese girl in Formosa, to whom he is still secretly engaged. He says it is his intention to marry her when he returns from Canton. That will not be for two years. Perhaps it is unkind of me, but I remark that many things can happen in two years. Canton is fabled to have the most beautiful women in China.

But they are not interested in Chinese girls. Neither of them has had a Chinese female friend since he was very young. They insist they will not marry Chinese and they enumerate the virtues of Japanese women which make them in every respect more admirable. Besides, they confess that they cannot speak a sentence of Cantonese.

Presently, Yamanada-san excuses herself with a "Sayonara!" and we shout after her, "*O Yasumi nasai!*"—"Good sleep to you!" But I think of that little parcel of a cabin, heavy with sea-sickness, and I wonder if it will be possible for her to sleep at all. It is long afterward when I go down to try it myself.

It is, in fact, one o'clock. Although all the lights in the cabin are on, Yamanada-san and the two Chinese women are asleep. Two of the Japanese men are talking in unhushed voices and the third is reading a paper-backed book that has on its cover a picture of a moga—a modern Japanese girl—and an equally sophisticated young man, embracing each other in approved American cinematic style.

There is no room to undress here, so I go outside, slip into a kimono and return with hope that the Japanese gentlemen will soon grow tired of talking and reading love stories, and will turn out the lights. It is another hour before the cabin is quiet. I venture to open the port window, and cut off the lights. In a little while I am asleep.

Half an hour later I am awake again. The room is bright and someone has closed the port. The husband of the two Chinese ladies is talking in a loud and persuasive voice. In his hands are two bowls of rice and chopped chicken. He is trying to induce the ladies to eat, for they have had nothing but those bananas all day. Neither of them is taking the slightest notice of him, but he is not discouraged. Occasionally he jabs a wife in the back and exclaims:

"*Sa! Ni-ni chefan bu-yao-ah!* This is a deplorable situation. You must eat or you will surely die. Come, now, a little rice inside of you will help matters a great deal. *Sa!* Come quickly!"

After an interminable interval during which all the solicitous man gets for his trouble is an occasional emphatic "*bu-yao*" from the women, he goes off to where he is probably playing mahjong with others like himself, who do not believe in sleep.

Again I put out the lights, open the port. About an hour later I am awakened by loud conversation between the two Japanese. From what I can understand of the talk, it has occurred to one of the men that the other was mistaken in an opinion he voiced earlier in the evening. They are silk merchants and the ensuing argument has to do with some new patterns which they are going to buy in Kwangtung.

The Chinese husband returns with his rice bowls. "*Ni hsueh-chao ah?* When are you going to get up and eat like a human? Verily, it is said that of all animals women are the most stupid"—He chatters on in that incredible Cantonese dialect.

Outside, the waves slap lustily against the sides of the ship. Through the port sifts a gathering circle of faintest light and there is one lingering moment of quiet. The Chinese retires, having finally abandoned his efforts to stimulate appetite in his females. The Japanese silk merchants begin to snore.

In a little while it will be dawn, and all clamor and activity. Then the Japanese will open the port wide to the morning air; then they will consent to cut off the lights; then the Chinese women may even get up and eat some rice and chicken. But it will no longer be possible for me to sleep.

II. Canton, Where the Chinese National Revolution Began, Plus Hong Kong and Macao

Introduction to Section II

Despite the impressive number of miles Snow traveled during his initial two-year stay in China, he had never gone south from Shanghai to Canton, the seat of the national revolution. So he planned, as he resumed his around-the-world trip, to fill this gap in his exploration of the geography underlying modern Chinese history. He also found it imaginatively satisfying to retrace the routes by which the West had discovered and come to influence the East. Canton had been visited by Hindu and Arab merchants in the tenth century. The Portuguese had traded regularly with Canton in the sixteenth century.

The Pearl River flows past Canton into a large estuary dotted with islands, one of which, Hong Kong, was ceded to the British in the nineteenth century. It quickly became an international port rivaling Canton. Macao, the older, Portuguese harbor in the Boca Tigris estuary, never developed as a significant trade rival, but it had achieved notorious supremacy as a "clearing house for the eroticisms" and a gambling center by the time of Snow's visit. Hong Kong and Macao, however, seemed to him only incidental. His primary interest was Canton, the origin of "the Nationalist revolution that still gives promise of uniting all China." He arrived in Canton sometime during the second week of October and stayed through the celebration of Sun Yat-sen's birthday on November 12. Since Canton was the earliest urban capital of the national revolution and hence the city longest ruled by the Kuomintang, Snow hoped to find in Canton evidence of the promise and problems of the emerging China.

The incongruous eclecticism of the Sun Yat-sen memorial described in the opening selection suggests Snow's view of the modern Chinese nationalist movement. It seemed to him to be made up of fragments of Western revolutionary thought not yet thoroughly assimilated into an authentically integrated Chinese national expression. But he also assumed that Canton's long exposure to foreign cultures and peoples made it the appropriate origin of Chinese national revolution. At this point in his career, like many foreign visitors, Snow still viewed revolutionary thought in China as principally a response to foreign influences.

His second article is about the island of Shameen's international settlement. It begins with an apparent tribute to foreign entrepreneurship capped by an ironic review of the events that led to the massive 1926 boycott of British goods, one of the most dramatic and effective early demonstrations of the depth and strength of the people's feeling against the extraterritorial power that had been ceded to foreign countries.

The *China Weekly Review* did not reprint Snow's piece on Shameen until he was already back in Shanghai, about ten months after he wrote it. Eugene Chen, the fiery Kuomintang official mentioned in the article, quickly took offense and telegrammed that Snow's references to him amounted to "an unmitigated lie. I have never lived in Shameen, under a British passport or otherwise, for two days or for any other period of time." Snow replied in the next issue: "As the story was written last October obviously it could not have been with the purpose of injuring Mr. Chen or of jeopardizing his political career in China, since at that time he was sojourning elsewhere and supposedly had definitely left the scene. . . . However, I do not see that there is anything disgraceful in a man's utilizing any legitimate means to avoid being killed or imprisoned by his political opponents in China."[1]

Snow was skeptical of the mythification of Sun Yat-sen then in process. Chiang Kai-shek's obvious political machinations to assume Sun's mantle ripely merited the frequent diatribes Chiang had received from the foreign press of Shanghai during the last two years of Snow's residence there. Chiang had drawn the press's criticism through his courtship and marriage of Soong Mei-ling (the sister of Sun's widow, Soong Ching-ling), his efforts to identify the widow with his cause despite her explicit public repudiations, and his building of the Sun Yat-sen Memorial in Nanking, Chiang's choice of a national capital in repudiation of the former governing body at Wuhan. Thus Snow was happy to discover and write about another Cantonese doctor who was a very loyal friend to Sun Yat-sen and who had left a heritage of more immediately beneficial public service. The Wu Hon Memorial Hospital was more clearly a success than the realization of Sun Yat-sen's airy *San Min Chu-i.*

Nevertheless Snow did feel it imperative to visit Dr. Sun's childhood home in Choy Hang before leaving the area. That Agnes Smedley should be one of the two Americans who preceded his visit to the Sun home that year is a notable coincidence, particularly since Smedley had almost certainly briefed him on the Indian nationalist movement and provided him with introductions to nationalist leaders whom he

1. *China Weekly Review,* September 5, 1931, and September 12, 1931.

was on his way to meet. Snow notes in his article that Smedley recorded her regret that "the original clay hut where Sun Yat-sen was born has not been preserved to show how he came from the poorest and humblest of people." He then also notes that "Dr. Sun was impatient with antiquities. He wanted no sentiment in removing that crude ancestral home when he returned from the 'outside lands' with money enough to build something more modern and comfortable." It seems likely that Snow intended Sun's understandable desire to put the restrictions of his impoverished youth behind him as a mild rebuke of Smedley's more romantic attitude to memorialize them. This probably was part of a continuing friendly quarrel with Smedley. Certainly Smedley's strong proletarian loyalties would have made it unlikely for her to represent the entrepreneurial skills of Tang Shao-yi, the ex-premier of China and patriarchal leader of the neighboring village of Tang Kai Chuen, with such warm appreciation as did Snow in his previous article.

Yet, like Smedley, Snow did believe in justice as a measure of the success of an emerging nation's revolutionary ideals. Shortly after arriving in Canton, Snow was introduced to G. Edward Lyon, an American lawyer unusually fluent in Cantonese who was winning acceptance in Canton's courts. The two met through Kan Teh-yuan, the editor of *China Truth*. It was Lyon who escorted Snow on his visits to the courts described in the articles included here. The case of the old man accused of selling imitations of Everready batteries was Lyon's case.[2] Snow wrote a separate story about Lyon, featuring his unusual success as an American lawyer in Chinese courts, for the *New York Sun*.[3] Apparently he felt that in the articles reprinted here acknowledging and explaining the role of an American lawyer in a Cantonese court would distract from the issue of how justice worked for the ordinary citizen. Thus he describes himself visiting the courts in the company of "a young Chinese barrister." He very likely also chose fiction as more effective than fact in the romantic story of his visit to Repulse Bay with a Chinese friend unhappily married to an American "five-and-ten store" girl.

Snow reports mixed grades for justice in Canton. Au Yang-ku, the young director of the Bureau of Public Safety, is described as modest, enlightened, and effective. His police force wins high praise. The

2. Snow, transcript of diary 1A: 69–71.

3. "U.S. Attorney First of His Kind," unidentified clipping dated December 3, 1930, Snow's scrapbook.

courts, on the other hand, have a long way to go. The possible saving grace is the youthfulness of the judges. Snow's lawyer friend notes that the government hopes "that these younger men, who are getting valuable experience, will form the basis for a sound, modern judicial system a few years from now." The modern Legal Code recently announced in Nanking and supposedly in effect in the courts and jails of Canton had clearly not yet prevailed against some of the traditional sources of power. Snow cites instances where political and military power continue to make the workings of the court seem flagrantly cruel and unfair. His story from Hon San-so, in particular, strongly suggests that the noble pronouncements of equal justice for men and women are as yet little more than hollow-sounding words.

Chronology 1930

October 9 or 10	Arrives Canton; Stays until after November 12
November 17	Arrives Macao, on boat from Hong Kong
November 18	Arrives Tang Kai Chuen and Choy Hang, by car
November 19	Travels Macao to Hong Kong

Canton,
Metropolis of South China

Where the Feverish Rush of Occidental Cities
Is Noted—Much of the Old Has Made Way
for Modern Progress

One reaches this city from Hongkong after a night's enchanted trip up the moon-slivered Chu-kiang. Romantic with its unreefed junk sails athwart the low bordering hills, it is a river like no other, gentle and exotic, beautiful as peace and warm from the southland rice paddies deep in the hinterland.

Chu-kiang to the Chinese, it is the River of Pearl to Westerners. Over it, per mile of length, moves five times as much traffic as over any other stream in China. Besides the race of sampaners who are born, live and die upon it, the Chu-kiang supports a dozen steamship lines, ferry service and countless river junks and fishermen. And it is historic, significantly so. Up its treacherously sand-barred channel the first Occidental ships felt their way into the realm of the Imperial Dragon more than four centuries ago.

Stirring events have occurred in Canton since then. Here the opium wars of the middle nineteenth century were fought. Here white men first wrested from Chinese their peculiar privileges of extraterritoriality. Here was brewed the first savage distrust that still hampers relations between China and the Occident. And here began the Nationalist revolution that still gives promise of uniting all China.

Long years of contact with the West have greatly altered the facade Canton presents to the visitor. It is a modern port you enter today, the most impressive yet developed under purely Chinese administration. The Bund is lined with buildings of Western style, some of them, it is true, beginning to sag a bit dangerously.

Your steamer sidles up to the Canton Bund. It misses by inches a score of cumbersome river craft, junks, barges and perhaps a motor boat or two. It sends a thousand sampans irritably scurrying from its berth along the stone quay. Gangways cover the distance to the shore, and the ship is at the mercy of an invading regiment of half-naked coolies avid for luggage.

Out in the harsh clamor of the street you are a little shocked with the strange noises, bewildered by this abrupt meeting with seething Asia.

Over a million people dwell here. It is densely congested. This you rapidly realize, once you have been swept into the surge and swell of Canton's humanity. It floods unceasingly over the city's forty-five miles of surfaced highways. It ebbs and trickles in and out of the uncounted labyrinth of ancient insect-breeding streets that have yet to know the blessing—or curse—of roadmaking reforms.

Canton is one of the few cities in the Orient that is charged with the feeling of metropolis. Unlike Nanking, Foochow, Mukden, even Hankow, where immense populations manage to be only villagers pretending at urbanism, Canton seems convincingly grown up. It may be because people talk so fast in this incredible dialect. It may be because they have a city-bred restlessness about their ways, and often walk as if they were really going somewhere. Perhaps it is only because the rickshas move more swiftly, though less comfortably, on hard, airless tires. Again it may be merely that a solitary laborer, digging a sewer in the street, will attract a crowd around him more quickly than he could anywhere else but in New York.

Generalizing, the Cantonese seem to be better dressed than most northerners. Certainly they wash their clothes oftener, likewise their bodies. Silk is cheap and not uncommon apparel among the more thrifty of the proletariat. It is a rare amah or household servant who does not boast at least one satin coat and pair of flowery silken trousers.

You notice here that women cling to those trousers, old-fashioned as they are, and that most of them have natural feet. Cantonese femininity seems to prefer foreign cosmetics to the native rice powder and vegetable rouge. Regardless of which is used, the application is rather too generous. Those modest examples of the lyric, fragile beauty for which Canton's women and China were both once famous are seldom seen any more.

Canton, foreigners assure you, is not the picturesque place it was before Sun Yat-sen started the asphalt crusades. Most lately lamented of the byways liquidated by the new passion for pavements is Jade street. Nothing is left of it but an ugly gash in a district bleeding with half-demolished buildings, through which the Government is extending one of its so-called boulevards. Dealers in China's most exquisite stone, for the artistic carving of which the Cantonese have long been celebrated, are now scattered to all parts of the city.

Ivory, Lantern, Lacquer and Blackwood streets have met similar fates. With the dispersion of the ancient craftsmen from their time-stained workshops, the delights of a visit to Canton are fewer. No doubt the new highways are a source of great satisfaction to officials who drive motor cars, but they have sadly disrupted the old spirit of shopping. It is all very bewildering. There is no one to tell you what happened to Fat Sen's lacquer shop, or where Long On has moved his jade lapidaries, or whatever has become of Sing Lo, whose place used to be at the head of Embroidery street.

And yet Cantonese lanes, even with their perilous modern traffic, remain one of the memorable experiences of China travelers. Roving through them is a journey through one endless bazaar.

Fruit stalls range for blocks, with their luscious tropic products glistening, satiny as dew, and at night tempting under flickering lantern light. There are pineapples, small, but sweeter than the well-advertised Hawaiian brands. There are hairy coconuts, yellow pears, citrony pomelos, and small bananas, golden, or the highly prized Tonkinese variety, silky black. Nearly always there are great quantities of the perishable lichee, inexpensive and good here, which in the north are in a class with caviar. Papaya melons, royal and musky, are a staple food of the Cantonese, and lusty scarlet persimmons, fat and dripping sweetness, are cheap enough for the coolies, who eat them on the spot. Most tender, most favored by epicures is the star-shaped *yang-to,* the "foreign peach," its winey flavor sealed in a waxy jacket and colored like early autumn leaves, too perfect to seem real.

From the number of restaurants and tea houses you see on every street you conclude that the Cantonese are well advanced in the art of eating. You are right. It is said that the Chinese race consumes 10,000,000 bushels of rice every twenty-four hours. You decide that fully one-half of it must be digested in Canton. Find five Cantonese sitting down and three of them will be handling chop-sticks.

Nowadays Canton has sprawled to such distances that even the unhurried visitor must submit to transportation in what the local residents fondly call "taxicabs." Most of them are hand-downs from private owners in the treaty ports and have seen their best years of service before they begin to jolt over Canton macadam. Their pilots are freelancers, roaming buccaneers of the road, who follow you for blocks and invite you to risk your life with them at prices outrageous even in the depreciated silver twenty-cent pieces used in Canton. However, there are two or three more or less regular garages near Shameen, the foreign settlement, where you can get a fairly recent model of an American car for 40 Canton dollars a day—the equivalent, at present, of about 10 American greenbacks.

Mustering your courage, you hire one of these, instructing the driver to keep his eyes off the scenery and convey you down Taiping Malou. That is the main stem of Canton. As wide as Fifth Avenue, it resembles it in no other way. Over it you go through crowds that still prefer streets to sidewalks. Policemen, on every corner, timorously assume the responsibility of directing traffic.

Their efforts are regarded with hostility by your chauffeur. Frequently he ignores their frantic gestures completely. He drives fast and in a straight line, swerves only after collision seems a certainty, and keeps his hand on the horn from the time you start till you arrive, a broken neurotic, at the end of your journey. By then you have decided that what Canton really needs is a klaxon that automatically goes on and off with the motor.

Barring accidents, in less than half an hour you are at the outskirts of the city, in a region known as Yut Sau Shan. Here is Canton's newest and finest temple of hero-worship, the Sun Yat-sen Memorial. High on a hill, the long obelisk, and just below it the octagonal meeting hall, its curving purple roofs suggestive of the Temple of Heaven, are nearly completed. They are not yet open to the public, but you can wander over the gardened terraces that slope abruptly, picturesquely, Orientally down to the busy streets below.

But that is not the purpose of this pilgrimage; you have come out to visit the "72 Heroes Monument," secluded in an extensive grove of firs and cryptomeria. It was built in honor of the exploit of "Dare to Die" revolutionaries, whose attack on the Imperial Yamen in Canton was one of the first attempts to overthrow the Manchu dynasty. Seventy-two of them, trapped in secret passageways of the Yamen, were captured and beheaded.

Until the recent construction of the Sun Ling, Sun Yat-sen's $3,000,000 mausoleum at Nanking, this was the unique architectural product of the revolution. Perhaps you would not say it is a freak; parts of it, considered separately, are well executed. It is the incongruous combination that strikes you as ludicrous. For instance, on a carved pavilion there is an Egyptian obelisk, while back of it is a stone reproduction of the Liberty Bell. Beyond this is a building remindful of the Trianon of Versailles, on the roof of which is imposed a pyramid of heavy granite. Topping it all, and gazing out from almond eyes over high Mongol cheek bones, is a ten-foot replica of Bartholdi's statue of "Liberty Enlightening the World"!

Cantonese from all over the world gave funds for this tribute to fellow townsmen who they understood had died for freedom. That was in 1911, when overseas Chinese still believed in a "republic" of China.

There is a story told about the memorial which has it that several of the largest contributors could not agree about the form. In the end they reached a complicated compromise including various ideas. When put into stone the result was the curiously grotesque thing you see today.

As you motor back through a soft dusk it suddenly occurs to you how this has a stranger, a larger significance. These men created something typical, a record true to China since the revolution. Nothing could be more symbolic of the far chaos and suffering, the stubborn conflict of beliefs, and the stupidity and selfishness that have torn China for the last twenty years.

The Island of Shameen
in the Pearl River

an International Settlement
Reclaimed from a Sandbar Which Now
Is the Site of the Foreign Concession

Many rice boats have floated down the Pearl River since it carried the first Portuguese navigators up to the portals of Canton. That event, according to Portuguese historians, occurred in the fifteenth century.

Unfortunately, for those who came after them, these early European visitors failed to make a favorable impression on the prideful Chinese. "Free Companions" they were, probably more familiar with piracy than honest trade, and the Celestials may have been justified in refusing to permit them to enter Canton.

Lagging two centuries behind the adventurers from Lisbon came the stolid Dutch, who sought legitimate commerce with this southernmost port of the Empire. They fared better; the Chinese offered them for purposes of trade and residence a tiny island adjoining the city. But the Dutch, doubtless more ambitious, haughtily refused it. Time proved their decision hasty. Today that land is the most valuable in Canton. Hollanders resident here now endure the jest of hearing it called the "Dutch Folly."

Not till early in the nineteenth century were white men permitted to dwell in Canton. Even then their colony, known as the "Factories," was kept outside the city's massive walls. Rapidly the settlement grew, despite the hostility of Manchu officials. By 1820 it included a number of Americans, Englishmen, and Europeans of various nationalities. It was the beginning of major Occidental influence in China, the initial thrust of modern industrialism in the East, the precursor of the Euro-Asian trading communities found today in all great ports of this country.

Long ago the "Factories," pathetic little streets of mud-ramparted compounds, were superseded. For more than seventy years now foreigners have done business from the esoteric isolation of Shameen, a green little blister clinging to the Canton Bund.

Separated from the mainland by a fifty-foot moat channel of sampans and putrefaction, Shameen is reminiscent of the difficult past. It is symbolic of the gap that still yawns between mutual comprehension of East and West. Aloof, dignified with its fine old banyan-shaded esplanades, it is full of a Victorian sort of solidity, oddly untouched by the swift newness of the Chinese city that lies beyond its two ridiculously brief but well guarded bridges.

If you are on deck in time you can see Shameen off to the left as your steamer pulls in toward Canton. But the view is hardly worth interrupting sleep. Dream on, for regardless of your own wishes in the matter your luggage coolies will be sure to lead you, when eventually you awake, to the foreigners' sanctum sanctorum. It is even conceivable that you may be grateful for this refuge at the edge of what appears to be all chaos, but in reality is nothing more disagreeable than a noisome Chinese waterfront.

From your boat landing it is only a few minutes to the French bridge, which joins the eastern end of the diminutive island with an otherwise all-Chinese city. Crossing it, you are saluted by a French marine, armed with a bayoneted rifle. And on the other shore is an Annamite, similarly attired, who repeats the gesture like a puppet, till you puff with a new appreciation of your importance in the world. Voila! You are in Shameen. Or, to be more precise, in French Shameen.

When the foreign opium dealers took over this concession in 1859 it was only a dismal sandbar that disappeared at high tide. The Chinese thought the Europeans mad to accept such a site. The Manchu Officials, who considered that they had played a clever joke on the white merchants, sniggered up their wide silk sleeves. But unlike the disdaining Dutchmen, the French and British viewed their grant seriously. Around it they erected high, stout, stone retaining walls. Between them they dumped enough earth to fill in an area of forty-four acres. And, much to the chagrin of the astonished Asiatics, they built and cultivated their colony till even the Viceroy admitted it was more habitable than any spot in the city of the "Broad East," Canton itself.

The cost of reclaiming Shameen was $325,000, in Chinese silver. Four-fifths of the amount was underwritten by the British; the balance was supplied by the French. Proportionately the settlement is owned today by France and England, each country maintaining its separate government for its little patch of territory. Other foreigners are tolerated as residents, but no Chinese, save menials, may dwell here. There is a considerable sprinkling of Americans. All told, the foreigners number 710, and require the presence of about 2,200 Chinese servants to look after them. Our consulate is in Shameen, as are also the consulates of Belgium, Italy, Japan, Portugal, Sweden, the Netherlands and, of course, the colony's co-proprietors.

No rickshas are permitted on Shameen, no automobiles, no horses. Unless you ride a bicycle, roller skate or succumb to the whimsicality of a palanquin, thereby inviting bemused stares from the residents, this is one place in China where you have to employ the means of locomotion with which foreigners in the Orient so often forget they are endowed—i.e., the human legs.

But walking here is pleasant. The three longitudinal streets of the island are pairs of wide footways, divided by long strips of green, shaded with great leaf-heavy trees, sweet with gardens' breath and overhung by a soporific quiet, sharply antipodal to the crowded *ma-lus* of China, only an archer's shot away.

Flanking the geometrical precision of office buildings and homes, substantial and European in architectural front and interior design, are rows of tennis courts, bowling greens and a cricket field. In one place there is a children's playground, while on their end the French have installed an edifying exhibit once intended as a zoo. Decadence has engulfed it, however, till the most ferocious of the remaining beasts is a loquacious, flea-bitten monkey, whose ludicrous attempts to scrape the few remaining hairs from his ancient rump afford a spectacle of perennial delight to the Chinese servant population.

Following the generous cement walk that encircles the island, you come to the Victoria Hotel, whence Thomas Cook and the steamship companies diligently direct all passing foreigners. In Canton there is now the eight-story New Asia, which offers certain advantages over the Victoria; namely, showers, running hot and cold water, an American restaurant, and floors that do not slant at a twenty-degree angle. But of these remarkable innovations pallid complexioned visitors seldom hear. Meekly they follow their guides, who from force of habit, or the promise of fat "*kumsha*," escort their charges to the Victoria.

The "manager" of this quaint caravanserai is a half-legendary Englishman named William Farmer. Not many of his customers ever succeed in facing him on the premises, nor are the evidences of his direction any more readily discernible. But in the grill room are some brave oils and pastels which are signed, in quite legible three-inch letters, "Wm. Farmer," so the individual undoubtedly exists. His gallery, by the way, is worth inspecting. There is none of this modernistic nonsense about it. Mr. Farmer thoughtfully has labeled each picture with a legend so large that even myopic folk cannot possibly mistake a Soo-chow canal for a drawing room scene in London.

Actually, the hotel for many years has been mostly owned and oper-ated by Chinese. Here, as elsewhere in foreign concessions, no Chinese can hold property in his own name. So the Victoria's Cantonese owner-mortgagers are obliged to keep their possession a sub-rosa affair and subscribe to the fiction of foreign management. Indeed, capital is made of this point, for in English language newspapers up and down the China coast the establishment boastfully advertises itself as "the only hotel in Canton under direct foreign supervision."

That statement fails to take cognizance of the Japanese, who also have a hotel on Shameen. But the Nipponese have never objected to the absent-minded British method of censuring the non-Chinese popu-lation of treaty ports as so many "foreigners and Japanese," so perhaps they see nothing misleading in Mr. Farmer's newspaper advertisements. Anyway, the Japanese "Shameen Hoteru" does not clamor for white patronage. It is a stern gray edifice that resembles a Chinese ware-house-pawnshop and little suggests the paper windows and June roses of Tokio's charming *yado-ya*. Behind iron-shuttered windows that are never opened the hotel flourishes, principally by obliging Japanese sailormen in romantic distress.

There is a Japanese sukiyaki house, also, which is well patronized by seamen and foreigners of all nationalities. Next to it is a Japanese beauty parlor. Here courtesans of Chinese politicians come to have their nails manicured, their bobbed hair waved, and their vague eye-brows all but completely removed. It is alleged by some that the real motive of their frequent visits is to promenade before the admiring male onlookers in front of the Victoria and the Sailors' "Y" in what the missionary ladies describe as their "sinful silks."

Wholly without relevance to the above gossip, Shameen is consid-ered the most attractive real estate buy in the neighborhood of Canton. Certain residences and business buildings here have been financed, or taken over, by Chinese capital, the property titles ostensibly remain-ing, however, in the hands of privileged foreigners. Shameen is the one spot where the bourgeois merchants—or Kuomintang officials—may rest their profits with serenity. It is the one place where money may be invested today with the reasonable certainty that the property will not be confiscated tomorrow. For Shameen alone continues unchanged in status, despite all vicissitudes of politics and the vagaries of what some-times seems to be rather loosely termed the "Government" of Canton.

Shameen guarantees safety of person as well as purse. Dethroned Chinese generals in the past have sought haven behind the protection of foreign gunboats here. Latterly the preference seems to be for Hong-kong, toward which an entire Government has been known hastily to retreat down the Chu-kiang without previous notice.

Sometimes, in emergencies, Shameen is still used. Eugene Chen, former Minister of Foreign Affairs for the Nationalist Government, found his British passport convenient when for two days he is reported to have hidden in Shameen while his enemies were scouring the alleys of Canton for him. Last summer, when Chang Fah-kwei's rebels were bombarding Canton, the Warlord-Governor, Chen Ming-hsu, hurriedly sent his wife and valuables to Shameen. There they were kindly received by the Chinese compradore of a foreign banking institution with which the Governor intrusts what is reliably said to be a large personal fortune—in Hongkong dollars.

Despite this official confidence in its tranquillity, there have been times when Shameen was not a healthy region. The latest of these was not so long ago, during what has become known to the world as the Shakee Affair. On that occasion a crowd of several hundred armed students, soldiers and agitators, excited by Red propaganda, led by Russians, marched to the foot of the British bridge and conducted a mass demonstration directed against the "Shameen Imperialists." Inevitably, trouble ensued.

Foreigners do not agree among themselves as to who fired the first shot, though unanimous in the opinion that it came from the Chinese. Some of them declare it was a Whampoa cadet. Some say it was a Russian. One "eyewitness" maintains that a frenzied chauvinistic student, aiming at a missionary who had once taught him English, started the tragic encounter. The British Consul-General swears over oath that it was a Chinese soldier. But despite all this excellent testimony, the Chinese still insist that the fatal bullet was sped by an English resident of Shameen.

The engagement lasted for about twenty minutes. Chinese soldiers, urged by their Russian advisers, tried to take the British bridge. A line of bluejackets held it with machine guns. From behind barbed wire entanglements, from within barricaded guardhouses stretched along the Shameen Bund, French and British soldiers and sailors returned the fire of the Chinese across the canal. About 120 Orientals were killed or wounded. Foreign casualties were slight, with a Frenchman killed and half a dozen British soldiers wounded.

Following this incident there occurred a strike of all Chinese employed on Shameen, and an extensive boycott of Great Britain and British goods. For six months the luxury-loving taipans on the island had to scramble their own eggs, sweep their floors, and light their own Havana cigars. It was terrible. Some of them found their domestic tasks so exhausting that they closed up their offices and moved to Hongkong. By the time the strike was settled the surviving foreigners were almost willing to forfeit their cherished extraterritoriality rights in exchange for Chinese cooks and some minions who would obediently answer "Yes, mastah!" to the imperious call of "Boy!"

Something like this may happen again, despite all that foreigners can do to prevent it. But a repetition seems less likely if slower belligerence, greater patience and more potent applications of common sense govern future relations of the Shameenites and the Cantonese.

Two Cantonese Doctors
Who Made Asiatic History

Twenty-four years ago two young Chinese doctors in this city pledged loyalty to each other, and mutually promised to work ceaselessly for the overthrow of the alien Manchu Dynasty, and for the spread of education and scientific knowledge among their countrymen.

One of them was Dr. Sun Yat-sen, founder of the Kuomintang, and for 14 years acknowledged leader of the only genuinely revolutionary party in China. During his life he was a character more pathetic and more politically ridiculous than Woodrow Wilson, but, since his death, history has chosen him as one of the great Asiatics of all time.

The other man, Dr. Wu Hon, is not so well known abroad. Less spectacular, less dramatic, he nevertheless made his contribution to the republican idea. Through all of Dr. Sun's fiascos, Dr. Wu never deserted him. And it was in support of Dr. Sun Yat-sen, in opposition to the imperial ambitions of Yuan Shih-kai, that Dr. Wu eventually lost his head, in Peking.

Today, Wu Hon is an honored name in the long roll of patriots listed among those early martyrs who died in the service of the Kuomintang. In the north, known as a politician, his own province remembers him as a physician, a surgeon, and one of the earliest modern doctors in China. In 1904, he established the first European hospital in Canton under Chinese management and operation.

After his assassination at the hands of henchmen of Yuan Shih-kai, the Southern Provisional Government temporarily took over that hospital. While Dr. Sun Yat-sen ruled here, new equipment was added to the institution, its school for the training of nurses and midwives was greatly enlarged, and it was renamed the Wu Hon Memorial Hospital. Until the $1,000,000 Municipal Hospital was recently completed, it was perhaps the best of its kind in Canton. Its school of obstetrics is still the largest in south China.

In 1922, the buildings and equipment were restored to the Wu family when the deceased revolutionary's son, Dr. Wu Pak-liang, returned from France, where he had received his M.D. at the University of Lyons. Since then it has been a privately conducted hospital, although the public clinic has continued to be of wide popular service, and at no time has been a profit-making enterprise.

Dr. Wu Pak-liang is now politically one of the most active men in Canton. He is a member of the Municipal Council, Director of the Bureau of Social Affairs and executive head of several other departments of the Government. Despite these activities, however, he still manages to spend from three to six hours at the Wu Hon Memorial Hospital each day.

Four other members of the family participate in the administration of various departments of the institution. Dr. Wu's brother, his sister, and his sister-in-law are all graduate doctors and each cooperates in the management of Wu Hon. His wife, who received her degree from the Hackett Medical College, is in charge of the midwifery branch, which is known as the Ta Keung School of Obstetrics.

The hospital has had an eventful history. At times its 40 rooms have been crowded with wounded soldiers, rushed bleeding from the front. It has tended Communists, and victims of the Communists; it has cared for military tyrants and for peasants who did battle for them; it has housed Nationalist troops wounded by machine-gun fire from English blue-jackets, and it has mended the broken heads of student agitators. But it is the school of midwifery that is perhaps more interesting, more socially significant.

"During the 26 years my father's hospital has been operating," Dr. Wu Pak-liang told your correspondent, "we have graduated over 1,100 students. These women have gone back to their homes, in all parts of this province, and have established practices of their own and set up a tradition of midwifery in south China. Some of them now have small hospitals; others have begun schools in their villages."

At present there are 340 students in the Ta Keung School. The majority of them are under 21 and while most of them come from the vicinity of Canton, there is a good percentage from other cities, other provinces. Dormitories in the hospital compound enable them to live here throughout their period as interns, which extends over two years. The course offered, the writer is informed by foreign medical men here, is comparable in modernity and thoroughness with that available at similar colleges in America. But, consider the difference in the costs!

The full tuition fee for one year is $60, Canton money—about $15, U.S. currency. For board and room the girls are charged the equivalent of about $2.50 in American coin. The tuition fee includes free use of the laboratories, libraries, music room, study hall—all the facilities of the school. Even the neat white aprons and nurse's caps which are worn as a uniform by all students, are supplied by the hospital. It is no wonder that Dr. Wu and his associates have to turn down the applications of several tens of girls each term.

"But you won't get rich quick that way, Doctor!" this interested visitor to the hospital exclaimed.

Dr. Wu said he was not interested in money. "It is my ambition to see the Chinese, as a race, equal to any in the world. I know of no better way to achieve this than to do all in my power to see that every child born on China's soil is brought into the world with all the aid of enlightened medical science."

The results of nearly three decades of effort at Wu Hon have begun to show results in Canton. There is less infanticide, there are fewer children's diseases, there are more sound, healthy babies, and there are fewer deaths at parturition than in any other city of similar size in China. Gradually the unsanitary and superstitious practices of the old crones who once were regarded as necessary evils in connection with every nascence, have been eliminated. Today their clientele is largely restricted to the water folk, or *tan-min,* who live almost exclusively in their various sampans and other small craft on the rivers and canals of Kwangtung, beyond the reach of modernization.

Justice Is More Advanced in Canton Than Elsewhere

but There Are Occasional Lapses!

Walking into the arms of the law voluntarily always fills me with an uneasiness that would appear to be born of a guilty conscience. And yet I have never made a million dollars, nor even killed a man. To my recollection I have been guilty of crimes no more malicious than tossing stones at new street lamps, or thumbing one's nose at a copper's back. Of course there is prohibition, in America—but that is different.

Nevertheless, as I enter the great pailou that opens into the compound of the Canton Lower Court, I am much agitated when two gendarmes suddenly smack their heels together, lift their bayoneted rifles above their shoulders, glare menacingly at me, and shout something that sounds like "Hrrmmph!"—which is a word I do not understand.

Fortunately, my companion, a young Chinese barrister grasps me by the arm encouragingly. "Never mind," he says, "That's their order. They salute that way every time a lawyer or an official goes through the gate."

If they do all that for a mere lawyer, I wonder what happens when a general comes to visit the Court. But I do not say this to my friend, who might misinterpret my remark as a thrust at the importance of his profession.

We walk into an open space, off which branch numerous lanes leading to various buildings of the Court. Ranged on long benches that reach into a little flower garden are perhaps 50 or 60 Chinese men and women, of all classes: merchants, bankers, coolies, amahs, and here and there a soldier. They are witnesses, waiting to testify before the magistrates and judges.

On one of these benches, which are open to the blue, hot heavens, I sit down with the lawyer, and wait for his case to be called. Opposite us some masons are tearing down the new wall of a building under construction. My friend remarks:

> Yesterday, after the workmen had finished that wall, the architect came round, for the first time in a week, to see how the building was progressing.

83

When he saw what had been done he was very angry. It seems that there was supposed to be a door, and two wooden pillars on this end, but the masons had left no openings. So now they are tearing it all down again to make a place for an entrance. This will be used as a waiting room when it is completed.

We are laughing about this when a merchant, sitting next to my companion, nudges him and asks what the joke is about. The lawyer tells him, and this fellow's mirth, which is a magnificent thing to behold, attracts the attention of most of the other Chinese in the compound. They all want to know what it is, and soon the story has gone round the whole group. One of the soldiers from the nearest courtroom has to come out and warn these laughterlovers to keep quiet so that one can hear oneself think.

Presently, a policeman beckons to us to follow him. We enter an alleyway between the buildings and after many twists and curves, are ushered into the presence of a magistrate.

It is a small room, at one end of which is a raised platform where the Court official and his Chinese clerk are seated behind a low wooden railing. There is a bare table in front of the bench, and this is for the lawyer's use. On each side of it are half a dozen chairs for observers and witnesses.

Framed and hanging on the wall directly behind the magistrate, is a photograph of Sun Yat-sen, under which is printed the text of his "last will and testament." The magistrate is dressed in a gown of dark maroon cloth, with a white collar, while the clerk wears ordinary Chinese clothes.

There is a rustle of papers and the Court is called to attention. The policeman, who is supposed to be a kind of bailiff, stands on one foot, leaning against the railing, his mouth open, his hat unremoved, and chewing on a piece of straw. Annoyed, the magistrate orders him to doff his hat and discard the straw, which he does, reluctantly.

This is a criminal prosecution against a Chinese merchant who has been manufacturing and selling an imitation of an American flashlight battery. It is a case of infringement of copyright and patent rights, which have been registered with the Chinese Government by the American firm, a client of my friend.

"Bring in the defendant," orders the magistrate.

The policeman shuffles off to obey. While he is gone, the magistrate glances through the evidence, which has all been presented in advance, according to Chinese procedure.

When the prisoner enters the room, I can scarcely suppress a laugh. On his shaved head there is a white, knitted skullcap. The back of his head is covered with old scars, while the front of it is marked with the depredations of what must have been a very severe case of small pox. From above his lips there depend two long shaggy strands of white hair, and from a mole on his chin half a dozen similar tokens of venerability tremble with indignation. He wears a blue coolie coat, short blue trousers, no socks, and a pair of leather bedroom slippers.

The magistrate questions him, but he vehemently denies everything of which he is accused. He declares he does not manufacture such a battery, nor sell it. He asserts that a card which bears his own name, and, among other items, lists the imitation which he is alleged to manufacture, is a forgery. The magistrate reminds him that he will be held accountable for all he says, but the little man continues to maintain complete innocence.

All of the evidence is taken down by the clerk, who writes in flowing script, with his long Chinese brush. There is no shorthand in the language, but the man works swiftly and only occasionally has to interrupt to ask that a sentence be repeated. It is important that he make no mistakes, for the defendant will have to sign this record when the hearing is over. In China, of course, testimony is not sworn in over the Bible.

During the proceedings the policeman has reassumed his one-legged, nonchalant stance against the railing. From time to time he emits gentle eructations, and, when he is inclined to do so, expectorates on the floor. Discipline seems to come hard to some people in China.

Finally, the magistrate closes the hearing. The records are signed by the plaintiff's lawyer and by the prisoner, who is led from the courtroom. Yet, still my Chinese friend does not know whether he has won the case. He must wait, perhaps a week, before a copy of the magistrate's decision is delivered to him.

If the man is found guilty, the verdict, together with the evidence in the case, will be handed to one of the judges in the District Court. If the latter approves of the decision, he may then sentence the prisoner, without further trial. Should the judge be in doubt, however, the case is given a further review in the District Court. Here the decision usually stands as final.

However, an appeal can be entered, in which circumstance there is a trial before what is called the Higher Court, of Kwangtung. One of the curious things about this kind of appellate court is that it frequently decides to increase, rather than decrease, the fine or sentence given in the lower courts. Thus, a defendant who gets off fairly lightly in the District Court generally declines to gamble with whatever whimsies may prevail in loftier judicial circles.

There are over 20 magistrates and judges holding sessions in the various rooms of the police compound. Both criminal and civil suits are heard. Some of the rooms are much larger than the one in which my friend's case was held, and there are crowds of spectators and witnesses at the important or sensational trials.

Although the magistrate before whom we have just appeared was middle-aged, these others are nearly all quite youthful in appearance. Some of them obviously are well under 30.

"Most of the judges and magistrates here now," my companion comments, "have passed the new examinations inaugurated by the Judicial Yuan of the Central Government. They are all well-trained men, and thoroughly conversant with the Legal Code recently promulgated at Nanking."

"But they are so young!" I exclaim. "Some of them cannot have had more than a year or two at the bar."

"They have not all had that," the lawyer admits. "Some have not practiced at all. But the Government is not worrying so much about the present as the future. They hope that these younger men, who are getting valuable experience, will form the basis for a sound, modern judicial system a few years from now."

It is doubtless a fine scheme—for the judiciary. One trusts that the public will live through it. And as for the foreigners, who are about to lose their extraterritoriality rights in China—well, such fellows always manage to get preferential treatment somehow. Witness my own case, for instance, how when I bid my friend good-bye, and walk through that imposing archway again, those two gendarmes smack their heels together, lift their bayoneted rifles above their shoulders, glare menacingly at me, and shout something that sounds like "Hrrmmph!"— just as if I were somebody of importance.

Some Cases of Military and Political Interference

No city in China has a more advanced judiciary than Canton, yet with all its "specially trained judges," when equity is inconvenient it is flagrantly disregarded, and even the right to legal trial is denied the alleged guilty.

In most provinces, in most cities, justice, as understood in the West, is a term of little meaning, for the military quite frankly holds the power of life and death over every man, and does not hesitate to exercise it. But in Canton, birth-city of the "People's Revolution," where the righteous Sun Yat-sen awoke the first stirrings of political consciousness in the common man, it is a disappointment to find that courts are often still subservient to generals and politicians.

There is, for instance, the recent case of Tsui Ming-chou, a well-known businessman who was arrested on a charge of forgery, at the request of Fan Ki-mow, Director of the Bureau of Finance. Held in jail for three months, he at no time was allowed to consult a lawyer, at no time appeared before a court. Many efforts were made by his friends to secure his liberation, or at least to bring him to trial. They failed. One morning a squad of Cantonese soldiers appeared at Mr. Tsui's cell and marched him double quick to a spot where he could watch the sunrise, slow and magnificent, lift over the hills of Kwangtung. For a while he hung in the breeze, suspended by ropes, from his thumbs and toes. Finally the firing squad finished him off.

After Mr. Tsui's death the Bureau of Finance took over his property—he was quite a wealthy man—and pocketed the money obtained from its sale. Conservative gentlemen believed that it was rather a stiff sentence for a forger, especially one whose guilt had never been proved in court. A few even recalled that the new legal code, which is supposed to apply in Canton, provides for a maximum penalty of five years imprisonment, for this crime. But no such heresies found expression in the Canton press.

Item two: The case of Chang Li-tsai, accused of the murder of Lai Hong, Director of the Ka Naam Tong Bank.

Chang, a promoter, had borrowed large sums of money from Lai, to finance business ventures which failed; shortly before his death, Lai had quarrelled bitterly with Chang. Other circumstances seemed to indicate that the latter might have killed the banker.

A long court trial was held, an autopsy performed on Lai's body; all the evidence was examined thoroughly. Chang Li-tsai was acquitted, the judges finding that Lai had committed suicide. Immediately after the trial, Lai Hong's family asked that Chang be rearrested. They proposed to establish that even if Chang did not murder Lai, he was at least responsible for the despondency that led to the suicide.

The court agreed that Chang Li-tsai should be detained, although he already had received an acquittal which would give him complete freedom in almost any other country. He has now been in prison for more than five months, without further hearing. Because Lai Hong's survivors are politically powerful it is generally believed that Chang's long internment is merely prelude to the same fate meted out to the unfortunate forger, Mr. Tsui.

Another case: Gendarme-Inspector Chang Sihai was accused by two fellow officers of having attempted to extract bribes, or "squeeze" for permitting them to patrol certain sections of Canton. Chen was arrested on October 15, at the order of Lam Sze-ching, Commander of the Canton Gendarmery. Ten days later he was taken from his cell, led to the execution grounds, and shot. There was no trial.

Confiscations of the property of individuals are frequent, of course, but the Government's treatment of Dr. Lo Hong-yuen, a former president of the Shanghai Mixed Court, was a surprise even to Canton.

Dr. Lo recently resigned the presidency of the Shanghai Court and returned to this city, where he took up residence in a house said to have been the property of his family for many years. Shortly afterward he received a message from the Military Headquarters informing him that, as the house was needed for billeting troops, he would have to evacuate.

Dr. Lo asked for time to find another house, but before he could move his possessions, a troop of soldiers arrived and presented a court mandamus ordering that his property be confiscated.

The house was occupied by Cantonese soldiers. Dr. Lo's wife and children had no opportunity to vacate; they are still living in a few rooms at the back of the premises. On the grounds that he had resisted the execution of a Government command, a warrant was issued for the arrest of Dr. Lo. But, warned in advance by friends, that gentleman sagaciously fled to Macao, the Portuguese settlement, where he is still in hiding.

Some Chinese declare that the measures taken against Dr. Lo are in the nature of political retaliation. There is basis for such a belief, for while he was president of the Shanghai Mixed Court, he incurred the wrath of high officials at Nanking because he declined to obey an illegal demand that a court order be issued, ordering the confiscation of the rich Sheng Kung-pao estate. The refusal cost him his position. However, others here believe that his Canton house has been taken over merely because certain military chiefs like his flower garden.

While other verifiable cases of this kind could be mentioned, your correspondent does not wish to intimate that they are characteristic. On the contrary, the opinion prevails here among foreigners and educated Chinese that the majority of court proceedings are conducted in a manner which would be considered equitable in most Occidental countries. Usually it is only when political jealousies and animosities are involved that the word "justice" is superseded by the word "power."

Despite such notorious occurrences as those listed above, it is perhaps true that civil authority in Canton has more nearly achieved its independence from the military than anywhere else in China, and it is at times evident that certain members of the judiciary are carrying on a courageous struggle against intimidations of the courts.

How 5,200 Policemen
Keep Order in Canton

Few cities in the Orient—none in China—have a more modern and efficient police department than the one which functions here as the Bureau of Public Safety.

There are, of course, people who disapprove of policemen, on principle. While no anarchist, the writer is at times inclined to sympathize with them. No one who values liberty can witness certain tyrannies and repressions periodically practiced by both foreign and native police in China without occasionally wondering if perhaps the public wouldn't be safer without its bureaus of public safety.

Canton's gendarmery, being the first defense of a Government jealous of opposition, naturally is not guiltless in this respect. It is a pliant organization of unusual power, some of the uses of which are extraordinary, if not actually unjust. But, as an instrument for controlling the whims of a somewhat unruly populace, this Bureau of Public Safety must be recognized as a finely balanced mechanism which commands respect—in a country where that word so frequently is said to have fallen into regrettable desuetude.

Fifty-two hundred policemen are required to maintain order in the Municipality of Canton, which embraces a population exceeding 1,000,000. These are not the ragamuffin, out-at-the-elbows, half starved ex-soldiers one sees patrolling many cities in the north. They are the antonyms of all those adjectives. They are smartly uniformed, athletic, competent young men who have been thoroughly trained in their duties as guardians of the law. They are all literate men. Many of the officers are college graduates. Some of them can converse not only in several dialects of Chinese, but in English, German, French, or Japanese, as well.

Credit for the excellence of the Canton police force is to be extended to General Au Yang-ku, the 36 year old Director of the Bureau of Public Safety. A graduate of Paoting Military Academy, once the most famous of its kind in north China, during the Revolution he distinguished himself as Commander of the 18th Division. Two years ago he was appointed to his present office, and given a free hand to develop a model gendarmery. The results are articulate. How they were achieved is summed up very simply by General Au.

"Whatever success you may find in our Bureau," he told your correspondent, "is most easily explained by the word discipline. In my own military experience I learned its value in handling men effectively; I merely applied that principle here."

But discipline is maintained only when men are well paid, systematically educated, and satisfied with their jobs. The real reason why General Au has a loyal, reliable force is because he has introduced reforms which recognize those requirements.

Formerly, dishonesty, neglect of duty, and general incompetence were prevalent throughout all departments of the Bureau. The men were too few, and they lacked capable officership. Physical training had not been emphasized. Little attention was given to the uniforms, and to general appearances. Methods in the departments were old-fashioned and there was an absence of scientific coordination. All this naturally accounted for a low morale.

Perhaps General Au got to the heart of this problem of discipline when he persuaded the Municipal Government to grant a wage increase for all employees of the Bureau. Monthly salaries, in Canton currency, are now as follows: $15 to $30 for privates; $30 to $60 for corporals; $60 to $120 for sergeants; $120 to $240 for lieutenants; and from $400 to $600 for captains. Board and lodging are supplied gratis.

No other Chinese police are so well paid, and few police of foreign countries. This is not said facetiously. The above amounts, due to low living costs for Chinese here, have a purchasing value of twice these sums, in gold in America, for instance.

Having secured his men living salaries, General Au next issued orders forbidding the acceptance of bribes or any kind of largesse. To the astonishment of all, these orders were enforced. Offenders were summarily dismissed. In grievous cases, severe punishment was administered. Very recently an officer was executed for misuse of his authority in extracting some "squeeze" money while on duty.

Meanwhile, a training school for recruits was established, under military officers. The course includes six months of rigorous instruction in military and police science, in physical training, and in general discipline and education. In this school tobacco and alcohol are taboo. Recruits receive nominal salaries while in attendance, and upon completion of the course are enlisted as privates.

Another institution, an Officers' Training College, has been founded by General Au. The applications of only middle school or university graduates are accepted for entrance, and additional examinations for mental and physical fitness must be passed. Those who are permitted to enter are paid by the Government while they study.

The college at present has 430 students, out of whom half a dozen are graduates of European or Japanese universities. There are 32 instructors, some of them army officers, some civilians. The term is for two years, and the curriculum includes foreign languages, the history and principles of political science, a general survey of police methods used in various foreign countries, mathematics, infantry and artillery tactics, and related subjects. Upon graduation, the cadets are given a period of practical training after which they are commissioned as lieutenants.

At the invitation of General Au, the writer recently visited this interesting college, and was particularly impressed with the scrupulous cleanliness and neatness, not only in the dormitories and lecture halls, but in the cadets, their uniforms and their equipment. There is a brisk, business-like air about this place. System rules here; system and discipline.

The Bureau of Public Safety has been reorganized, partly after American patterns, partly after the Japanese and European. The Director's aim is to combine the best features of each of them. In the fingerprint department, American methods are used; in the traffic department, the European scheme has been favored; in the criminal investigation department, the British model is followed. Uniforms amalgamate various items from the Japanese, the British, the Americans—and yet somehow manage to look as though they were indigenous to China.

In order to inculcate loyalty and comradery in the force, Director Au has borrowed freely and profitably from the experience of Western countries. Athletics are not only encouraged, but participation in them is required. Police meets are frequent. A modern gymnasium and athletic field is well patronized by the men. Free movies and other entertainments are offered in these recreation grounds. There is a police band, equipped with an expensive set of American musical instruments, and directed by a Chinese graduate of an American fine arts school. A monthly magazine is published by the Bureau, and the men are encouraged to air their complaints in this journal. The cadets publish an annual and print their own weekly paper in an establishment operated by themselves. And, something rare in China, the Bureau publishes a year book which gives accurate and comprehensive statistics, charts, diagrams and photographs concerning the activities of every department.

"Your accomplishment," the writer remarked to General Au, after spending a day visiting the various offices under him, "is something remarkable. The spectacle of such efficiency in China startles me."

The Director of the Bureau of Public Safety expressed his *hsieh-hsieh*, but, à la Chinois, deprecated his own success.

"We have only begun," he said, "Come back two years from now and we may have something to show you. By then we hope all our men will have been systematically drilled in training schools—both the privates and officers. By then we will have introduced most of the methods used against criminals in Western countries. And by then we hope to have police who will be the equal of those anywhere in the world."

Melancholy residents of Chicago, please take note: there is no ban against American immigration to Canton.

The Hard Lot of
Women Prisoners in Hon San-so

A pale hand thrust timidly through an ironbarred door and plucked gently at my sleeve. I turned, to look into the face of a girl who could not have been more than 17. Swiftly she spoke, in a voice troubled with tremors of fear, of appeal—perhaps hope.

Observing that I did not comprehend her words, which were in Cantonese dialect, she reached into the side of her gown and from her bosom drew out a letter, clutched it uncertainly for a moment, and then handed it to me. In the dim light, I stood and gazed at the long envelope, trying to put meaning into its great sprawling characters. Suddenly the warden shouted, from down the draughty corridor, to come along. I stuffed the letter in my pocket, and walked on, giving a farewell reassuring nod to the young prisoner.

With such an introduction, one is tempted to carry on to the romantic end, wherein the hero (in the first person) returns when the moon is pale, swims the moat, clambers up a twenty-foot ladder, releases the dark-eyed damsel and carries her away to a shining new life of freedom and happiness ad infinitum. And it might have happened, had not so many similar letters been pushed toward me before I got out of the Hon San-so, the Canton Police Jail for Women.

Apparently all the incarcerated ladies were innocent, if one could believe their petitions. The one which I accepted, and later turned over to a Chinese lawyer, was a tearful document. To quote from it, as translated for me, will be enlightening to those who would know why women go to jail in China. This was the young prisoner's plea:

> My husband, Wu Fat-sen, thinks I am an adulteress. But he is mistaken. He is older than I, and he is jealous and suspicious because he fears I may be attracted to a younger man. One day he came home and found me laughing and talking with his friend, Mr. Ng Pu-shih, and he went into a great rage. He accused me of being unfaithful, with no more evidence than that.
>
> Moreover, I have been put into jail, just on his word, and without any trial whatever. For four months I have been here, and no friend, not even that craven Ng Pu-shih, has made any attempt to have me set free. If I could once appear before an honest judge, I am certain that I could establish my innocence.

You who read this, take pity on a broken-hearted girl who has been very much wronged! Please use your influence on my behalf!

There was more to it, with some rather embarrassing details of the treatment she had received from her irate husband after that good man found her in the company of Ng Pu-shih. That lawyer who now has the letter had promised me that he will get her a trial.

In the Hon San-so there are sympathetic companions for the alleged incontinent wife of Wu Fat-sen. Twenty-three women are said to be imprisoned here for the same offense. Through the aid of Chinese friends with me, I questioned many of them. Nearly all denied their guilt. Nearly all declared that they had received no trial. And most of them were hardly more than children—girls of 18, 20 or 21.

Each of these had her carefully written letter of appeal, prepared in advance with the pathetic trust that some stray visitor would interest himself in her case, and help to secure her release. But the warden warned us against taking such petitions. It was against prison regulations. He permitted us freely to converse, however, with as many of the prisoners as we liked.

A few girls frankly admitted that they had deviated from the path of marital rectitude, but justified themselves on various grounds. In one case, that of a slave girl, the prisoner maintained that her owner had beaten her regularly for the past two years, ever since she had become his concubine. He was 24 years older than she, and she could not love him. But had he treated her kindly, she would never have run away, she admitted, and gone to the house of a young man who offered her refuge. She now has had 14 months in which to cogitate over her conduct, but still steadfastly remains defiant.

In one cell there was a girl who said she was 16 years old. Her crime was desertion. After three months of living with the 42-year-old husband to whom her parents had married her, she had run away with a childhood sweetheart, a boy of about her own age. Both of them were arrested, at the request of the girl's mother-in-law. The woman paid— with a sentence of eight months in Hon San-so. The youth was released. And the outraged husband now has another wife.

I talked with a young woman who had been jailed for soliciting on the streets, without a license. She was a pretty creature, with long dark hair, bright, intelligent eyes, and the fine satiny skin of southern Chinese. But the gown she wore was in tatters, and for shoes she had straw sandals.

"And you are guilty of the charge against you?" I asked. She replied, politely:

"Yes, one is a law-breaker because one hasn't the money to pay those thieving police their squeeze every time one gets a patron."

"But you cannot have had so very many patrons. Come, tell me, how old are you?"

"Seventeen."

"Your parents must be greatly disturbed because you are in jail."

She laughed. There was not a trace of sentiment in her answer. "Parents? Father and mother? One has none. One is a *tan-min.* One is a child of the river."

In the same cell with this friendless waif there were three others, of ages varying from 18 to 27. Here in this parcel-like room, ten-feet long and eight-feet wide, they eat, sleep, and exchange their aching thoughts. When it is dark they try to close their eyes, and when it is dawn there is nothing for them but that those eyes should be opened. For there is no illumination in here when the sun slips under, and neither is there a shade for the single barred window, to keep out the day's first light, that streams in from our world of comparative freedom.

It cannot be said that the room was bare of ornament, for over on one wall there was a picture of Buddy Rogers, the American movie star. It shows him standing in front of his new "bungalow"—a home such as none of these girls could quite believe really existed, for they had never seen anything remotely like it. On the opposite wall there was a quasi-nude of another satellite of filmdom, a lady who I believe is known as Mae Murray.

We questioned each of the other girls in this cell at Hon San-so. The first one had been a concubine of a wealthy merchant, a lovable fellow who, upon suspecting her of misconduct with one of the servants, had her locked up for six months to cool her ardor. Scornfully the young woman denied the charge. She informed me that she regrets justice in China does not enable her to go before a court and prove that her master is a liar, a villain, and the offspring of ignoble ancestors. She asserted that she had no intention of returning to him when her liberty is restored to her.

The second girl was in for having stolen her neighbor's baby. She admitted her guilt and said that she had appeared before a magistrate who had treated her fairly. She explained that, since the death of her only child, a year before, she had been much distraught and was subject to hallucinations on the subject of other mothers' babies. It appeared that she had recognized in her neighbor's infant the face of her own dead son and, in a moment of insanity, had run off with him.

The case of the third prisoner also involved a baby. This woman, thin and emaciated in appearance, had been interned at the instance of an action brought against her by a brother-in-law, who accused her of selling her youngster to a friend. She maintained her innocence. With her husband dead, she related she was destitute, and without money to care for the child. She had simply given it to a wealthier woman, who had promised to return it as soon as the mother had money enough to feed it. She thought that, given a chance to appear before an upright judge, she could prove that no money had been exchanged.

I cannot know how many of the tales told by these women are true; certainly one might expect distortion, exaggeration, perhaps complete fabrication. Yet it is more than probable that behind each of them there was a substance of truth. The fact that the Cantonese who accompanied me found nothing strange in the imprisonment of women for infidelity indicated that the practice is not uncommon here. But the modern Legal Code, recently promulgated at Nanking, and supposedly functioning in this city, definitely does not permit that. It provides that every woman shall have the same legal rights as men. Indubitably, some of the cases at Hon San-so were victims of those possessing *shylick,* that omnipotent term in Chinese that means political power, and before which, unfortunately, even finely phrased legal codes at times are still of little avail.

But the inmates were not all here for refined indiscretions and misbehavior. Mixed with alleged unfaithful wives and dissatisfied concubines were others, of a type more readily recognizable as criminal. There were some women who had been convicted of engaging in the *"Mui-tsai,"* or slave child traffic, against which Kwangtung now has a prohibition law that is occasionally enforced. There was a number of petty thieves, several women guilty of fraud and perjury, and some young ladies who had undertaken to flog their mothers-in-law.

No long terms have been served here since 1925, when the Reds, during their brief reign in Canton, released all the prisoners in the lower court jails. Dangerous and incorrigible felons are now kept in the Honan Penitentiary, which is considered to be a safe distance from the scene of possible uprisings in the future. There the sentence begins at two years, and ends, not infrequently, only with death.

Hongkong, England's Own
Little Corner of China

Which Refuses to Become Anglicized—
a Beautiful and Mystic City by Day and by Night

Hongkong is an island, as everybody knows; but it is also a mountain. It rises swiftly from a base rimmed with moonlit waters and is only twenty-seven miles in circumference. In sharp grandeur it culminates loftily at a place which a British Governor named Victoria Point. How inexplicably droll and dull that name sounds, hovering above a scene so exotic and aflame with light!

The illumination, then, starts at the peak and in a thin trickle drips down toward the blaze below. Your eye can follow the line of the peak tramway that clambers doggedly up the granite slope, wrapping itself to the narrow footholds as it swings over a deep precipice, now gripping precariously to a boulder or two, and now digging its teeth boldly into the unsheltered shoulder of a long ridge as it nears the summit.

The lights near the top are few and scattered, the homes of men of wealth, Europeans and Chinese, who can afford a motor car that will stand the strain of part of the daily climb and a squad of chair bearers to complete the journey. Your eye moves down and the lights grow denser: street lamps, the subdued illumination from curtain-hung windows, and the lenses of motor cars staring through the night with their long beams slanting. Down, down, till you hit China street and a million lights, shop fronts and offices, trams and buses, motor cars and every peddler and ricksha with a swinging lantern.

The river, full of its own life, mirrors some of that ashore. Little formless splashes of amber gather and disperse and regather in fantastic shapes over the bay, that majestic bay that is ten miles square and into which the proudest ocean liner may move without a tremor. Junks glide past, their sails pale silver and their crews, wavering shadows on the high decks, silent. Sampans, with their single bobbing lanterns, move, small and dark, across the water, the *laodahs* sculling slowly. Along the bund a dozen ferries, alive with gleaming windows, and beside them river boats, larger and like the demon Krim, with a thousand eyes; and the moon full and close to the Peak, and the gray clouds drifting—Hongkong at night.

People say it is the most beautiful harbor in the world. But that is said also of others. I do not know; there are so many harbors that I have never seen. And I am not sure that this is beauty.

My ship drew up to the pier and was made fast by some shouting, half-naked coolies who stood panting and grinning when their job was done. I had come from Canton and on board I had met again a Chinese friend whom I had not seen for two years. He was now with the Kwangtung Government, but he knew Hongkong. He said he came down once a week and he proposed to show me the town. A Chinese, if he is so inclined, can always show you things in a city where you might live for years and never know.

Up Peddard Street we walked, through blocks of stone buildings, gray and shadowy. They were of the type the English erect everywhere in the East, with solid, ponderous facades, deep long windows and doorways that are forbidding and cold.

We reach Queen's Road. It is still early evening and the crowds are moving down toward Queen's Theater, where there is an American talkie. "All the world loves lovers," says the sign in front of the cinema. "See Charlie Farrell and Janet Gaynor in the thrilling drama of love and youth and high society." You do not see so many foreigners, for there are only 12,000 in Hongkong, while there are 650,000 Chinese. But many of the latter wear European clothes and speak English, not American. It is always amusing, though I do not know just why, to hear a Chinaman speak with what people call an English "accent."

There are a great many "Point Fives," as the British say, or "Anglo-Chinese," as they call themselves. Eurasians. Some of them are lovely, the girls with their skin light gold and wide timid eyes that have in them naive wonder and confusion, the young men tall and swarthy, darkly handsome. They intrigue you with their English self-assurance and their color of Asia.

Up and down Queen's Road rumble buses, motor cars and trams. Young Chinese, dressed in flamboyant blazer coats and sporty trousers, drive motorcycles, with their girls looking flushed and a bit frightened, sitting saddle fashion on the seat behind them. Four soldiers, little men, Cockneys, march unsteadily down the side of the road and look appraisingly at young Chinese girls, who take no notice of them.

There are English stores, with conservative show windows; there are Chinese drug stores and quick lunch soda fountains; there are candy makers, magazine stalls, lace shops and Indian silk stores with their owners watching hopefully each passerby. Further on, the jade and ivory and lacquer shops cluster close to the amusement centers, and there are curio shops with such a variety of fine things as you could not find without visiting ten different establishments in a Chinese city. Here the owners, safe from oppression under British law, do not hesitate to gather and display a quantity of rare and rich articles.

"Have you been to Repulse Bay?" my friend asked.

"Yes, but not at night. Let's go."

We got into a motor car and drove further down Queen's Road and then turned and suddenly began to climb. There were streets like those in Chinatown the world over: narrow and winding, flanked by flat-faced buildings of drab cement and with little balconies on which sat paunchy Chinese, shaven of head, lightly clad and smoking water pipes. All the streets rise steeply from Queen's Road. At the foot of each of them stand sedan chairs and their bearers, hawking for trade, as soon as you turn toward the peak.

As we reached the edge of the city the road leaped upward, lacing into the granite ribs of the mountain and keeping a tenacious hold as we followed, high above it, the line of the sea. Far out we could see the junks, vague, ghostlike, seeming not to move and as though caught in a rapturous calm. Below us the surf beat softly and the spray leaped like feathery silver dust. There were the long green estates of the taipans, with here and there an English cottage or a rambling baronial house. There were stretches of woods and a fresh scent of wild green things.

Repulse Bay. It is a crescent of alabaster such as you find on the Kahuna side of Oahu in the Hawaiian Islands. The waves creep up to it gently and end, with sudden flourish, in a swirl of surf, sparkling and phosphorescent. Behind the bay climb emerald terraces, formally laid out in flower beds through the center of which is a wide stone stairway that leads to the hotel.

Inside there is an orchestra and a ballroom that reminds you of that hall where sailormen, adrift in New York, seek their romance with scrawny little girls who buy their evening gowns on Tenth Avenue. But the gowns you see here on modern Chinese girls are not like those. They are of rich velvety stuffs with a gloss like fur, or of thick silks that strike your fancy, or of Eastern brocades in patterns that no white woman could wear. Their dresses are long, have sleeves and high collars that give a royal dignity to the lotus-slender figures of their wearers.

"They are beautiful," my friend said quite simply.

He had been abroad long enough to have acquired an air of detachment in judging the values of things in his own country. "I think," he remarked, "that there is nothing on earth so wistful and exquisite as the beauty of Chinese women. They are like something carved in mellowed ivory that has mysteriously been brought to life."

We were sitting at a table watching the dancers, and I gave a sidelong glance at him. Such a speech does not come naturally from a Chinese; I thought he must have memorized it and was repeating it for effect. But no. He was not even looking at me; he did not care whether I agreed with him or not. I concluded that he must be in love.

"I think you are right," I said. "When a Chinese woman is really lovely she is something to shatter the ambitions of a versifier. There is a tragic tenderness to her beauty, a flavor and a fragrance. I know of nothing that is remotely like her unless it is a spray of jasmine and April. She reminds me—"

"Wait."

I thought I had been going quite well, but he stopped me and looked at me, smiling oddly. He saw that I was perfectly sincere and then he said:

"What I cannot understand is why a Chinese, with so much to charm him in his own race, should want to marry a foreign girl."

There was a strange intentness to what he said that puzzled me, though he was still smiling. And then, as through a mist, a recollection came to me. For the first time that evening I recalled that he had an American wife. I had never seen her. They said she wasn't much; a five-and-ten girl.

I said nothing. What could one say? He had made a mistake, but it was worse than that; he had to live with the mistake for the rest of his life, for the Chinese rarely divorce. We finished our drinks and left, driving back through the scented night. The moon was still there, and the radiance of the Peak, and the deathlike stillness of the junks in a calm sea. But the night had lost its glamour.

Macao, Picturesque Port
on the South China Coast

Which Was Founded by the Portuguese Four Centuries Ago, Inaugurating Sino-European Trade

Here in this Portuguese colony by the sea is a city made to order for the spinner of credulity-taxing travel yarns. It has all the elements of truth that is stranger than fiction. A background of stirring history, of romance, high valor and emprise, with a thrust of pathos added by the present day decline of its ruling race. A foreground of the choicer vices, featured by unrestricted indulgence in opium and gambling, preludes which lend zest to the ancient pleasures of wine, women and wrong.

It is more than four centuries now since the intrepid and rascally Vasco da Gama, sailing into the sunrise in search of slaves and a new trade route to the Orient, laid the foundation for the once great overseas empire of Portugal. After him, hot on the trail of his reports of rich undeveloped commerce, came Portuguese merchants, avid for the fabulous wealth of the East. Some of them reached southern Cathay as early as 1516. Ten years later they had a small settlement on the peninsula that is now Macao, and by 1557 they obtained permission from the Chinese to build godowns and residences for the purpose of conducting permanent trade relations between China and Europe.

For almost two and a half centuries Macao was the only Occidental foothold in the Celestial Kingdom. Gradually the Portuguese annexed additional privileges, until their settlement took on the complexion of an extraterritorial grant. They fortified it and a few small neighboring islands, and began to assume jurisdiction over natives who drifted through their gates. Not till 1887, however, following China's defeat in a war with France, was a treaty effected which recognized Macao as a Portuguese colony.

A little over a century ago this was still the leading Euro-Asian trade mart. Opium and gambling had not yet become its chief commodities, and Latin padres made it the headquarters for all religious and cultural proselytizing in the Orient. The Portuguese court, gratified with the fat tributes sent home from this far-away outpost, was generous in bestowing titles upon merchants responsible for the prosperity. But times changed. Other Europeans got closer to the heart of trade when they opened commerce directly with Canton. And then England fought a war with China and in the middle of the nineteenth century secured the colony of Hongkong. That was the beginning of the end of Portuguese commercial eminence in China.

Today the Government of Macao derives its principal revenues from such intriguing items as poppy smoke, fan tan, mahjong, roulette, raffles, horse racing, lotteries, alcohol, and the enterprise of some 2,000 young persons euphemistically referred to as sing-song girls. It is a kind of clearing house for the eroticisms. Vices may exist elsewhere which are not found here, but it is because they cannot be made to flourish on a paying basis. A facile imagination is required to conceive of an environment more calculated to encourage the gentle arts of corruption.

With a population of less than 100,000 this little spot of land annually earns about $5,000,000 for its European exploiters, approximately 70 per cent of which is said to be sent home to the Portuguese Crown. Inquiring journalists are not warmly received in town, and it is hard to get official information on anything. But there are always means of circumventing such reticence. In Macao everyone knows everybody else's business, including that of the Government.

A few weeks ago Gov. Barbarosa renewed the lease on the gambling rights for another year, but made the usual attempt to keep the transaction secret. Within twenty-four hours it was known to all that Lu Chuck-suin had paid $1,600,000 for the monopoly, the highest amount ever collected from it. Equally well known is the fact that in 1929 the Government made in excess of $1,200,000 from the manufacture and sale of opium. The lotteries and raffles add from $400,000 to $500,000 annually, while $50,000 is derived from the activities of the numerous and energetic *filles de joie.*

It is hard to say whether Macao's commercial decay resulted from the legalization of her shabby iniquities or whether that policy became paramount only after so much trade had shifted to Hongkong that new sources of income had to be secured to make up losses in remittances to the home Crown. Certainly the easy money from opium and gambling acted as a soporific, lulled the Portuguese into a false sense of economic security. For perhaps 50 years, while their British rivals were swiftly building a great modern port forty miles away from them, the rulers of Macao sat idly beside their shallow water harbor, content with their large annual surplus of silver Taels. But ships calling at Macao grew fewer and fewer. Finally, eight years ago and too late, an attempt was made to regain some trade by building a deep-water harbor at a cost of $10,000,000.

The project was a failure. Times were hard and the King demanded more than usual from his China agents. Lacking funds, the harbor was never completed. What was done remains today mute testimony to the indifference of home authorities toward the future of a possession which, since its establishment, is estimated to have furnished between 250 and 300 million dollars in revenues.

Macao's status is now almost solely parasitic. It is one of the purest forms of exploitation surviving in the world today. Aside from its dwindling exports of fish, vegetable oils, dried snakes, tobacco, and firecrackers, it appears to produce little but opium and degeneracy. It preys upon the weakness of its resident and transient population. The Government has been called "a group of organized croupiers directing a chance game in which they cannot lose," and the description is not inapt.

But treasure is rarely taken out of China without a few Chinese deducting their share of the loot. Macao is no exception. Here the chief profiteers are the Lu family, now attaining the third generation of supremacy. The Lu Chuck-suin who holds the gambling monopoly is at present manager of the Lu interests, which are extensive in the colony. He is the eldest of twenty-eight sons born to the founder of the fortune. It is said that in the authorship of this abundant lineage the prolific old gentleman collaborated with six different concubines. Even so, it remains an achievement which succeeding generations may well aim to emulate.

Lu influence also dominates the syndicate which controls the local sale of Government opium, and it holds investments in public utilities. The most important of these is the power plant, installed and operated largely by French and British. There is a telephone service, also managed by foreigners other than Portuguese. The city has no waterworks, and is dependent for its supply upon wells, and upon the Chinese carriers who transport water in buckets and wagons from outlying districts.

Lu Chuck-suin owns the Riviera, a semimodern foreign hotel where tourists are kept, and he is also proprietor of the newest Chinese hostel, a six-story building proudly known as "the skyscraper." Some import and export houses and small merchandizing firms are in the hands of

Portuguese, but most of the business is dominated by Chinese. A great many shops, selling the usual articles of Chinese bazaars, line the Old World cobbled streets and flank the gambling and opium establishments.

Many of the prominent merchants and politicians are "Macaonese," a term of special application to the offspring of Sino-Portuguese marriages. It has been said that the Portuguese more readily intermarry with Orientals than any other European race. This is probably true, but in considering that there are more Eurasians of Portuguese extraction than all others in China combined, one should remember that the little Latins have been here two centuries longer than most Occidentals. A hundred years may show some interesting amalgamations with other nationalities.

This "Macaonese" element of the population is about 7,500. Excepting the army, and perhaps a hundred or so officials imported from Portugal, there are few full-blooded Portuguese in Macao today. A number of the Catholic priests and nuns who have charge of educational work in the colony are of mixed Chinese and Portuguese ancestry, but it is a circumstance which appears to arouse no curiosity on the part of the populace.

For defense and policing there are about 500 white troops and an equal number of blacks, brought over from a Portuguese colony in Africa and officered by dashing young fellows from Lisbon. Some of the soldiers acquire Chinese women, occasionally with benefit of clergy. I am not informed regarding the conduct of black mercenaries in that respect, but it is assumed that they follow the example of their superior officers. African loyalty, by the way, was given rather a severe test last spring when an obstreperous and somewhat inebriated Portuguese sergeant organized a comic revolution.

The sergeant, together with a considerable force of enlisted men, suddenly mutinied and managed to get control of one of the principal fortresses. Greatly excited, the commander gathered his remaining adherents, who seem to have been principally of ebon hue, and made plans to oust the rebels. Marines were also landed and the lone gunboat got ready to bombard the fort. Meanwhile, the Chinese inhabitants stood by, indifferent as to the outcome, but prepared to be highly amused by what promised to be a good show. They did not get it. When, after two days, the commander finally assailed the traitorous enemy, he found most of them had quietly gone to sleep. It was a government victory.

This occurrence reminds me how a Chinese military official in Canton remarked that China could easily demand and secure the retrocession of Macao. It was his belief that, on moral grounds, Portugal had forfeited the right to govern the colony through her open violation of China's national laws of prohibition against opium and gambling. (The fact that these laws are observed hardly anywhere did not disturb my friend.) He spoke of the facility with which Cantonese naval and air forces could capture Macao in the event the Portuguese refused to return it peacefully.

"It would all be over," he reflected, "in a little while. The Portuguese have only one airplane, one gunboat and 1,000 soldiers. I have estimated that it would require not more than twenty minutes for us to take the city. We could hold it easily against the entire Portuguese navy."

But China really has no need for Macao. Although it still has some utility as a harbor, it would be healthier if the Chinese built up a wholly new free-port city of their own, as they are now planning to do either at nearby Tang Kai Chuen, or at Whampoa. Besides, it ought to be remembered that not all the surplus from the colony's revenues goes back to Portugal. Some of it, I know, has been used to silence the attacks of Chinese editors of my acquaintance. Considerably more is said to branch off toward official and influential pockets in China. And if this friendly and sagacious policy is continued, it is doubtful if agitation against "iniquitous Macao" will result in a formal demand for retrocession, at least not in the near future.

Tang Kai Chuen in South China
Home of Ex-Premier Tang Shao-yi
a Village Which Is Clean
and Where Opium Is Barred

Overhead the sky is turquoise, unflecked by a cloud. In the lucid air, some sunlit mountains deepen their thrust against the horizon, and stand as detached things, full of the illusory beauty of distances. They are the kind of peaks, with their trailing wisps of shade and color, which you fancy do not really exist beyond the dreams of Chinese painters, until you have roamed a little of China and come to believe the verities of your eyes.

In the valleys, nearly all is dry and brown. The autumn harvest is done; the rice has been marketed. Bending over the sun-baked rice paddies, leavening the soil for new plantings, are sturdy brown children, dressed in clean blue lambu, in wide trousers and coats that are rarely buttoned. Against the heaven's glare, their shaved heads are protected with the straw helmet of the southland, the *tai mao-tze,* pointed and full brimmed, suggestive of a minaret with its bulbous lower swell sliced off.

But most of the fields have been deserted. It is a season of agrarian inactivity and the poorer peasants have joined the road builders. For this is Chung Shan, the "model district" of Kwangtung, and there are many new highways under construction. More than seventy miles of them now reach into the villages, linking them with the Portuguese colony of Macao, and with fishing ports on the gracefully curving coast of the Tung Tsao, the Eastern Sea.

Coming across the country in a motor car hired at Macao, you see many hundreds of the road makers of Chung Shan. They are old folk, men and women, bald and toothless. They are perspiring mothers, with babies tied to their backs in crimson shawls, and hard-flanked virgins and well-muscled youths burnt the color of bistre by the hot winds from the sandy soil. They are boys and girls only a few years beyond nursing age, some of them hardly as tall as their sunhats are wide. They are all peasants to whom the equivalent of 10 cents American money is worth working ten hours a day to obtain.

Over a shoulder each of them wears his pack yoke of bamboo or teak from the ends of which depend straw baskets filled with earth for the roads. Little fellows have poles to suit their strength and they move along in a quasi-trot with the conscious pride of emulating their elders. In high uncertain voices they join in that song of burden bearers throughout China, a curious four-toned chant heavy with the strange patience of labor.

You have driven perhaps twenty miles from Macao when there is a branch in the road and you follow a tangent that skirts under a green hill, on which there is a garden, unexpectedly lush and tender in the dusty landscape. Bougainvillea spills down the emerald slopes and fat chrysanthemums flank the stone-flagged pathways. In the midst of a cluster of exotic trees there is a brown turret that looks as if it had come over from a castle in France. That, you are told, is the newly constructed watch tower of the village of Tang Kai Chuen. But its real utility seems to be one of ornamentation for the garden, which belongs to Tang Shao-yi, ex-Premier of China, astute business man, and friend of Herbert Clark Hoover.

Literally, Tang Kai Chuen means "Tang House Gathering," and nearly all who live here are relatives. Most wealthy, most venerated, politically most powerful, is Tang Shao-yi, secular head of the Tang clan. He is also a member of the council which rules over Chung Shan. Two years ago this entire district was created as a special area by the national Government, because it contains Choy Hang, the village where Sun Yat-sen, late leader of the Nationalist revolution, was born. Chung Shan is now a kind of national park, governed independent from the provincial authority, by a council composed of local men chosen by the Kuomintang.

Tang Kai Chuen explodes one of the credos popular among foreigners—that it is impossible for a strictly Chinese village to be kept clean. No one would say that it is not of typical Chinese pattern. The lanes are narrow and winding and follow the line of least resistance. The buildings are of clay brick, with facades of yellow tile that end in cornices carved and curved according to the delicate architectural principles of the celebrated Chang Teh. Sewers are open channels lined with stone, and no different from those in use half a millennium ago. And there are many seemingly unattached, untended fowl and pigs and tiny children, who roam the village and bask in cool corners at sunny noons.

But modern concepts of system and hygiene have been introduced.

The streets are swept daily by the Department of Sanitation and, in addition, each resident, each shop owner is answerable for the appearance of his property frontage. Actually, you walk down ways that have been scoured with sand and water till they glisten. And along the main thoroughfare, where an ancestral temple and some market stalls built more than a century ago are newly painted and in good repair, wheat and rice are spread out to dry on ancient stone pavements that are as spotless as a New England hearth.

Tang Kai Chuen has other virtues. No opium is sold or smoked by the habitants. Peasants from other villages who have acquired the habit are sent here for reform. There is a Department of Public Safety, but you are informed that no crimes have been reported for the last six months. Although the population is only a little more than 10,000, Tang Kai Chuen has two hospitals, a number of primary schools and a middle school. Elementary education is compulsory and even the hot water carriers are said to read and write.

You go up to an end of the village, and opposite the magistrate's dwelling there is an open field where several hundred boys and girls are competing in a semiannual meet. An oval, marked into lanes with white chalk, is the target of all eyes, for there is a relay race between the fleetest youth of Tang Kai Chuen and a neighboring village. In the center of the field youngsters are participating in other events. There is a volley ball match. There are broad jumping, high jumping, pole vaulting and various tricks on the turning bars. Over on one side you see a platform decorated with blue and white bunting and hung with Chinese and Kuomintang flags. Twenty-six silver cups gleam in the sunlight and beside them stand four khaki-clad Chinese Boy Scouts, Troop No. 1 of Tang Kai Chuen. Behind the cups, on the platform, sit the magistrate and four of the village elders, watching the sports and enthusiastically applauding every winner.

Many of these children speak a little English, for they are the sons and daughters of Chinese who returned to their village after having accumulated fortunes in the laundry and restaurant business in Australia, in America and in the Philippines. Most of the Chinese now living in Hawaii are members of the Tang clan or of one of the other old families in the vicinity of Chung Shan.

On the surface, Tang Kai Chuen looks quiet, peaceful, dignified, altogether the sort of place an opulent overseas merchant might choose to retire with his thoughts and legitimate sons. But the drowsy appearance is deceiving. Tang Kai Chuen lately has been disturbed by sinister rumblings suggestive of a real estate boom. For this is one of the sites mentioned by the national Government as a possible free port to be opened in competition with Hongkong, the British colony where most of the trade of south China is now concentrated. Villagers are beginning to refer to their dwelling as Tang Kai Wan, or "Tang House Harbor." Land prices have risen so that on paper many of the peasants in the neighborhood count themselves Rockefellers in the nascence. It is said that land near the waterfront now is quoted at $35,000 an acre.

Once you have seen the splendid bay, the scheme to develop a harbor here does not seem so fantastic. At present, there is a natural anchorage about five miles wide, and protected on north and south by a range of low hills that end abruptly over the water. Much dredging would have to be done, for the sea bed is a tough shale. But the expenditure of $5,000,000, which is roughly estimated as the cost of making the harbor available for ocean steamships would be justified if only a part of the rich commerce of Hongkong could be diverted here.

There are, however, numerous drawbacks to the realization of the plan. Most prominent is the complete lack of shore facilities to take care of the transshipment of goods to the interior. An expensive hundred miles of railways and a costly bridge would have to be constructed between Chung Shan peninsula and the mainland, to connect the harbor with Canton, and to tap the agricultural hinterland. Probably the project eventually will be identified as more of that commodity for which government hot air artists are famous. But meanwhile the landowners of Tang Kai Chuen continue to find it agreeable to imagine they already are citizens of the great free port of Tang Kai Wan.

Perhaps the most energetic promoter of the scheme is the sagacious Tang Shao-yi, whose efforts cannot be altogether altruistic, as he is said to own tracts of ocean frontage, besides valuable property in the village. Mr. Tang has succeeded in interesting high officials of the provincial and national governments in the purchase of his real estate, transactions which are reported to have considerably enhanced his fortune.

He is also concerned with the development of several industrial enterprises in the locality. Among these, one is unique. It is an oil refinery, the only plant in China extracting kerosene and gasoline from crude oil. At present it has a capacity of 500 barrels a day, but when completed will produce 10,000 barrels. Most of this will be secured from shale, exceptionally rich deposits of which are available on the nearby island of Hainan, where the company has options on several hundred thousand acres of land. The plant is under the management

of two American petroleum experts, and has been financed principally by Chinese bankers of Hongkong. Others interested, besides Tang
Shao-yi, include some prominent officials, one of them Chan Ming-
hsu, Governor of Kwangtung.

Mr. Tang has not confined his activities to his native village. As a
member of the administrative council he has undertaken numerous
other projects throughout Chung Shan. Years ago, even before Sun
Yat-sen, he was the first to urge the building of surfaced highways and
he devised the road tax which at present enables their construction. He
helped organize a company to produce light and power and he was
instrumental in modernizing the local flour and cotton milling industries. It is true that from these enterprises he has made money, but
private capital is not considered iniquitous in Chung Shan. Nowhere
is a shrewd businessman more venerated than in this district which has
produced so many of them.

The people of his village seem to love Tang Shao-yi and certainly
Tang loves his village. Not long ago he made of his garden on the hill a
park open to the public. If you go there on your way out of Tang Kai
Chuen you will be sure to find a stray infant or two, or a palsied
octogenarian enjoying the shady paths of this estate. You may descend
a steep rock-lined walk yourself, past English hedge and Chinese peach
and plum and cherry trees, and in his arbored sanctuary you may find
Tang Shao-yi reading the Confucian Analects, or an English edition of
Tolstoi.

Then, because he is said to be a hospitable man, he may ask you to
sit with him for awhile. And as you sip jasmine tea near an old devil's
head that hangs above his door, he can discuss brilliantly any subject
from Ch'ing vases and T'ang poets to the Kellogg Pact, Chevrolets and
compound interest.

You leave Tang Kai Chuen reluctantly, and with a lingering backward glance, as though you would like to take something of it with you.
You understand that it is a place where truths are so simplified that life
for the common man is accepted easily, obviously. And perhaps you
are a little covetous of that sureness, that seeming peace. These are the
rustic graces, the virtues of villages; they will not thrive in cities and
towns. That is why all the young Whittingtons who leave here in
search of fortune come back before they are too old. For verily, unless
the menace of a free port becomes a reality, Tang Kai Wan always will
be the sort of place an opulent overseas merchant chooses to retire to
with his thoughts and legitimate sons.

The Little Brick Home of Sun Yat-sen in the Village of Choy Hang, South China
Is Today a Revered Shrine of the Kuomintang

Sixty years ago, on November 12, Sun Yat-sen was born in this dozing village, inside a rustic hut made of clay bricks and straw. Today, five years since his death, there is no more honored name in all Asia. His apotheosis is nearly complete. For in the modern China that rejects saints and devils and brands religious loss as foolish superstition, Sun Yat-sen is a new kind of god—the god of Chinese nationalism.

I was in Canton on the last anniversary of Sun's birth. Wherever the Kuomintang flag was flying—and this year that included most of China—November 12 was a holiday. In Canton it was almost a holy day. Government offices, factories, department stores, all but the smallest shops, were closed. Schools were out and soldiers halted their preparations for new punitive expeditions against the perennial rebels.

On Tai Ping Lo, on Yat Ping Lo, on other broad boulevards of Canton, Chinese pailous had been erected and from their grave arches swung photographs of Sun Yat-sen. Beneath them passed thousands of Cantonese on parade. Schoolboys dressed in white uniforms and carrying placards bearing words from the "San Min Chu I," the catechism of Sunyatsenism. Schoolgirls, marching in the sensible dress introduced by Madame Sun Yat-sen. Government officials, clerks, stenographers, wearing the simple semi-military Chung Shan coat. Hundreds of members of the Kuomintang, young men most of them, and all bowing and saluting the "late leader" as they marched beneath the great red and blue and white pailous. Cadets, from the government military training school, smart in their Sam Brown belts. Bands, music, singing. And fat merchants in their private motor cars.

At another hour in the day I stood with Chinese friends in the hall of the Nationalist party during the memorial ceremony to Sun Yat-sen. Two thousand bared heads bowed once, twice, three times in silence before the portrait of the peasant lad from Choy Hang. At the same moment, in every village that held a local branch of the Kuomintang, over every province in China, other Chinese were making the same gesture of respect.

In cities of the north I had often attended these meetings. Every Monday the same ritual is performed with fewer elaborations. But even in Nanking it often seemed to me that for most of the participants it was more formulas, necessary but in itself of no significance. Here in the south as you get nearer to the tradition of Sun Yat-sen the proceedings take on the depth and zeal of a creed. I felt this especially during the reading of Sun's will.

"For forty years," Sun declared in this last testament,

> I have devoted myself to the cause of the people's revolution with but one end in view, the elevation of China to a position of freedom and equality among the nations. My experience during these years has firmly convinced me that to attain this goal we must bring about a thorough awakening of our own people and ally ourselves in a common struggle with those peoples of the world who treat us on a basis of equality. The work of the revolution is not done. Let all comrades follow my "Plans for National Revolution," "Fundamentals of National Reconstruction," "Three Principles of the People" and the "Manifesto" issued by the First National Convention of our party and strive earnestly for their consummation. Above all our recent declarations in favor of the convocation of a national convention and the abolition of unequal treaties should be carried into effect with the least possible delay. This is my heartfelt charge to you.

Signed a few hours before the leader's death in 1925, that statement is now memorized by every schoolboy in China. It is a Gettysburg address and a Declaration of Independence rolled into one. It has become known, in half a decade, to as many living men as any historic document of human liberty.

No wonder, when I visit Choy Hang, I am a little awed in the home of a man whose words and spirit have been used to such wide influence over the continent of Asia. I am prepared to make the triple bow before entering the gate and I half expect to find two soldiers waiting there to enforce the kowtow.

But no theatrics greet the pilgrim to this shrine. From the wide sandy plain of Chung Shan, the "model district," our motor car swoops out of a wreath of dust and halts at the edge of the village of Choy Hang. Opposite is a two-story gray brick house, with a long veranda on the second floor and an inclosed porch on the first. It is surrounded by an open courtyard around which runs a low wall pierced by a very plain gate over which is an inscription in small characters, "Sun Wen Home."

In the yard some urchins dressed in cotton bibs that cover them only in front are playing a solemn game in the dirt. Over in a corner there is a leafy shade tree, some southern variety of the acacia and around it half a dozen robust ferns and healthy flowering plants are potted in blue urns set on marble Chinese pedestals.

"That tree," says an English-speaking Chinese who has come out of the house to meet me, "was planted by Dr. Sun after he graduated from Queen's College at Hongkong. He say would live till revolution completed." This doesn't look well for China. It appears that the tree will last for many years to come. But I keep this observation to myself, for the Chinese is jolly, and there is no purpose in making unpleasant suggestions to a man of such obvious good will toward all.

"I am Mr. Lok," he tells me. "I know Sun Wen in Honolulu, years before. Now I getting old. I come back native village for retire. Government asks me take care Dr. Sun's house. I got little else to do."

Like many Chinese who have lived in America, Mr. Lok has a habit of talking like a telegram. It is not pidgin-English for he is an educated men. It is merely efficiency in words. He speaks rapidly and almost constantly, and he laughs a great deal. He is short and fat and full of good-natured, nervous energy.

"Come in, come in!" he invites, and takes me by the arm. We enter a stone-floored room, one end of which has been turned into a kind of family altar. There are two large brass incense burners and above them are portraits of Sun Yat-sen's mother and father, of his brother, Sun Mei, who helped educate him in Hawaii, and of himself. They are all draped in red embroidered silk, and some framed mottoes by Sun hang beside them. The rest of the walls are covered with photographs of Sun's comrades, honorary shields, scepters and some scrolls done in the exquisite calligraphy of scholars.

Along the sides of the room are ranged ten or twelve stools of Chinese blackwood and some marble-topped tables on which rest teapots in padded heat retainers. Several old women are sitting hunched and gnawing watermelon seeds. One of them is Sun Yat-sen's sister, three years his elder. When I am introduced to her she smiles and rises to shake hands. It is a little startling to discover that she has bound feet. Now I remember that when Sun was 14 he rebelled against the foot-breaking ceremony practiced on his younger sister, and in reprisal broke the mud feet off one of the village gods, after which he rather hurriedly left town.

All the other rooms in the house have been kept exactly as they were when Sun lived here during his early revolutionary activities. Nothing has been taken away, nothing added, except a few photographs contributed by Sun's friends. Several are interesting groups of the old Tan Meng Hut secret society, forerunner of the Kuomintang. Some were taken while Sun was conducting his anti-Manchu propaganda abroad and the Son of Heaven had put a price of $500,000 on his head.

Mr. Lok is talking. He is nearly always talking. And it is a pleasure to hear his rush of words and information. "In this picture Dr. Sun was schoolboy, Honolulu. Here very famous motto written by Dr. Sun." He reads it in Chinese, then translates, "It means, 'Easier to know than to do.' Right, eh? Of course. Dr. Sun always right. But look here! This letter written by Dr. Sun twenty years before. This manuscript first draft people's constitution. Dr. Sun used these medical books when . . ."

And so on. Mr. Lok guides me through every room, and for each article there is some anecdote, some stray phrase by Dr. Sun, ordinary words most of them, become memorable only because he said them. Finally, I am taken over to a carved table and a chair which I am assured was the "only place Dr. Sun ever really rested." He could not have had that pleasure very often. He must have fidgeted much, for his life was ever in peril. A Frenchman once said to me that the real price every great leader pays for his fame is the inability to relax his thighs.

As I am about to leave, Mme. Sun, her eyes friendly behind silver-rimmed spectacles, moves over to me holding the family guest book between fine thin hands and wrists encircled by jade bracelets. She asks me to sign my name. "Two of your countrymen have been here this year," she says, and opens the book to their signatures. One of them was Agnes Smedley, who wrote in her round, swift hand, "I am sorry that the original clay hut where Sun Yat-sen was born has not been preserved to show how he came from the poorest and humblest of people."

The little house formerly was in a corner of the courtyard and would have been picturesque if left standing. But Dr. Sun was impatient with antiquities. He wanted no sentiment in removing that crude ancestral home when he returned from the "outside lands" with money enough to build something more modern and comfortable.

The other American had been mildly laudatory. He wrote: "At last, a lifelong ambition has been realized! I have reached the home of the Greatest Man of All Time!"

Out in the dry white dust of the roadway again, we walk through Choy Hang, Happy Valley. There are the usual candid pigs and naked children ambling about as if they had nothing to do and a great many lives in which to accomplish it. Roosters yawn and crow and small boys throw sticks at the birds. Otherwise, it is not a lively place. In five minutes we have seen everything and it is hard to believe Mr. Lok when he declares the population is 2,500—until further inquiry produces the information that 2,000 of them are living in foreign countries. "Let a man live in America twenty years, he is still a citizen of Choy Hang," I am told.

Now, the flesh that was Sun Yat-sen lies under the purple roof of a $3,000,000 mausoleum in far-away Nanking, and not many of those who climb to it, up a mile-long flight of steps, even remember where he was born. But the people of "Happy Valley" do not forget. They say the spirit of a Choy Hang man always returns. They say all that was immortal in Sun Yat-sen stays here, unworldly now and resting under the banyan trees he loved as a boy.

III. Indo-China and Yunnanfu (Kunming)

Introduction to Section III

In Edgar Snow's description of his landing at Haiphong, on November 23, 1930, he notes that French Customs officials were searching for concealed books by such dangerous authors as Lu Hsun. Three years later Snow would edit a collection of modern Chinese writers that featured Lu's work, *Living China*. Agnes Smedley had become a close friend of Lu's immediately after she arrived in Shanghai in 1929. She hosted a secret but defiantly well-attended birthday party for Lu Hsun just before Snow left Shanghai. Although Smedley almost certainly provided Snow with introductory letters to the Chattopadhyaya family in India, he was apparently not yet sufficiently known or trusted in her revolutionary circle at the time of the party to be invited.[1]

Also disembarking at Haiphong were Bill Smith, an engineer for Anderson, Meyer & Company, and Pierre Bloy, an aviator and former manager of Coty's Chicago factory. Bloy was a friend of chorus girls and show people from the States and the Continent.[2] The three got "slightly squiffed" on cheap, good wine at the Hotel de l'Europe before going to see a second-rate musical comedy, at which Snow found the audience more entertaining than the production. He distilled the rambling observations of his diary into the description of a corpulent Frenchman and his sensitive Annamite companion, which appears near the conclusion of his Haiphong article. Later, Snow and Bloy went dancing at a hotel where many Eurasians were present. This seems the likely occasion for his lightly thinking of love as a "leavener of color prejudice," though in his diary he noted that Bloy and other French bachelors seemed more interested in married European women than in the eligible Annamite or Tonkinese.

The next afternoon Snow interviewed the Haiphong manager of Standard Oil, who was outspokenly critical of French rule. That evening he and Bloy paid twenty-five dollars to be driven to Hanoi. Snow stayed there little more than a week before beginning the three-day train journey to Yunnanfu.

1. Janice R. MacKinnon and Stephen R. MacKinnon, *Agnes Smedley: The Life and Times of an American Radical* (Berkeley: University of California Press, 1988), 151–53.
2. Snow, transcript of diary 3: 1. Snow gives Bloy the name "Coudray" in *Journey to the Beginning*, 42.

While in Shanghai, Snow had written an article on opium use in China, "Celestial Poppy Smoke," for *Asia* (March 1931) that was subsequently excerpted by several other magazines. He had followed that writing with a disillusioning investigation of a much-touted Japanese experiment at controlling opium use on Formosa.[3] In Hanoi the heavy fragrance of opium became for him the odor of decadent French colonialism. The French used the same bland denials to turn away charges both of the addictive nature of opium and of the oppressive nature of colonialism.

On the second day of Snow's train ride to Yunnanfu, the relative comfort of his car was invaded. Weary, hungry peasant soldiers, ragtag remnants of a force of fifty thousand men, had been coerced into escorting a rich caravan of opium-laden mules from Yunnan to the consuming centers of Shiuchow, Wuchow, and Canton. The force had been organized to break a yearlong blockade by the Red forces of the south, but it was touted as a "punitive expedition" against the Kwangsi bandits. The close of Snow's story of the official neglect and abuse of these peasant troops understates, but reveals, his professional commitment: "It was true that travel with them had not been a comfortable experience. But after all it was not comfort I sought here, but incident, and they had given me an abundance of that." Their story became one more item on his lengthy list of the tragic human consequences in the devastating traffic in opium.

Journey to the Beginning was published in 1958 as America was beginning its tragic slide into the quagmire of the Vietnam War. In this autobiography Snow tells of meeting French-educated Annamites through a Chinese merchant on his 1930 visit. The Annamites gave him copies of the demands of the organized Vietnamese resistance against the French. He also describes smuggling reports of this incipient rebellion past the French censors to Hong Kong, and he quotes from one of his dispatches. No stories resulting from those dispatches seem to have appeared in the *New York Sun,* and Snow does not mention either the Chinese merchant or such documents in his diaries. It is possible that he considered it too dangerous to put such information in writing that might then be sequestered.

However, while in Hanoi, Snow did read the newspaper *La Volonté Indo-Chinoise* and noted in his diary its strong editorial criticizing the

3. "Formosa, the Island of Monopolies," *China Weekly Review* (October 25, 1930): 277–78 (see Introduction, section I).

government's policy toward the Communist movement. He noted its report of the execution of twelve Communists over three days, November 23–25, 1930. He also interviewed M. Garreau, chief of the foreign service, about the resistance. He learned that the rebellion had begun with an Annamite troop in Ven Bay early in the year. In June peasants had demonstrated against landlords in Dalat and other cities of Cochin. In September, five thousand armed peasants had marched on Vinh, the provincial capital of North Annam. The French responded with bombs and machine guns, killing one hundred fifty and wounding six hundred, but the march continued. The peasant demonstrations against the landlords spread, and the French retaliated by sending troops to occupy and police the major cities. The French claimed that sixty revolutionary leaders were living in Canton. Only recently Governor-General M. Pasquier's ship had been sabotaged as he prepared to sail from Haiphong. The boiler was ripped out, and the engine was damaged. Pasquier was forced to return to Hanoi, but then "turned the incident to his own glory by suddenly deciding to accompany the aviators Goulette and Laouette," who were attempting to set a new flight record between Indo-China and the Continent.[4] None of this, however, kept Snow from writing, with what now seems embarrassing assuredness, that in contrast with the Indians and the Chinese the Annamites and the Tonkinese "look as though they had never been anything but a subject race, and worse, as if it had never occurred to them, that they might be anything else."

But Haiphong and Hanoi, fascinating as they were as test cases of French colonialism, were still only a sideshow compared to the travel adventure that loomed center-stage in Snow's imagination. In the third article of this section he describes plotting his escape from the confining office of the *China Weekly Review* by poring over Maj. H. P. Davies's map of the region, reviewing Dr. Joseph F. Rock's articles in *National Geographic,* and talking with Col. Theodore Roosevelt about caravan life: bandits, golden monkeys, and blue sheep. Yunnan, remote and strange, thus gathered "tumultuous" magical associations for him.

The sad state of the narrow-gauge French railway that carried him from Hanoi to Yunnanfu seemed an ironically appropriate comment on the defeat of French colonial ambition. It had been overwhelmed not by armed native rebellion but by the extraordinary challenges of mountainous terrain, a severe terrain that isolated peoples and com-

4. Snow, transcript of diary 3: 9–14.

munities. Thus, it afforded effective protection to ancient feudal corruption and arbitrary rule against the spread of modern corruption and the arbitrary rule of European colonialism. Snow admired the bold planning and ingenious engineering of the railway but saw no reason to regret the thwarting of French imperial and commercial interests.

Snow found Yunnanfu filthy, frustratingly inefficient, and dangerously barbaric. He was shocked, but fascinated, to find a city unchanged in many ways for a thousand years despite being closely connected for the last thirty years with modern civilization by railway. But the surrounding mountainous country offered many glorious surprises, and sometimes these surprises were enhanced by myth and history. On December 29, three weeks after arriving in the city, having bought the provisions and hired the personnel necessary for a caravan to take him to Tali, Snow abruptly changed his mind. He persuaded Mr. Wang, the interpreter from the American consulate, to hire a car to take him to Anningchow, where Snow retrieved his goods, and broke his contract with the muleteers who were packed and ready to leave. As they passed by Pi Chi Shan [Jade Phoenix Mountain], Wang told him the story of amorous denial and jealousy associated with the mountain. Snow must have been at one of his lowest moments of frustration and despair, but later, before his typewriter, recognizing that he and Marco Polo probably had heard the same story made all his frustration seem only the necessary irritation within the oyster that produces a pearl.

Snow arrived in Yunnanfu on December 6 but did not begin his caravan trip until January 31. Making the arrangements necessary to travel by caravan from Yunnan to Burma with reasonable safety proved far more difficult in practice than when he had dreamed about the trip in the *Review* office. The difficulty of those decisions became the subject of this section's final article, but Snow refrained from giving details that might antagonize those on whom he depended for help.

Upon his arrival in Yunnanfu events had moved quickly and with seeming good luck. Harry Stevens, the American consul, immediately called on Snow and invited him to stay at his home. He informed Snow that Dr. Joseph Rock, one of the two Westerners who had written with authority on this region, was arranging for a caravan to leave Yunnanfu and travel at least part of Snow's intended route. Stevens took Snow to meet Rock the next day, and Rock readily invited him to join his caravan.

But neither Snow's relation with Stevens nor with Rock developed as smoothly as these early meetings promised. Snow was originally very flattered at Rock's friendliness and more than a little awed by his scholarly achievements. He also envied Rock's success at marketing his writing. He remarked in his diary that *National Geographic* paid Rock $1,500 per article and gave him a book contract guaranteeing $7,000 for a two-hundred-thousand-word manuscript.[5] On December 13, Snow noted in his diary that Rock could not leave until after Christmas. A week later Snow began to feel that the Stevenses, particularly Mrs. Stevens, who had apparently not been consulted before her husband invited Snow, were beginning to resent his prolonged stay. Stevens was also unduly fearful that Snow might write disparagingly about him. He persuaded Snow to promise not to write about him at all. On December 23, Snow moved from the Stevens home to the shabby Hotel du Commerce. By this time Snow knew of both Stevens's and Rock's more guarded views of each other, neither of which were very complimentary.

On December 22, on Rock's recommendation, Snow had hired Ho Chi, Rock's discharged cook, for a caravan to Bhamo. Rock was not ready to travel with this caravan, but he apparently advised Snow on the details. The next day Rock sent a note saying that the caravan had arrived in the city. With Ho Chi's help Snow then purchased supplies and made final arrangements. He had doubts, however, about making the long trip alone. He listed the following reservations: "Possibility of robbery & kidnapping; chance of delay by magistrates who refuse to give permission to pass through their territory because of unsettled conditions; my inability to make self understood in Chinese; insufficient funds in case of emergencies; consciousness of having done no work since my arrival in Yunnanfu 20 days before; and likelihood of inability to do anything for next 40 days."[6]

His *work* was writing. Since his diary indicates he had in fact typed on several occasions before this date in Yunnanfu, his comments were probably characteristically harsh self-criticism over not sending out much finished copy. At any rate, on December 29, Snow gave in to his anxieties about the trip and decided not to go.

Rock also recorded this "most unpleasant experience with that Mr. Snow" in his diary. He charged Snow with arbitrarily breaking his

5. Ibid., 9.
6. Ibid., 25–26.

contract and failing to pay the muleteers sufficiently for their lost opportunity. Snow was an "uncouth American youth . . . only learned in ill manners." Rock noted disparagingly that Snow bought potassium cyanide instead of potassium permangamate to disinfect fresh vegetables on his trip. He could have killed himself and his cook at their first meal.[7]

Despite their differences and antipathies Snow and Rock were drawn to each other. As Snow learned more about Rock's past he tried to fathom the significance of his "curious mixture of conviviality & seclusiveness." He posed a question about Rock pertinent to himself: "What force is it, unseen by us, which urges men into voluntary withdrawal from crowd and kind? It must be some trace of atavism mixed with a driving pull toward the thrills of living that are found nearest the greatness of nature which despite all men's genius, still reduced his total accomplishment to nothingness in the great high spaces of time & perpetuity."[8]

But as early as December 10 he began noting traits in Rock that he would have to allow for in their future relation: "Susceptible to flattery. Easily led on to conversation by playing on his vanity . . . Does not like criticism. Thinks J. B. Powell is a Bolshevik." Rock's suspicions of Powell stemmed from Powell's publishing of an article by Jack Young that raised unwelcome questions about Rock's activities.[9]

By January 3, at tiffin, Rock had apparently forgiven Snow. Rock informed Snow that he expected his own caravan to leave by January 20. Snow spent a week mulling over his own decision. Finally, after a frank face-to-face talk with Rock, Snow decided once more to travel with him. Again, however, the question did not long remain decided.

Snow was invited to move in with a couple named Parker, who ran the local YMCA, on January 12.[10] That day he received a note from

7. Joseph F. Rock, diary 16: 4–6.

8. Snow, transcript of diary 3: 12.

9. Ibid., 14.

10. Snow had little good to say about his stay at the Hotel du Commerce except for meeting the "most engaging personality" of his Yunnanfu stay, a middle-aged French painter, Madame Besant, more a commercial artist than a potential Velázquez or Corot, but with "a deep sorrow in her eyes that are nearly always hidden beneath those long lashes." One day Snow walked into Madame's room when she was painting a nude Chinese courtesan laying on a leopard robe smoking opium: "The rich contrast of her white flesh against the velvet softness of the leopard robe gave her the appearance of a kind of forbidden nocturnal flower unfolding in an erotic dream. I understood at once why Madame had chosen to paint her at night." Deep in her opium dream, the model gave no sign of resentment at Snow's entrance

Stevens: two Seventh Day Adventist missionaries would be traveling to Tali two days later, and Snow could join them. While Snow was considering that, Rock arrived and abruptly announced, "Well, I think you had better not go with me." When informed of Snow's other opportunity, Rock pouted, "Go with them. They're not *naturalized* Americans. . . . You don't like naturalized Americans, I understand." Then he turned on his heel and left.

Snow felt aggrieved and angry himself and wrote requesting an explanation from Rock. He met the missionaries and was pleased to find they were not the evangelical type, but he was not ready to leave until he received his mail and an expected check. January 13 was Rock's birthday, and at tea in honor of the event Rock told Mrs. Parker "an unclear story" of the cause of his previous day's behavior. At dinnertime he sent Snow a note that did not mention his "blow-off" but did invite Snow (again) to travel with him. That evening Snow visited Rock, agreed to the trip, and noted in his diary, "Well, that's that—till tomorrow at least."[11]

When January 20 came Rock postponed departure until January 25, by which time he was ill in bed. Even on January 31, when he and Snow finally left Yunnanfu for Laoyakuan, he threatened to back out of the trip altogether. On January 20, Snow also discovered to his surprise and dismay that a Japanese dentist, who had been drilling one of his teeth during more than one visit, was planning to "put a gold tooth in my head." He could only hope to have this "hideous thing" taken out when he reached Rangoon, but he feared "this devil has left very little of my tooth!"[12]

On January 24, Snow recorded his fear at what "Consolidated Press will have to say about all this procrastination. I can never explain to them the long delay. And I am sure I shall never get sufficient copy out of the trip to make it worthwhile from their viewpoint. My God, but

---

into the room. Mme. Besant worked with intense quickness, but clearly gestured for Snow to remain. After about ten minutes the model finished her pipe, stretched, and fell asleep. Besant quickly finished her painting and explained to Snow: "I didn't intend to paint her like that. I asked her for [a] simple standing nude. But she refused—said she'd be bored unless she could smoke. It was only after she started that I recognized an unusual picture. I painted it as swiftly as I could and it is finished now." She then invited Snow to dine with her, savoring the thought of her subject "lying on my bed in that supremely exhausted physical bliss" (Snow, transcript of diary 2: 22–24).

11. Snow, transcript of diary 4: 3–4.
12. Ibid., 10.

it's awful—this fearful waiting, waiting. I do wish I'd gone on, the solitariness be damned. It would be better to be with bandits than biting my nails here in this filthy hole."[13] But the day of departure eventually came and, finally taking his leave, Snow could "wink slyly at a brown, pleasant old woman leading a morose old buffalo, and . . . say to her that Yunnanfu, after all, has been rather an amusing experience."

Chronology 1930–1931

November 23	Arrives Haiphong, 10:45 A.M.
November 24	Leaves for Hanoi by car, P.M.
December 4	Leaves Hanoi, 8 A.M., by train for Lao Kay; Stays overnight
December 5	Arrives Ami-chow, 7 P.M.
December 6	Leaves Ami-chow, 6:30 A.M.; Arrives Yunnanfu, 5:45 P.M.
December 7	Moves to Stevens's home
December 8	Meets Dr. Joseph Rock; Receives first invitation to travel with Rock
December 23	Moves to Hotel du Commerce
December 29	Cancels caravan; Retrieves baggage from Anning-chow
January 8	Accepts Rock's second invitation to caravan to Tali
January 12	Quarrels with Rock; Receives different invitation to walk to Tali; Moves to Parker's home
January 13	Agrees, again, to travel with Rock
January 24	Postpones departure scheduled for January 27
January 29	Caravan leaves, A.M.; Rock and Snow to catch up the next day
January 31	Leaves; Arrives Laoyakuan, 5 P.M.

13. Ibid., 11.

Haiphong, the Great New Port Built by the French in Northern Indo-China

Which May Look French, but Is Oriental

Sheep, rice and Chinese form the chief cargo carried by the little vessels, of 500 tons, that toss over the 450 miles from Hongkong to this northernmost seaport of France in Asia. It costs $2 more to ship a fat sheep than a Chinese pays to travel in steerage. The human in the hold takes up greater deck space, but the sheep's food is more expensive. Sometimes the sheep die, and the company has to figure in that when computing its rates.

"*Mais non,*" remarked the French skipper from the bridge of the S.S. *Canton,* on which I was a passenger, "*Mais non,* we do not mix ze sheep and ze Chinese—onless eet becomes necess, bu We put ze sheeps in ze front, ze Chinese in ze back. But when zere ees too much beesness from ze sheeps, zen we put zem in ze back also." His florid windbeaten face grinned and he slyly tugged the beard which made you think of him, somehow, as an artistic villain.

"Of course," he continued, "ze sheeps zey do not like eet—but zere is no other place to put zem. You see?"

I saw. There were perhaps a hundred Chinese stowed in the hold, men and women lying on the same long mat-covered platforms. A great wire netting stretched the width of the ship between them and the engine room. They were not all poor folk, though a great many looked as if they had come fresh from the rice paddies of Kwangtung, bent on immigrating to a warmer land that brought surer reward to honest Chinese effort. Some were dressed in southern silks and gay patterns of satin, their hair gleaming, with slippery elm and a few so fat that you at once associated them with affluence and wondered why they were traveling in such fashion.

But it is always thus in China. Chinese willingly sacrifice comfort and convenience and cleanliness if they can save a few dollars thereby. Occasionally, I have recognized merchants of considerable wealth, men whose fortunes might go into five figures or six, traveling deck passage. They curl up on their strip of matting, cozy in nothing but their underclothing, and apparently are quite happy. I suppose that is the kind of real democracy which we cannot understand. Or it may be merely Chinese miserliness.

Yet I have envied these deck passengers when we get into a port in the East. They pick up their little bundles wrapped in blue cloth and their baskets filled with teacups and teapots and hot water bottles. And without bothering about porters or customs officials or the everlasting distribution of gratuities they march swiftly down the gangway and are soon about their business. Meanwhile, you are being put through a cross-examination by officious, stupid and exasperating hirelings.

The customs men at Haiphong are notoriously inquisitive. They hand you three long forms to fill out, and then they ask you questions in French—for you pass out of the English belt when you leave south China—as if they would like to catch you up on something. They cannot see why an American newspaper man should want to come to Haiphong, and they do not with much subtlety disguise their suspicions that you may be, after all, a Red agitator with fake papers. So they take up your passport and inform you that you will have to call for it at the police station next day. Nor are they disturbed by your protest that you wish to go up to Hanoi that night.

And the customs examination of your baggage, it is a thorough-going business. It is not like China, where a man looks at you and sees that you are a foreigner, smiles and says, "All right, sir." Here you have got to produce the keys to your bags and your trunk and have the contents dumped onto the pavement, where there are many other people crowding around you. The point is that after they have satisfied themselves that you are carrying no arms, ammunition, opium or narcotics and that the books you have are not by Lenin, Trotsky, Gorky nor Lo Shun [*sic*], you have to bundle all your clothes away in chaos and a stinging heat.

Haiphong. It is a Chinese name, but beyond that there is not much to show that it is in territory over which, up to the time of the French, Chinese had held a suzerainty since the reign of Kubla Khan. The streets are wide, so that you could lead half a troop on line through them, and they are well paved.

It is a clean, white-washed, palm-dotted city, "like a town in southern France," as they tell you, which is something they seem to regard as its chief virtue. Its newness astonishes you, for you have been used to the antiquity of Chinese towns, and a place that is less than four or five hundred years old is difficult to realize. Haiphong is less than fifty.

When the French took over Annam and established a "protectorate" in Tonkin, following the war of 1884, in which China lost her claim to these provinces, they looked at once for a port which would be to the north of their Eastern empire what Saigon had long been in the south. They decided upon Haiphong. It was then hardly a name, only a few fishermen's huts reaching down toward the sea. Now it is a city of 100,000 people and except for the native quarter it is Europe transplanted on Asiatic soil.

I like the French in the Orient. They are mad, many of them, it is true, and they often make a great deal of money in ways which are not quite honest. But they are gay and vivacious and they can nearly always amuse you with their talk. In the ports of the East, so heavy with humdrum and inarticulate men, that sort of person is charming. Moreover, he is generally in love. And you cannot help admiring a man who can keep romance intact in environments that are all against it.

But I do not like this French city of which they are so proud. It may indeed be like a town in southern France. But it is not France, and it seems silly to go on pretending that it is anything more than a second-rate imitation. It is [as] absurd as the belief that a Parthenon would ever look right in America. Or a Chinese monastery. I do not like to see things uprooted and thrust across an ocean or a continent merely to suit strangers in a strange land.

I know it is not a very practical viewpoint. But I am a traveler and avid for the picturesque. I suppose if I were a French resident and owned a motor car I should appreciate those broad highways and be gratified that there were such splendid shops like those in Paris. Even were I a wealthy Annamite with wives to drive round in imported motor cars or to follow me grandly down the boulevards in rickshaws my opinion might be otherwise. But there are not many rich men among the natives and for the rest it is hard to see how they benefit greatly from motor cars in which they cannot ride, clubs into which they cannot enter, the French modistes whose gowns they cannot buy, or the iced aperitifs which Frenchmen sip beneath striped awnings in front of the Hotel de l'Europe.

The natives are naive. They regard the sidewalks as places where one sleeps when the heat is over. They regard the fine streets as thoroughfares for the pedestrian and sullenly look upon speeding motor cars as intruders. But the most useful purpose which they seem to have found for both sidewalks and streets is for target practice with the bright crimson betel juice. All Haiphong is stained with it, from the wharf to the end of Boulevard Paul-Bert, and beyond to the rice fields.

The Tonkinese wear a gown that flares out and ends at the knees. It has a low collar that is fastened at the throat, but the rest is buttoned at the side, like a Chinese garment. Indeed, that is what it is, except that the Chinese have not worn such a style for twenty-five years. Beneath this there are long Chinese trousers which are held up by rolling the waist band into three or four thicknesses.

A Frenchman took me to the Municipal Theater, where a Paris company was doing very poor musical comedy. The chorines were too old and a little haggard, they sang in French which my friend declared was wretched, and I felt that they would have gone better with more clothes. But the audience was intriguing.

In front of me there sat a middle-aged Frenchman, nearly bald, very wide at the hips and with a double chin. He found the play rich in mirth, and he laughed often, a loud, coarse laugh which had in it a quality oddly disquieting. Now and then, overcome by his own enthusiasm, he would turn to speak excitedly to the Annamite girl beside him.

Her figure was trim and supple and had in it the delicacy of youth not yet mature. She had rather a good face, there was a nice balance to her features and she had lovely, slender hands, one of which was clasped tightly over a snuff bottle. Her little shoes lay beneath the seat, for she was sitting on her feet, as is the Annamite custom. She sat quite still and she did not smile.

She did not understand French and it was evident that she had no regrets about it. When the corpulent gentleman seated next to her turned to explain a rapt phrase from the stage, she greeted his translation with no sign of appreciation. She was not impolite, she did not look stupid, so that you concluded she was merely utterly indifferent. But in her eyes there was the stubborn hurt look of a sensitive child who has been made to eat something which was repulsive to her.

In the audience there were other French colonials with their native wives or mistresses. Some had brought along their children, swarthy little things with a frightened look in their eyes, as though they already knew the troubles that lay ahead in their hybrid lives.

I said to the Frenchman with me that it looked as though the white men were being absorbed by the natives. Love was a leavener of color prejudice, and after all was perhaps the most disastrous weapon against imperialism. The Frenchman shrugged his shoulders, and replied: "Oh ce n'est rien! These things are not enduring or important. And it is not love, my friend; it is a matter of comfort and convenience. I tell you a man gets lonely and morbid out here without a woman. If you were to live here for a while you would understand."

After the theater we went to the Hotel du Commerce where the Frenchman introduced me at a table of pretty Eurasian girls. The floor was large and there were too many people. It was dusk when I left and walked down toward the canals, where the natives live.

Annamites and Chinese and Tonkinese leaned in dark doorways and smoked cigarettes or indolently sipped tea. In the streams little sampans, like swarming night insects, lay motionless, tied to the banks while the family squatted in the bow round a brazier over which simmered the evening meal. An old man hurried by with a bamboo yoke on his shoulder, from the two ends of which hung pots of hot rice, chopped meat, steamed rolls and bits of boiled greenery.

Presently I came to a doorway that looked like the rest, except that there was a little garden before it, and a table with some chairs. So I sat down with a China teapot and a handleless cup full of a pale fragrant tea. The cries of the night, the clumpety clump of wooden shoes on the cobbled streets, the smell from somewhere nearby of burning sandalwood, the slow arc of a temple roof massed dark against the sky, the reflection of a lantern-lit tea-house glimmering on the canal and seen through the garden gate; it was the Orient.

Hanoi, Chief City of the French "Protectorate" in Tonkin, Annam and Laos

Where Everything Is Gay—on the Surface

We arrived at the Hotel Metropole in a motor car which we had hired at Haiphong. We—there was a young French aviator with me, whom I had met on the ship coming down from Hongkong. It was a nonstop journey and the Annamite chauffeur had seemed possessed with a passion for speed. Haiphong, about ninety miles down toward the mouth of the Red River, we had left at 10 o'clock and we reached Hanoi at 11:45 P.M. It was the fastest trip I had made, except an airplane flight to Hankow, and I felt a trifle shaken when at last we rolled up the spacious Boulevarde Henri Rivière.

The Hotel Metropole is a four-story building of white stone, with high ceilings and long shuttered windows, and it rambles over half a city block. Officials of the secondary status stay here, and traveling men and tourists. It is, I believe, the only public place where society dances in Hanoi (if you exclude the sidewalk cafes). Here you see the wives of French army officers, the wives of French officials, and a few brilliant and seductively gowned Congais, or Eurasians, in the arms of men who are generally not their husbands. It is all very gay and on Saturday nights, when dancing lasts until 2 o'clock, it even partakes of a breathless abandon. Everybody drinks too much but does not become obnoxious, the army officers grow warm but seem happy in uniforms which it appears they wear for all occasions, the French ladies are charmingly French ladies in gowns that are completely decolleté, and the orchestra plays Steinka Razine so often that its yearning fugue stays in your mind long afterward.

The corridors of the Metropole are cavernous, high and dark. When you walk down one of them, on any floor, you notice a heavy odor that you do not at once recognize as opium because it seems to have in it a vague submerged fragrance. But presently you perceive it comes from the rooms of female smokers who spray their rooms with Narcissus Noire. It is not for the purpose of deceiving anyone, but so that when they light a fresh pipe the opium smell will break over their weary nerves, strong, penetrating and invigorating.

"It is the climate," a French apologist explained to me. "White men need something to buck them up against dysentery, bronchitis and consumption. And opium is not at all harmful if taken in moderation. I myself have used from fifteen to twenty pipes a day for the last ten years. Tell me, do I look the worse for it?"

He was with the Government in a post of some responsibility and a friend of mine in Shanghai had given me a letter to him. After his ready confession, I felt that he could answer and would not be offended by a question I wished to ask.

"Is it true that most of the officials use opium?"

No. I should say not over a third of them. The younger married men generally avoid it. But if a man stays a bachelor for five years he is fairly certain to become a smoker. That was the way with me. I have been out for fifteen years. And among the friends of my early days who are still here I know only two who do not smoke. Of course men have been ruined by the habit. *Oui, c'est bien fâcheux, vraiment! Mais mon ami!* You must know that there are those who make fools of themselves at any pleasure.

One afternoon my official volunteered to show me Hanoi. The French, when they have time, are always pleased to show you Hanoi. They are proud of its white facades, almost Grecian, and of its buildings with nearly Doric columns and of the botanical gardens and the Municipal Theater.

The city is divided into three districts: the French quarter, the native quarter and the Citadel. The latter is a large walled inclosure, fortified and containing government barracks, French and native. It was built long before the French arrived but has been considerably extended and strengthened. In it the 6,000 foreigners of Hanoi could defend themselves almost indefinitely against rioters or revolutionaries. Thinking of that, perhaps, many Frenchmen in recent years have built their homes in this neighborhood.

Hanoi is an old city. For years here on the right bank of the wide Red River, that flows down from the tumultuous mountain ranges of western China, the Tonkinese gathered for trading purposes, and before them tribesmen held their markets and festivals on this plain. After the Chinese conquest, in the thirteenth century, it grew to be a far-scattered collection of adjoining villages each under its native chief and all under a king who once ruled here. Shrines and temples, Confucian and Taoist, were established by Chinese monks and Mandarins sent from the northern Celestial City, Chinese civilization was introduced by the Khan's diplomats and soldiers and the Analects of Confucius became fused with the indigenous culture of Tonkin.

But in the native quarter that now flanks what was once the French "concession" there are few reminders of Chinese rule. The buildings are one- and two- and three-story structures, with barren facades that are as shabby as their occupants and as uninstructive as the eight-toned language which they speak. They tell nothing of the past and give you no hint of the future. They are completely of the present East, that present which is overrun by Chinese contractors putting up square boxes with tin roofs in what they fondly call "foreign style."

A tram line runs through the native quarter and as the sidewalks are scant you are forever hearing the accursed things clanging at your heels. There are rickshaws, too—"*pousse-poussée*," as the French call them—that also dispute your right to the middle of the street. And when a Frenchman comes hurrying through in his Renault you are forced to the conclusion that the indigenes erred in not making their streets a few feet narrower to exclude these mad fellows bent on anni-hilating space and time.

Monsieur, who was still with me, felt that we ought to see the Confu-cian temple on the shore of Petit Lac. He thought it a remarkably graceful piece of architecture. (It is odd how you often find people who have never been in China with a much deeper appreciation of things Chinese than many of the folk who have lived there most of their lives.) Petit Lac lies in the heart of Hanoi, a blue oval of calm water which the French have banded with wide boulevards lined with acacias and oaks and now and then a banyan. In its center there is a crumbling Chinese pagoda, thrusting upward like a last challenge which the European conquerors thought of no consequence when they were removing the rest of the Chinese influence.

Monsieur and I go into the lake temple and walk softly so that we will not disturb the pious at their prayers. It is not purely Confucian, but like most temples advertised as such—about half of it is devoted to shrines for Taoist gods—of Wealth and Happiness and Mercy (who is a goddess) and Fertility. Wealth and Fertility seem to be getting most of the incense and offerings of rice and flowers. But there is a young Annamite girl, intent and all stillness, kneeling before the matronly Kuan Yin and I feel as though I were prying into a confessional as I wonder what strange push of the fates has brought her here to beg Mercy to intercede.

It is evening. Over in the French park a military band is playing. The music of the horns and trumpets marches boldly across the lake, but the reeds tremble and hesitate as though afraid to venture very far, so that the effect is confused and amusing. We listen for a moment, and then laugh. Something brushes past me, scent and the rustle of silk. I turn and see that it is the Annamite girl who has been in communication with Kuan Yin. It troubles me to think that the goddess may have been irritated by my laughter and refused to grant the maiden's wish. To amend matters I buy some sticks of powdered sandalwood, light them and set them as tapers of joss before the immutable old lady. Then my companion and I move on, fearful of distracting the others.

We get into a motor car and drive over the broad highways of the French town. This part of Hanoi, which is now the largest in area, grew out of what was once the French "concession" before France established control over Tonkin in a form quaintly known as a "protectorate."

"No, Tonkin is not a colony, you know," the Frenchmen tell you. "For this reason you do not have so many advantages as in Cambodia and Cochin-China, where the administration is entirely French."

It is difficult for the stranger to discern how a French protectorate differs from a French colony. You can hardly picture a State wherein a people has been more completely relieved of its autonomy. In Hanoi all important posts are filled by Frenchmen. When the legislative bodies are not assembled in Saigon the Governor-General of Indo-China resides here in what the French unblushingly refer to, and with justice to its magnificence, as the Palace. The Provincial Government is under a French Resident-Superieur and the city under a French Mayor. Headquarters of all the principal Government departments—finance, judicial, interior, communications, army, and so on—are located here. Their directors are, of course, French. The banks, telegraphs, railways, telephones, light and power and the opium monopoly are owned by the French, and they also control virtually all major business and industry. It appears that native participation in the Government, except for trivial local offices, is limited to enlistment in the Indigenous Army.

Now, it seems absurd for anyone to dispute that Hanoi is the political and commercial capital of French imperialism in Tonkin and Annam and Laos. It is to the north, with its port of Haiphong, what Saigon is to Cambodia and Cochin-China in the south. Yet the Frenchmen insist that such is not the case. Then they remind me of the Japanese.

We rode for an hour through the spacious avenues, tree-lined and with broad walks flanked by deep gardens behind which were many large homes, some of them charmingly laced with old ivy or roses rambling up their fluted Corinthian columns. We saw numerous schools and we drove past the Indo-Chinese University, to enter which a student must speak French as the language of daily life. There was a long street of shops, with rich Parisian windows with creamy white fronts, but when it reached the Petit Lac it became lined with Chinese and Japanese and native stores and tonsorial parlors. A mile further along, on this same road, you came to a part of the city less populous, and after passing a monument to Francis Garnier (he who subjugated the Indo-Chinese) you began to see the Government buildings. They all looked recent, they were clean and white and in the starlit night they shone with a rapt splendor.

When we walked back toward the Metropole it was over a narrower street, up and down which Annamites and Tonkinese shuffled darkly and without smiling. There is something about these people that hurts you. In them there is the strangely distressing quality that you see in the eyes of those who have resigned themselves to stronger men. They look as though they had never been anything but a subject race, and worse, as if it had never occurred to them that they might be anything else. They are not like the Indian in whose black eyes there seems to be an attitude of waiting, nor are they like the Chinese, who take all men with a philosophical sense of humor, nor like the Japanese, whose pride is something deep and ennobling. They seem to be utterly beaten. They move sullenly aside when you pass too close to them, and they cower. They have no spirit.

Entering the Notorious Yunnan
Province in South China

and Planning a Caravan Trek across
This Mysterious Bandit Ridden Region

Yunnan [South of the Clouds] is a name around which there clings the windy, blustering promise of high Asia. It is a far place and it is west, and it rolls down from the towering splendors of the Tibetan snow ranges. It is a wild, rough country and it is inhabited by wild, rough men, wind-burned men in homespun who ride sturdy ponies or drive shaggy yak over the stormy summits and across the dark, swift-flowing rivers. It is a name of tumultuous magic. It conjures for me the same visions that roll out with the lyric sounds of Tarkand and Urga, of Kashgar and Kabul, of Lhasa and Samarkand, of distant glamorous names from the badlands of the world. If those worlds intrigue you, then it is probable you have a passion for maps. I have.

Two years ago, when I was an armchair traveler in Shanghai, I first made a deliberate search for Yunnan on my map of Asia. I found it, filling in the southwestern corner of China and bounded on the north by Szechuen and Tibet, on the west by Burma, on the southwest and south by the Shan States and Tonkin in French Indo-China and on the east by Kweichow and Kwangsi in south China. In area it is about the size of Poland and its latitude corresponds roughly to that of northern Mexico. It is nearly all mountainous with an average elevation of between five and six thousand feet. But it holds some of the world's loftiest peaks, the Amnyi Machen range in the northwest, rivaling the Himalayas with known heights of over 25,000 feet and others yet unmeasured. Yunnan is the second largest province in China and because of its isolation is perhaps less generally known, even to the Chinese, than any other part of the country. There are many regions which have never been explored.

Searching for more information on Yunnan I found that little had been written. There were Dr. Joseph F. Rock's interesting articles in the *National Geographic Magazine,* and his remarkable pictures, but they did not tell you much about how one got from here to there. The only comprehensive book that had been published on the province was by

A Yunnan peasant harvests opium from a poppy.

Major H. P. Davies, written many years ago. It had been out of print for over a decade, and copies of it were rare and hard to procure. For a long while I could not get hold of one. But I was able to buy his large scale relief map of the province and over this I sat enthralled. It was a wonderful map.

It showed you where the mighty Yangtze Kiang, from the great heights of Kokonor, rushed down through Tibet and entered Yunnan between gorges 18,000 feet above the sea. It showed you where the Salween and the Mekong, close by, and at the same terrible heights, flowed swiftly carrying the snows from the eaves of the world. It showed you the Kingdom of Mi-li, and Lolo Land, both autonomous States, surrounded by Chinese territory but through the centuries never conquered, never absorbed by China. It showed you regions inhabited by the head-hunting P'uman and Ak'as encountered once by a white man who never returned. It showed you the strongholds of the twenty-three principal aboriginal tribes scattered through the deep forests of the north and the fertile jungles of the south. It was a map that was the result of years of hazardous pioneer travel, and behind which lay the abandoned dream of British India for expansion to the north.

On Major Davies' chart I followed the railway that entered Yunnan from French Indo-China and I saw that it reached as far as the capital, Yunnanfu. From there travel was accomplished only by caravan. Mountain trails led off in several directions, some climbing up toward Tibet, some wandering into the Shan States and Burma, and others clambering over the ranges to Chinese provinces in the north and in the east. It was fascinating to trace these routes to their various terminals and contemplate what a journey over one of them would be like. It looked so easy, and yet it looked full of adventure. It became more difficult to put down the urge for such a trip each time I thought of it.

My eye always lingered longer on the Burma frontier. It intrigued me to think of leaving China that way. It stirred me to conceive of such a neat plan for defrauding shipping companies out of passage money for what is considered the inevitable long swing round Singapore. And I thought of Marco Polo, of course, and the old lure to cross his track through Central Asia crept over me. The road to Burma became a fixed idea with me and an ambition.

About this time Theodore and Kermit Roosevelt led their expedition into western China in search of the Giant Panda, which they eventually shot down in Yunnan. I saw Col. Roosevelt when he was in Shanghai and had two long talks with him. He told me something of the adventures of the Kelley-Roosevelt expedition. He described their camps on the wind-swept, snow-driven plateaus. He told of crossing the Yangtze on a single thread of rope and the Mekong on an improvised raft. He mentioned a near encounter with bandits and a visit with the Abbot of Yungning. He told of the golden monkeys they had got in Szechuen and of the blue sheep in Yunnan.

He depicted the picturesqueness of their caravan life and of long treks over majestic peaks and through dense forests. It was absorbing. His testimony satisfied me that it was the kind of thing I wanted and I made up my mind to follow the line I marked out to Burma.

A year and a half have elapsed since then and now at last I have arrived on the Yunnan frontier. Ahead of me is a two-day journey through turbulent hills and untamed tribal country up to the Yunnanfu plateau, 5,000 feet above the level of the sea. Behind me is the day's journey from Hanoi, which takes you through the most fertile valleys of French Indo-China.

The Yunnanfu train leaves Hanoi once a day, at 7:30 A.M. There is no night train. You roll out across fields still drowsing in the mists and with no workers yet tilling them. At first it is all paddy, gently laid out in placid squares that seem fitted over the earth like strips of stained glass. The sun comes up, but it has little warmth until mid-morning. The air is chill and the sky a murky gray.

From Hanoi the country appeared one vast plain, limitless, with no mountains and no forests. But when you have been on the train for perhaps an hour you begin to see the first faint rim of hills, and then clearly you discern a mass of palest blue, and another and another. Soon the railway is flanked with them on either side, though they keep well back and for a while vague, until the sun, roused at last, beats over them, marking them sharp against a clearing sky with the clouds shattered and dispersing.

You begin to climb gradually, though you know it only by the decreasing vigor of the green terraced rice fields and the growing sharpness of the air. The villages are smaller now, and are seen less frequently. Occasionally there is a peasant's new hut, with mud walls and roof of thatch, set in the midst of a clearing but recently torn from the avaricious clutch of tropical vine and tree. There are distances when the train parts masses of pale yellow pampas grass, with slender stems and tufted heads bent melancholy and low with the wind, like Chinese ladies languishing in a T'ang painting. A flock of wild geese, screaming, passes overhead and soon folds into the emptiness of space. And suddenly there is a lake, dark but not sinister, because on it float white lilies and around its shallow edges are fringes of blue hyacinth and lotus. A scent of gladiolas in full bloom drifts through the window and out again and then a fragrance of burning wood comes to linger.

A small station is reached. It stands on the edge of a coffee plantation and the train stops to pick up a few of the peasants who have been laboring there. They get on board silently, with their arms full of bundles and baskets. A Tonkinese, neatly dressed in European clothes, enters the first-class compartment. His eyes are soft and mild; about his manner there is an air of apology. One would say that he is a government clerk; a family man, with perhaps three or four sons, the sort of native who passes the plate in the indigenous Catholic Church.

It is dusk when the train reaches Lao Kay. There are French soldiers loitering on the station platform, for this is a town heavily garrisoned, the headquarters for the border defense. A man takes up your passport and tells you it will be returned the next morning. You get down from the creaking car, stiff from your journey. Some Chinese coolies in station uniforms come up, tie your luggage to their bamboo yokes and motion for you to follow them to the hotel. As they move off, the street is dimly splashed with lantern light and you hear their weary sing-song chant drifting across the dark paddy fields:

Hei-ho, hei-ho, hei-ho. Ho-hei, ho-ho, hei-ho ho-ei.

And you know that in the morning, and for many mornings to come, you will be hearing that same patient cry of labor over and over again, for tomorrow you will be in China.

The Railroad Journey to Yunnanfu
Is Filled with Scenic Thrills
on a Line That Is One of the
Engineering Marvels of the Orient

The two-day rail journey from the border of French Indo-China up to this capital city of farthest China is a steady strain on the gaunt locomotives from the time they start, just after dawn, till they arrive at the end of a stage a little after dusk, with stacks bent and seeming to droop like the weary animals of a caravan.

It is a remarkable railway, conceived with such audacity as to leave you at the end of your trip breathless and admiring. Starting at Haiphong, the port city of north Tonkin, it rolls up to the foot of mountainous southern Yunnan, takes hold with its talons of steel, and proceeds to pull itself up and ever upward, clinging to rocky pinnacles, burrowing through them in long tunnels, slashing into the precipitous sides nearer and nearer the clouds till at last it emerges high on the Yunnan plain and more than a mile above the delta of the sluggish Red River, back to the south and east, near the sea, where it began. Ten years of labor were invested in the railway and 40,800,000 gold dollars. It is 539 miles from terminal to terminal, of which 395 miles are in China. One can readily believe the legend that for this latter section, during the construction of which nearly insurmountable obstacles were encountered, every mile of track cost the life of a Chinese coolie.

From Lao Kay the ascent follows the valley of the Nan-hsi, which river tumbles down through gorges and over rapids and falls of swirling surf, from distant heights where it has its sources near Yunnanfu. The hills are at first low and cloaked in verdure thick and tropical, banana palms and giant ferns, with here and there wild date trees and tamarinds, or an orchard of orange trees, laden with large golden fruit. There are a few paddy terraces cleft from the semi-jungle by hardy hillmen who somehow manage each year to push a little deeper into the tangle of roots and crawling ferns, winning a bit more of the soil to their service.

Then the river becomes swifter and the valley narrower, the hills sharpen and grow taller until sometimes there are long stretches when the sun shines through only for a brief interval at high noon. Struck suddenly against the sky, in sharp silhouette, you see on a mountain top the creeping forms of men and beasts, your first glimpse of a Yunnan caravan. One of the muleteers takes off his wide hat and waves it defiantly against the sky so that you think of him as a gladiator heading the braves of some dead Khan.

The mountain locomotive puffs and snorts and shoots red cinders into the solemn woods as it digs deeper into the rocky heights. There is a moment of suspense when you cross a lank bridge with no guard rail, its legs resting on huge boulders, straddling a snarling stream a hundred feet below. Infinity looks up at you, blankly, as for a mile or two the track huddles close against the wall of the cliffs with a sheer drop to the torrent that you can hear, but cannot always see, far beneath you. There are numerous tunnels, some of them several thousand yards long, which have been cut through solid rock; there are heart-stopping moments when the train, bursting from the darkness of one tunnel, leaps immediately across a wide canyon, only to bury its nose at once into an embankment on the opposite side; there are hairpin twists and one long snaky ascent where for an hour the track advances, then retreats, and then marches ahead again, gaining 600 feet and an elevation whence, like Confucius on Tai Shan, you "look down and feel the smallness of the world."

All one day and the next the train climbs, patiently, stubbornly, indefatigably, with an engine hitched on fore and aft. It keeps high on the banks of the Nan-hsi Ho, which through the centuries, each year a bit more, has worn its bed lower and lower into the towering gorges. You do not often get above these peaks, but occasionally when you can see beyond the nearest of them there is nothing to greet you but troop upon troop of the same thing. The same interminable winding valleys embraced by the same endless succession of hills massed blue against the sky until finally they are lost in the funnel of perspective. There are few plains, but when the river widens a bit and checks its mad haste, or when the scene for a while slopes gently, you observe the industry of peasants who have laid out waving green beans, or fields of tawny wheat, striped neatly over the valleys, like patches on the seat of a pair of trousers.

It is a superb, daring exploit, this railway. The breadth of image behind it and the faith in its purpose reveal boldness and emprise. But for those Frenchmen who originally planned it as a political adventure it is admittedly a failure. Their dream is dead. France's hope to annex

Yunnan to her dominions in Indo-China (the motive with which construction of the line is said to have begun) did not materialize, and there is little reason to believe now that it ever will. So the *Companie Française des Chemins de Fer de l'Indo-Chine et du Yunnan,* which still operates on the concession which France wrung from China after defeating her in the war of 1885, has lost most of its political significance.

Nor has the line been sufficiently profitable to justify the enormous cost at which it was built. The opening of the railway, which it was believed would result in rapid development of commerce and industry in eastern Yunnan, has apparently made small change in the lives of the phlegmatic, indifferent Yunnanese. Traffic on the line has declined steadily, the cars moved last year actually being only a little more than a third of the number handled five or six years ago. Civil war, unchecked outlawry, heavy and yet heavier taxation, the enormous waste of the inefficient, corrupt governments which have controlled what military power has been in the ascendancy, are largely responsible for the diminishing exports and imports of Yunnan and the resultant disastrous effects on the prosperity of the railway.

Disgusted with the wretched misgovernment of the province, the French at present aim to do little but maintain their roadbed, philosophically hope for better days and keep a skeleton service operating between the two ends of the line. Skeleton is a word chosen carefully. For this is railway travel stripped of all comforts. No other line in China, not excepting those so badly used by the war gods in the North, strings together such a mongrel lot of cars, with bent, sagging frames and wheels flat and lopsided, to call them, when they teeter crazily up to a station platform, *Le Yunnan Express!* But the French sense of humor is, of course, well known.

It is said that the concessionaires have learned from bitter experience that it is folly to run any better rolling stock on the China side of their line. Invariably it is commandeered by the military, who draw no distinction between passenger cars and sheep wagons, whether the commodity to be transported happens to be men, mules or horses. In six months the new cars are the same writhing, groaning mass of steel and timber as those which have been similarly maltreated for many years.

A Regiment of Defeated Chinese Soldiers, Sacrificed as a Convoy

for Opium Shipments, Overruns All Classes of Railway Carriages Entering Yunnanfu

The Yunnanese are not an affluent people, but if they were no one could induce them to squander more than the scant minimum required to carry body and bones and bundles from one place to the next. It seems probable that they would be quite willing to balance themselves on a pair of wheels hitched to the tail of a train, provided that by this process they could save some additional coppers for investment in the important pleasure to be derived from a few pipes of opium. As it is, they ride fourth class, in cars that are nothing but freighters. Perhaps occasionally there will remain in one of these cars a broken remnant of what was once a seat, but most of them have been removed by former passengers, who piously carried them off to be placed before the ancestral altar.

One car in each train offers slightly less primitive arrangements for finicky folk, mostly foreigners; it is a combination first-, second- and third-class day coach. But the traveling soldier recognizes none of these artificial barriers created by iniquitous capital. If he chooses, and if he happens to be in sufficient numbers, he invades this sanctum of the Westerner, seats himself on the cushioned leather seats, lights his water pipe, grins, and tells the worried little Chinese conductor, who feels he really ought to collect something for the *cause celebre* of his employers, that he may please go to a specific devil. Whereupon the conductor shrugs his shoulders, lifts his hands in a futile gesture of appeal (a habit he has acquired from the French), looks at you as if to ask what can one do about it, and demonstrates the correct answer by doing nothing.

I write from experience. The afternoon of the last day to Yunnanfu, I am told, is in some respects the most interesting part of the trip. I am in no position to deny it, for during the latter part of the journey I was unable to attend to the scenery. My time was absorbed by a dozen ragged soldiers who had drifted into the first-class cubicle, and, like great, weary, clumsy dogs, draped themselves on the floor, over the seats, on my baggage and against various parts of my anatomy.

145

Do not understand that they were surly or sullen or insolent; they were not. They were good-natured in the rough, generous way of Chinese peasants, and offered me tobacco, opium and an orange. When I would explain that I had paid for and was entitled to the use of a certain part of the carriage they would deferentially leave a little circle around me. But then the tides of sleepiness would sweep over them again and in a moment three or four nodding heads would be inclining toward my shoulder.

They were a miserable lot. Their uniforms, what was left of them, were in tatters, their faces were swollen with the heat and their bare feet were cracked and bleeding. Five of them were wounded and had dirty bandages that only partly covered their infected injuries. They were young and had in their eyes the confused look of children suffering an experience they do not understand. I was moved to pity them.

Nevertheless, they brought in odors of verminous inns, their faces were caked with dirt and sweat, and their deep-chested coughing filled me with dismay. It was not for this that I had paid 40 piastres to ride with the esoteric. But, like the Chinese conductor, I could do nothing about it; there were too many of them. I contented myself with brushing them away, as you do with summer flies, when their tired bodies swayed toward me.

There were others in the second and third class, crowded so that it was impossible for any one to move; any one, that is, except the soldiers, who did not hesitate to clamber up and down the aisle, over each other's necks, arms and legs. Managing to poke my head out of the window, as now and then we neared a station, I saw that gray-clad figures infested the train from engine to caboose. They sat in the windows, with their feet dangling over the side; they were perched on the car roofs and bulged from the platforms; the sides of the fourth-class carriages seemed to swell with the throngs packed inside. If the French could have collected fares from all of them their amortization problem for the year should have been solved. The thought pleased me and I grinned.

"Where have you come from?" I asked one of those sprawling on the seat beside me.

"Kwang-si. We were at Nanning."

"Oh! You were the troops sent against the rebels Pei Tsung-hsi and Chang Fah-kwie?"

"Yes. We were defeated. They had better guns than we."

"Oh!"

"Yes. If it weren't for that we would have beaten them easily. The Yunnanese are good fighters and brave men."

"Oh? Then you will perhaps get a better gun and return to crush Pei and Chang?"

"I? Ah, no, honorable foreigner. Not I. I go back to my village as soon as I have received my pay at the capital. You see, I am not a soldier. I was forced to go to Kwangsi. An officer and a squad of men came to fetch me from my father's field. They told me that I would have to fight for the Revolution and the Three Principles or that I would be shot."

"And the others, will they return?"

"Oh, no, they are the same as I. They want to get back to their families quickly. We have seen enough blood and butchery. Half of our number was killed in Kwangsi." He was silent for a moment and then he laughed. "Some of these fellows," he said, "are as homesick as kittens. They act as if they were not off their mothers' breasts yet." He pointed to a lad who looked soft as butter and lay in an exhausted sleep between two soldiers smoking bamboo water pipes. "We caught that young one weeping like a baby last night."

No wonder they were tired. They had been traveling for forty days, on foot, over the broken trail that scrambled up and down and across rocky mountains and dry, hot valleys and malarious streams. They had no bedding and for food only rice. They had been well treated by the Miaos, the Shans and the Lolos in the tribal villages they passed; but for their generosity more of them would have died of thirst and famine. At the Yunnan border they had been disarmed, their officers had disbanded them, without money and with bare rations of rice, and they had been told to report to the capital for their pay. The capital, nearly 400 miles away, and about half of the distance on foot! Yes, no wonder they were tired.

I knew about the Yunnan "punitive expedition" to Kwangsi. And I knew the motives behind it. Not patriotism nor loyalty to Nanking had energized the military council to drive 50,000 peasants from the fields and start them marching toward the Nanning stronghold of the rebels. No, it was nothing so silly as that. But for a year the so-called "Red" generals in the south had blocked the great Opium Road from Yunnan to the rich consuming centers of Shiuchow, Wuchow and Canton, and the result in Yunnan had been a severe economic slump. That route had to be reopened.

So there they marched, those backwoods lads, and between them, and beside them, all the way, went a caravan of 1,000 mules loaded with the celebrated poppy juice of Yunnan; there they marched, the mules and the men, to crusade for the Revolution and the People's Three Principles of Dr. Sun Yat-sen. The men came back, some of them, but the mules went on and the opium reached Canton. But the Revolution and Dr. Sun's *San Min Chu I?* Oh, it remained the same, except that it dripped with a little more blood, the blood of 25,000 young Yunnanese who died at Nanning.

It was crisp and the air had a tang like delicious champagne as we neared the capital. But my uninvited guests in their cotton garments were cold; they shivered and huddled closer together. I stepped over them and looked out across the plain of Yunnanfu. It was broad and as far as one could see was a deep velvety green, yet in the distance was a rim of mountains still, which lay high and dark against the sky.

As I watched, the black dragon rose from below those heights and began to gobble the sun. And as it slipped from sight it left behind it a wake of hammered silver and crimson. This soon turned to saffron and stained a white flying cloud so that it looked for a moment like a bishop in his chasuble about to pronounce benediction. Then it burst into a wild red flame that spread down the plain and set afire the tops of some weeping eucalyptus trees. And then I saw it for a moment marked upon an avenue of poplars, ancient but straight, and above them upon the long voluptuous swell of a temple roof blazing with yellow splendor.

The train grunted and groaned and stopped with a jerk. Rousing themselves, the soldiers took off their hats when they told me good-by. It occurred to me that these were good men, ending a tiresome, hazardous journey into which the world had buffeted them unwilling, and that they were arriving here, still a long way from home, sick, with no money and no food. It was true that travel with them had not been a comfortable experience. But after all it was not comfort I sought here, but incident, and they had given me an abundance of that. It was more, I thought, than I had given them. They had asked for nothing; one ought to help them out.

I looked around, found a bottle of wine, a basket of fruit and a box of cookies. I gave them these and each of them a Yunnan dollar. They seemed to think it was a great deal and their awkward gratitude embarrassed me. I suppose it is merely because I am a sentimentalist that the amazement in their queerly radiant eyes should have seemed to me poignant and distressing. It was certainly nothing else that brought an ache to my throat and sudden tears to my eyes. I wished them good luck more brusquely than I had intended and in a little while I followed them into the streets of Yunnanfu.

The Story of Yunnanfu—Ancient Chinese Legend of the Fall

of the Chou Dynasty and the Rise of the T'ang Dynasty Which Acquired Yunnan

Many years ago, about 4,000, when the Celestial Empire was ruled by the House of Chou, there was a young prince who possessed a wonderful horse. It was of pure gold. Its eyes were rubies and it had wings like Pegasus that would carry it round the world in a day. It was by means of this radiant charger that the Chou Prince circled his father's realm and was able to report on the lives of the mandarins, whether virtuous or otherwise.

Now, one day the Chou Prince discovered an elderly mandarin who was shamelessly living in sin with twenty and three concubines, instead of the twenty and one to which his rank entitled him. The prince was indignant with royal wrath. He severely admonished the old libertine, and since the prince was rather a long-winded fellow it was almost dark when he remounted his steed and charged off through the clouds toward the capital.

Of course he had been obliged to take with him the two whom he had released (since that was the custom of the times) and their weight hampered the progress of the golden horse so that he could only do about 300 miles an hour. Then, to make matters worse, one of the maidens kept sliding onto the horse's tail until the prince, afraid that she might fall off and be abducted into the harem of another unscrupulous official, had to put her on his knee and hold her with one arm. And since the other girl suddenly began to weep and complain that she was going to have one of her fainting spells the prince could do nothing but put her on the other knee and hold her with his other arm.

Meanwhile, in the capital, the Chou Princess sat waiting for her husband. She was very much annoyed because the rice had got cold and because her pet jade phoenix, which was so fond of the golden horse, had been acting sullen and dejected and wondering why the Chou Prince didn't come home. The princess, I am afraid, was a cynic. She supposed that her husband would come back with some cock-and-bull story about having saved another lady. As if the place were not already cluttered up with them. So that when finally she saw him splendid as a god come riding through the sky with a lovely maiden curled up on each knee she was quite angry.

"My dear," she said, when he arrived in the Jasper Pavilion. "I think you had better send those little hussies back to their homes. You know there is no more room in the harem what with those six you brought in from Soochow last week and with the four you rescued from that evil general in Tangchow only day before yesterday."

But the prince smiled, tickled her beneath the ear and said that there was always room for two more. After all, it was solely to defend the virtue of the Empire that he housed these unfortunate creatures at all, since every one, of course, knew that he loved only the Chou Princess. The princess, however, remarked that she was not impressed by his pretty speech; she seemed to recall having heard it a number of times before. Moreover, she told him, the rice had been cold for an hour and she was just about to ask him why if he truly loved her he had not come home last night, when the prince, still smiling, tickled her under the other ear and walked off through a moon gate into his private quarters.

The princess stood for a moment biting her exquisite lips, but since this was an unsatisfactory vent for her anger she decided to go in and have the concubines beaten for the second time that day. As she neared the golden horse she paused and thought bitterly that if only this beast were dead it would put an end to her husband's foolish gallivantings across the sky. And then she noticed that the prince had neglected to remove the golden key from the horse's chest. It was this key that controlled the marvelous mechanism which enabled the horse to fly and the princess was not long in recognizing her opportunity. Quickly she moved toward the animal, turned the key that set him free, and cried "Fly away you beautiful brutal thing! Fly away and never return!"

And then because she did not wish to see anything so lovely for the last time, she walked to the side of a lotus pond and stood looking into its dark waters. She heard the thunder of the horse's hoofs and then the beat of his great wings stirring the air. She sighed, she had already begun to regret her hasty action.

Suddenly she heard a familiar cry and with terror she looked up. Perched on the glittering back of the imperial mount its silken plumes spread wide and flowing sat the princess' jade phoenix, the most talented bird in the world. Overcome by grief, the princess started to run after them heedless which way she went. And the further she ran the deeper she became immersed in the lotus pond till presently she disappeared altogether and only the echo of her sobbing hovered over the water.

Great was the Chou Prince's sorrow when he learned that his princess had been drowned and his horse and the phoenix had fled. He ordered a search for the golden steed and the jade bird over all the land. But though every valley was scoured and every mountain scanned, nothing was ever seen of either of them.

Years passed, and with them the glory of the House of Chou declined. The officials, no longer in fear of surveillance from the flying prince became more and more debauched and neglected their duties in order to devote all of their time to carnal fancies. The Empire suffered and after lingering on for several hundred years the celebrated Chou Dynasty finally crashed. But men did not forget the legend of the golden horse and the jade phoenix and often peasants at sunset scanned the skies for a glimpse of them.

Then almost 3,000 years later there arose a great general who brought into the Empire of the T'ang Dynasty many of the far independent states of Central Asia. Among them was the Nan-chao Kingdom which is now the Province of Yunnan. And the T'ang general, reaching what is today called the Yunnanfu plain saw in a distance two lofty peaks so curiously shaped as to intrigue him deeply. Upon inquiry he learned the mountains were sacred, for upon one of them had once descended a golden horse, which had turned to stone, while upon the other had dropped a green jade phoenix, which had undergone a similar miraculous transformation. So the T'ang general being by nature a pious man descended from his horse and performed the kow tow and all of his men did likewise. For at last it was known what had become of the imperial pets that had flown into the darkness so many hundreds of years before.

Then the general stood up again and addressed his followers saying, "Here where the shadows of the Chin Ma (Golden Horse) and the Pi Chi (Jade Phoenix) lengthen at the day's ending we will found a city dedicated to the wonders of the past. Let us be guided by the wisdom of our long-burned sages in creating this city which will one day be celebrated throughout the realm of the Imperial Dragon.

And so it may have happened, for at any rate when Marco Polo visited the spot more than three hundred years later he found it to be a flourishing city known as Yachi. He did not, it is true, comment upon the uniqueness of the twin hills at the edge of the plain nor of the fanciful tales woven around them. For Marco was a practical man. He observed how "the people worship idols, use paper money and are subjects of the Great Kahn." After which he hurriedly passed on to trade and commerce, subjects nearer his heart. Still it must have been that Marco saw those hills and heard the stories but putting it down to native superstition thought no more about it.

The Yunnanese, perhaps because the story pleased them, or perhaps because the monks said it was so, did not forget. They built temples on Chin Ma Shan and Pi Chi Shan and into their carving and their embroideries worked the motifs of the fabulous beast and the bird. And an imperial governor, only a few decades ago ordered the erection of two beautifully arched pailous on one of the main streets of Yunnanfu calling them Pi Chi and Chin Ma. Today, when you enter the city, you see them marked gracefully against the sky and beneath them are tied little bits of paper and twine and now and then a stick of burning joss put there by wise folks who spend their lives propitiating the good spirits.

Now time and rough weather, the Yunnanese say, have contrived to break the back of Golden Horse Mountain so that now you cannot recognize where the tail begins or the head.

But there are the old monks in the monastery high up on the cliffs and if you ask them about it why they will take you to the exact spot where the resplendent beast, centuries ago, charged down from the heavens and first touched this mountain with his hoofs all ringed in flame. And if you are still unconvinced, then the priests may lead you to an inner shrine and show you in the dim candle light an ancient red lacquer box sealed with wax, which holds in it some of the golden hairs from the mane of Chin Ma.

How Two Powerful
Rival Generals Marked Time
While Their Compromise Candidate Ruled
the Vast Barbaric Province of Yunnan, China

This is a city of trails' endings. It is the terminal of a railway and the beginning of a caravan. It is the last contact, and the first, of East with West, the gateway to old Asia and to the wild frontiers of China. It is an absurd and hopeless confusion of nineteenth-century Chinese imperialism and grotesque young nationalism, of bewildered aborigines and a telephone system that does not work, of paper money and strings of brass cash, of opium caravans and innumerable beggars, of smoldering paper prayers and electricity that gives no light, of savage dogs and furs and old embroideries. Here stands a city with one foot warily feeling toward modern times, but with the other firmly implanted in an environment that has altered little since Kubilai Khan first wrapped it into the Empire.

Yunnanfu is unique. Although it lies well into southern China, it belongs to the north, as do most of the provinces of Yunnan. Its Chinese inhabitants speak *kuan hua,* or what is known as "Mandarin," the dialect of Peking. They eat and drink much the same stuff as the northerners. Their customs and festivals are similar. Here it is necessary for a Chinese to use *wen li,* the classical written language, in order to be pronounced erudite, here you may see old gates and pailous and yamens with their golden roofs arched in the Peking tradition, here the young and fashionable courtesans still have rigidly bound feet and wear their hair in the high pompadour, unoiled, that was popularized many years ago by singing girls in the north.

This happens because the original Chinese immigrants were nearly all soldiers and exiles from north China. Yunnan was the last province to become a part of China proper, a comparatively recent event in Chinese history. Although made tributary by T'ang conquest in the eighth century, it was not till the Mongol era more than 500 years later, that the Nan-chao Kingdom was destroyed, its tribal adherents subjugated, the Burmese and Shans driven back in the south, and the Khan's warriors commissioned to consolidated Yunnan as a Chinese province.

Except for the Chinese soldiers left to colonize and intermarry, the population of Yunnan for long remained almost entirely aboriginal. The land was regarded with unmixed horror as remote and barbaric by the Court at Peking, and offending officials were often banished to it as a punishment worse than death. Then, in the fifteenth century, an unseated Ming emperor fled here with most of his followers, who settled near Yunnanfu. They came to be known as the *ben-ti-jen* and it is from them that many a Yunnan Chinese, whether he is a hot water carrier or an affluent opium merchant, insists he has royally descended.

But though the Chinese have rapidly populated most of Eastern Asia, they have come slowly into Yunnan. The hills are high and the mountains numerous, the plains are few and many of them fever-laden. The tribesmen are often hostile and regard the Chinese as invaders. Today it is said that at least half of Yunnan's estimated 10,000,000 population is still non-Chinese. The various aboriginal domains, which cover about three-fourths of the province, are many of them virtually independent, although nominally subject to Chinese authorities scattered along the main highways and caravan routes.

These tribes are the most engaging subjects in Yunnan. They are a mystery. More than twenty, they speak languages mutually unintelligible, varying in manner of dress, habits and religion. Until recently none had a written language, so that they have no history except myths and legends. Ethnologists cannot explain them. The little study that has been made indicates that they are each a remnant of a race that once flourished in Central Asia and then was swept southward, by conquest and migration, to decline in this remote forbidding corner of the earth. It is possible that among them is the oldest surviving race of man, but it is improbable that anyone ever will be able to prove it.

Under the Empire little effort was made to Sinicize the tribes. The Chinese regarded them as slaves and treated them as such. They held them in the contempt which they hold for all "outside" races and considered them their social and mental inferiors. They took no interest in these "barbarians" except to see that they paid their taxes and kow-towed when a mandarin passed by. They were not allowed to compete for the examinations and until recently were not admitted into the schools. Today the great majority cannot speak Chinese. But lately some, particularly those with a bit of Chinese blood, have been educated in Chinese schools and foreign missionary institutions. A few have become officials.

One of the latter, it is surprising to learn, is the Governor, Lung

Yuen. He is a Lolo, one of the more numerous Yunnan tribes. It appears that he holds office by virtue of the fact that though there are two other military men more powerful than he, mutual distrust and jealousy prevents either of them from mounting the throne. I am informed, however, that this anomalous situation will not prevail for long, as the two generals are preparing for a decisive clash, the result of which will be Lung Yuen's return to the life of a private citizen. But it is improbable that the system of the government will be materially affected by this change.

Since the downfall of the Manchu dynasty, Yunnan has been left largely at the mercy of militarists, and bandits who aspired to become militarists. The saying, common among Yunnanese, that "a government official is only a bandit who has been successful" in many instances is literally true. It is quoted with meaning when the Governor's name is mentioned, but since nobody is foolish enough to offer testimony on his past (an indiscretion which would certainly merit the executioner's knife) it is rather difficult to piece together the story of his pre-potentate days. He rose from the comparative obscurity of the hills and temporarily became noted as a suppressor of bandits. In fulfilling those duties he gathered considerable military power. When the opportunity arrived it was only a matter of carrying out a graceful coup d'état, after the Yunnan manner, to establish himself by force on "Five Flower Hill," the Governor's yamen in Yunnanfu.

Mr. Lung has been Governor now for over three years, with one embarrassing interval. About two years ago he was betrayed by some of his military subordinates, whom he had displeased with certain of his rulings, and he was compelled to abdicate. With the mercilessness Chinese show toward fallen greatness, the Governor was bound, put into a bamboo cage, carried through the streets of the capital and into the mountains, where it was planned to torture him to death. Some foreign friends intervened, however, and managed to induce the plotters to spare his life, on the premise that Lung Yuen would participate no more in affairs of state. But the new Governor lasted less than a year. To the astonishment even of the Yunnanese, who are well seasoned in such surprises, the Lolo tribesman came back into office. He returned, however, a humbler man. With no troops now, he is dependent entirely upon the whims of the military rivals who, as a temporary compromise, decided to make him Governor again.

The two leading generals in the province are Lu Han, who led the ill-fated Yunnan expedition to liquidate the most recent Kwangsi rebellion, and Chang Feng-chung, garrison commander of the capital. They are both, to employ a euphemism, political adventurers whose careers are as picturesque as those of any of the more widely known satraps of New China. Chang Feng-chung I frequently saw racing through the crowded streets of Yunnanfu at full gallop, with a dozen panting coolies preceding him to shout, "*Ma Lai!* Make way for a distinguished official!" He was formerly a peasant and, it is everywhere alleged, was once a bandit. He has forty-one ponies and, it is said, twenty-two concubines. I have seen him, on his way to the park, followed by at least eight of them, pretty, painted girls with bound feet.

His distinguished fellow general, Lu Han, rose from an equally lowly station in life. I have not heard any one suggest that he was a brigand, but he seems to have been in the military racket ever since the revolution, a profession which the Yunnanese regard as closely allied to the former.

(Editor's Note—Since this was written, Gov. Lung Yuen and Gen. Chang Feng-chung have fled from the capital. The Yunnan Government is now in the hands of Gen. Lu Han.)

Life in Yunnanfu, South China
Where the Government Is Oppressive
and Life Is Safer for the Foreigner
Than the Natives

Gen. Lu Han, the present Governor of Yunnan Province, is feared by the people and cordially hated by all. In organizing his "punitive" army for Kwangsi he impressed thousands of men from the streets and from the fields taking them, with little training and no experience, to die a futile death against the much superior "Red" army of Chang Fah-kwei. Some of the men were taken without being allowed to notify their wives and children, many of whom have now been sent into beggary. Aged parents had their sons snatched from them without warning, and, their only means of support gone, died of sorrow and starvation. One old lady, blind, and a pauper, committed suicide when the militarists took both of her sons. Many cases of this kind could be listed and none of them puerile gossip. I have investigated enough to know that they are substantially true.

Organically the government is based on the pattern designed for the provinces by the Kuomintang. It has its executive committee, its council, its chairman of this committee and that. Most of the officials, I believe, are members of the Kuomintang, recently organized locally, and all of them are of course ostensibly approved of by the Central Executive Committee at Nanking. But the whole edifice is arranged to suit the convenience of the war barons, the perhaps half a dozen men who run the province. Nepotism and bribery are taken for granted in securing even petty offices; I know one fellow who paid $1,000 (Yunnan) for a job as a local deputy tax-gatherer and others who make no secret of having contributed sums almost as large for insignificant offices.

It is fantastic, this Government, original and ingenuous. Nominally it maintains a stanch loyalty to the Three Peoples' Principles; in practice it violates all of them. It honors the Principle of Livelihood of the People by forcing them to grow opium, by taxing their harvests, and by failing to prevent the ubiquitous bandits from robbing their caravans within sixty miles of the capital. It upholds the Principle of

Nationalism by permitting tribal chieftains in the southwest to settle "boundary disputes" with Burma so that each year more and more Yunnan territory goes under British administration. It defends the Principle of Equality by tolerating the sale, barter and exchange of girl children into a system of slavery.

This description hardly does justice to the tragic make-believe of the Yunnan Government. A full exposition of all its quaint qualities would fill a large and illuminating volume. Such an account would have to mention the several hundred cases of men and women executed without legal trial, of men jailed for refusing to accept worthless Government currency, of girls forcibly taken from their homes to become the mistresses of debauched militarists and similar unpleasant truths.

But I do not wish it to be construed that Yunnanfu is unsafe for foreigners. Quite a number live here, British, French, American and Heaven knows why, Greeks. They are not unhappy. They have their troubles, but they are always quick to assure you that, anyway, they have a wonderful climate, which is perfectly true. And usually they are well protected. In times of trouble it is for the foreigners that the officials are concerned and not the Chinese.

Normally both the Chinese and the tribesmen treat you with a deference and an awed respect such as your white skin and long nose gets you in few parts of China nowadays. At the moment, it is true, the young vigilantes of the Kuomintang are endeavoring to create hatred against the foreigner, on the naive platform that they are responsible for the opium curse in Yunnan. Sometimes these ardent patriots will call you "foreign pig" on the street, if they think you do not understand Chinese. But the majority of the population seems to be utterly indifferent concerning who introduced opium into Yunnan; what they wish to know are the devils responsible for the constantly increasing price.

The aliens live unto themselves here, as always in China, with the missionaries (except the jolly French padrés) disapproving of the commercial people because they drink, smoke, play bridge on Sundays and thus are no specimens to be paraded before the Chinese converts, while the commercial people disapprove of the missionaries because they do not drink, smoke, or play bridge on Sundays and because they teach the Chinese that they are as good as white men.

So if you are a Servant of The Word you do not go often to the crowded suburb where you are apt to collide with the Business Persons. Or if you are a Business Person you avoid the districts frequented by the servants of The Word. But should you, by chance, meet somewhere in one of the shops, then both of you remark what a delightful experience it is, and you say that sometime the other has got to come round for dinner at your place. But when you part both of you think, with a sigh of relief, that the threat will never be carried out.

To be sure, life in Yunnanfu presents its other minor irritations. Now and then an opium-drunk cook murders his master or mistress, but this does not happen so often that it may be said to be customary. Occasionally some ruffians kill another ruffian not far from your door (as happened while I was here), but this only gives you more reason for rapping the government at the dinner table. Sometimes a Frenchman may marry an Annamite girl, or bring her up to live with him, and there is the nettling problem of how to regard her socially.

And the odors on the streets, *Mon Dieu*. But soon one becomes inured to them and carries a handkerchief ready for each pungent surprise. It is true that most of the inhabitants have goiters, some of them admirably well-grown, but after you observe how much character they sometimes give to the wearer's face then they no longer seem repulsive, but have a kind of monstrous beauty. The dogs, and there are thousands of them, like the female mendicants, make it necessary for you to carry stones with you for self-defense; but the beggar ladies have never been known to bite.

It seems to you cruel that they let the unwashed infants, with nothing to cover their little bodies, wallow with the pigs, but after a time even this inhumanity leaves you callous. Most of the women, I believe, you do not find very exciting. But when you see a perfumed singing girl, all silken in her thigh-tight trousers and close-fitting bodice, her jade face immutable, come fussing down the street on her lotus-bud feet, then it is pleasant to conjecture whither romance summons her.

"Yet there are two things," a sensitive British lady said to me, "that the years do not make it any easier to take complacently. And one of them, I don't mind telling you, is the natives' habit of expectorating to windward, when you are windward."

"And the other?"

"And the other is the natives' habit of expectorating to leeward when you are leeward."

But there are compensations, as I assured this depressed lady, even for that.

Beyond the crenellated walls, lovely with age and neglect, you ride on your sturdy Yunnan pony out into the open plain, and over roads that are a thousand years old. You go through the endless rice fields that hold a subtle peace and you follow the long ridges of green, each parting its mirrors of water flashing brilliant in the sunlit, but never very hot, day. And never very far away rising from the blue horizon, you see mountains that are blue still, and beneath them, clear as the eyes of a young girl, is the long, clean, expanse of a great lake.

And then, because despite all of its wretchedness there are moments, alas! when you love China, you wink slyly at a brown, pleasant old woman leading a morose old buffalo, and you say to her that Yunnanfu, after all, has been rather an amusing experience.

IV. From Yunnan to Burma by Caravan

Introduction to Section IV

In this section's opening article and later in *Journey to the Beginning*, Snow describes his travels with Dr. Joseph Rock as far less troubled than they were.[1] Rock's indecisiveness plagued the early days of their trek. Later, on the night before their arrival in Tali, where they would part, a foolish quarrel over a slight incident poisoned their relationship for some time. Despite their mutual antipathy, they retained respect for each other. Months later Rock visited Snow in Shanghai, and years later he was a houseguest of the newly married Snows in Peking.

After numerous delays, described in the introduction to the previous section, the journey began harmoniously. Rock and Snow drove from Yunnanfu to Laoyakuan and stayed the night in a temple. Snow bedded down beneath the "somewhat dusty gaze" of the gaudy "god of fecundity and wealth, holding in one hand the golden tael, symbol of prosperity, in the other a gilded baby." Rock's Nashi guardsmen's evening songs added a romantic aura to the bright moonlight.[2]

But after only one day on the trail Rock halted the caravan at Lufeng. His chest cold had deepened, and his reservations about traveling loomed larger. The next morning, February 2, Rock decided to return to Yunnanfu. Snow was to go on with half the mules and five of Rock's men. Snow had developed a line of skin eruptions on his back, arms, and legs, but he nevertheless spent the day trying to persuade Rock to continue. They took to their beds, however, with Rock persisting in his decision to return to Yunnanfu. For both of the men sleep was fitful, and sometime during the night Snow once more tried to persuade Rock that he would regret turning back from the caravan that he had been so long planning. This time he succeeded. On the morning of February 3 the full caravan resumed after breakfast; Rock rode in a sedan chair and Snow astride a "stubborn beast" of a mule for whom he had "no affection, no praise whatever."[3]

Three days later the caravan paused for a day at Chiu Hsiung, where Rock and Snow could stay in the relative comfort of a mission. Snow's diary identifies the woman who ran the mission as Miss Mor-

1. *Journey,* 54–59
2. Snow, transcript of diary 4: 18.
3. Ibid., 21–22.

gan, a relative of Senator Morgan. She was in the United States for medical treatment when Rock and Snow arrived, but one of her Chinese nurses effectively treated Snow's skin eruptions. Rock, in a gesture of friendly concern, also persuaded Snow to hire a sedan chair to be available at need.[4]

All was still going well two days later when they arrived in Lu Ho Kai. In the afternoon, Snow wandered from the temple where they had pitched camp, lay under a eucalyptus tree, and pleasurably summarized in his diary his life since leaving Shanghai. After listing the names of the more exotic places he had visited, he wrote: "All the richness of my youth seems bound forever to these names and adventure and romance, found unexpectedly with them." In 1951, an older, more skeptical Snow wrote in red pencil in the margin, "*Merde.*"[5]

On February 12, their caravan arrived at Hungai, the last stop before Tali. During the night, some unexpected noise awakened Snow. For the first time since beginning the caravan, he had failed to put his gun and his purse under his pillow. With the aid of his flashlight he got up and retrieved them from a nearby table. His movements woke Rock, who peremptorily demanded to know what Snow was doing. Although Snow explained, Rock remained suspicious. He checked his own baggage with his flashlight and questioned Snow: "Why should you get up in the middle of the night to get your gun? This is funny business. . . . All right, if you are going to sleep with your gun, I'll take mine to bed with me too. What do you think of that?"

Surprised and resentful, Snow wrote in his diary, "Here was a man who had lucidly exhibited his cardinal obsessions: his money and himself. . . . The facts that he has no wife, no relatives, no one who is dependent upon him, sharply accentuates this weakness of his. He has developed an instant skepticism; he is the victim of his own selfishness, his egotism. He has become, at heart, a misanthrope." Snow's own single state was much in his mind since he recently had learned of the marriages of his brother and sister.

In the morning Rock asked if Snow had searched one of their men's suitcases for a missing book. Snow took this to be a crude, obvious means of accusing him of going through Rock's own belongings. He angrily renounced Rock's suspicions: "I am astounded to think that you would think me capable of such a thing, after you have known me

4. Ibid., 27–28.
5. Ibid., 30.

as you have, and slept with me, eaten with me, laughed with me over troubles we have shared together." After Rock backed off slightly, but did not apologize, nothing more was said. Snow had his own suspicions. He later added a note in his diary suggesting that Rock had probably been snooping in Snow's diary. His suspicions were probably sharpened by Rock's parting shot two days later.

The two barely spoke to each other again except to conclude their necessary business arrangements for the caravan. They separated the night they arrived in Tali. Snow was invited to stay at the missionary home of the Kuhns, and Rock camped out on the grounds of the salt gabelle office. Snow went to Rock's camp to settle accounts and with passive resentment paid what Rock asked, though it was more than Rock's original figure. Snow's business concluded, he got up to leave saying, "Well, I may see you again before you leave; if not, good luck! Good bye." When Snow had reached the outer court, Rock shouted after him, "And thank *you* for all the trouble you've taken for me! *Thank you* for acting secretary to me for three weeks!" To which Snow replied, "Yes, of course. But most of all I thank you for suspecting me of being a crook!" And he left, grateful that he was "no longer dependent upon such an ungracious individual for further help or guidance."[6]

Snow appreciated the domestic comfort of his four days and five nights with the Kuhns at the China Island Mission—a hot bath, Sunday morning breakfast in bed, a hike up to the snow line of the mountains, and even an earnest inquiry into the Kuhns's fundamentalist views. These were decent, generous, dedicated people whose beliefs were literally incredible to Snow, but the puzzle fascinated him. Amid the distractions and complications posed by the Chinese New Year celebration, Kuhn helped Snow arrange a more modest caravan for the next stage of the journey. And when Snow's departure was delayed a day because of the tardiness of his cook, Ho Shih Fu, and the muleteers, plus Snow's dissatisfaction with the horse they brought for him to ride, Kuhn stood by Snow, helping him fire Ho Shih Fu and offering his own mule for Snow to ride in place of the rejected ungainly nag. Thus Snow left Tali on the morning of February 18, rested and eager to tackle the final three weeks of his journey. He was happy to be on his own at last, free of Rock's presence and of the nagging petty thievery and lack of discipline of Ho Shih Fu.

6. Snow, transcript of diary 5: 1–12.

The inns on the trail from Tali to Yungping went from bad to worse. Snow left some of the more gruesome details of disease that he encountered out of his newspaper columns. But he added colorful dramatic details to his description of his stay at the Ching Tsing Tze Mohammedan mosque in Yungping. Rock had told him that he had previously stopped at the mosque, but that he doubted that Snow would be able to do so. So Snow felt something of a challenge. He did meet with some initial resistance from the worshipers, but, in contrast to the account in his article, as soon as he produced his card showing he was not a foreign missionary their resistance melted. His visit to the magistrate after dinner is also described much more laconically in his diary.[7]

At Sha Yang, Snow again attempted, at some length, to express his feelings about the nomadic life he had led since leaving New York. Rock was still a vivid presence in his imagination:

> There is a joy in this life; I understand Rock's love for it now. Leading one's own caravan, enjoying a special thrill of responsibility for the life of your men and yourself, riding into the morning mist, an hour ahead of the sun, driving yourself, on foot, over hills that tax the utmost strength in your limbs, and arriving toward sundown in a new valley, knowing not what room will hold your cot at night, and hoping only for quiet, well-earned sleep. These are the simple, primal thrills that no city dweller, no one who clings to the pavements can ever feel.

He recalled all the "sour advice of the stay-at-homes. . . . I've not got but enough for three months of sparse living ahead, but I would not have missed any of the things I've blundered into for the best advertising man's job in New York!"[8]

When he arrived in Yungchang, a relatively large town, Snow was distressed by the filth of the public accommodations. He called on the Booths, Canadian missionaries, but their mission was in the midst of repairs. They had no room for him. Finally he took a room at a public inn and subjected it to the epic cleaning process he described in his article below. He decided to lay over a day in Yungchang. The series of cleanings took place over both days, aroused considerable public notoriety, and attracted notably curious visitors. On the second day, the innkeeper's brother and his five-year-old son called on Snow. The pale-faced boy had a cigarette hanging from his lips and a bad rash over his

7. Ibid., 35–36.
8. Snow, transcript of diary 6: 2–3.

body. Snow gave the boy a dose of salts to be swallowed and one to be applied to the skin. Then he pounded the boy's chest and told the father his son would die in a month if he did not stop smoking cigarettes at once. Surprised, the man complained that the boy cried unless he had at least two cigarettes an hour. To which Snow replied that crying was better for him than nicotine.

But the man's primary mission was to resolve a bet with his brother: Did Americans really line their coats with gold? Snow told him it was true, but that he had none of these coats with him. His traveling outfit was made in China. The innkeeper paid off his five-dollar bet, and the boy continued to shorten his life smoking cigarettes. Later, Snow exchanged a can of Bartlett pears, which Mrs. Booth thought a great treasure, for homemade bread, marmalade, and peanut butter; the next morning he resumed his journey.[9]

Two stories Snow tells in this section are romantic fiction, disguised elements of Snow's private life, dealing with home, marriage, and travel. The first of these tells of the innkeeper, Mme. Loi, offering him her daughter, Me Le, for a bride. There is no mention in his diary of such an incident. Throughout his caravan journey, however, Snow did see plentiful evidence that human beings could be bought much more cheaply than mules or horses. He did not write these articles until after he had completed his caravan trip and settled in Burma. The story of Me Le seems strongly related to a romantic incident that Snow experienced in the British Compound, just after the end of his trip, at Bhamo. This relationship will be discussed in detail at the beginning of the next section, which is devoted to Snow's travels through Burma and India.

The second of these stories concerns Snow's purported visit to the Sawbwa of Kanai. While no such visit appears in his diary account of his stay at Kanai, much earlier, in Tali, Snow was introduced to a magistrate. Like the Sawbwa, this magistrate prided himself upon being modern and well informed about contemporary world events, and he urged Snow to stay with him and tutor his sixteen-year-old son. The pay would be good and the board excellent. Snow would be put up in the magistrate's own *yamen*. Unlike the incident he describes in Kanai, there were, however, no Maru dancing girls, and after a hasty glance into other unswept rooms of the yamen, Snow politely refused.[10]

9. Ibid., 11–12.
10. Snow, transcript of diary 5: 17.

This story also seems likely to have been stimulated by Snow's musings about his future and will be referred to again in the introduction to the section on Burma.

Snow follows the story of Mme. Loi and her daughter with a description of his ride through thickening caravan traffic and impressive mountain scenery into Tengyueh, where he would change caravans again and choose between two routes into Burma. He closes the column with yet another brief, romantic, and probably fictional image of a young Chinese lady, astride a bright-red dragon-rug on a white-and-black pony, as elegant and beautiful as a young empress. She is riding out the gate as he rides in; she lifts her smiling eyes as she bows, in response to his raised and flourished hat. "That is what I remember about Tengyueh."

No hint of this young woman appears in his diary. She is probably a tribute to the Shangri-la fantasies engendered by his travel in these remote and, at times, truly astonishing places. However, he does record in his diary many other pleasures of his visit to this faraway city that do not appear in his articles. Tengyueh's streets were wider and cleaner than any he had seen in Yunnan. He was charmed by the semitropic vegetation—roses, lilacs, jasmine, and clusters of bamboo, even in the middle of town. "Against his instincts," but happily for his sense of comfort, he called at the British Consulate and was invited to stay in the castlelike, two-and-a-half-story structure. Built of hand-worked stone, it was set on one hundred eighty acres, surrounded by a wall eighteen inches thick. Snow slept on a mattress for the first time since leaving Yunnanfu and enjoyed a leisurely breakfast in bed for two of the three mornings he stayed.

Stanley Wyatt-Smith, the British consul, was a gracious, congenial, well-informed host, and the source of Snow's enthusiastic exposition of Shan culture in his article below. Wyatt-Smith introduced him to George Forrest, the pioneer botanist, who preceded Rock in Yunnan and passed on to Rock invaluable information about the culture and the plant life of the province. The stout, red-faced Scot, then fifty-eight, helped Snow with the caravan arrangements for the final leg of his journey. Snow even hired Forrest's cook, Wang, who could produce, in fifteen minutes, in the heart of the jungle, a five-course meal climaxed by a delicious century pudding. Snow refers to Forrest only as an unnamed "Scotch botanist" in his published article. Perhaps he did not want to risk stirring up Rock's antipathy again by any public acknowledgment of his professional rival.

During Snow's first evening at the British consulate, dinner was begun and followed by drinking and storytelling, mostly about "sex and reminiscences of Shanghai cabarets." Snow records in his diary that he "discovered" a real affection for the city that he thought he would not see again. The good company and domestic comfort enticed him to stay an extra day, and the next evening his satisfaction reminded him of when he lived in the China United apartment building in Shanghai, "which was after all my most pleasant experience in dwelling places in China. . . . How deeply I wish that I could be back again in Shanghai, just for tonight." The pleasures of travel for Snow came in many different guises. On the morning of his departure, he sent the mules on ahead and had a late breakfast with Wyatt-Smith. It was 10 A.M. and two whiskeys later before he took to the road.[11]

While in Tengyueh, Snow had gathered extensive notes about "The Kashins" [*sic*] from Wyatt-Smith's library. Once in Kanai, Snow transferred those notes into his diary. He had, in fact, been warned that Kachins had been raiding caravans, though not by the Sawbwa of Kanai. And he did have a dangerous confrontation with threatening Kachins, though again he took certain liberties with the facts in telling the story to his distant American public.

It is true that he thoughtlessly and impatiently went on ahead of the caravan, until he found himself suddenly uneasy about the vagueness of the trail and his distance from support. In his diary account, however, the crackle of twigs first made him aware of a single, frightened Shan, who warned him of the danger of nearby Kachins. In Chinese the Shan asked Snow to accompany him out of this dangerous spot, indicating that Snow's being a foreigner offered them both some protection. Before they could move far, they were intercepted by four fierce Kachins running toward them, apparently unimpressed by Snow's foreignness. When they were within six feet, Snow fired his automatic twice. The gun's noise had the desired effect. Surprised and frightened the Kachins fled.

But the experience didn't end with Snow doubled up in laughter as he describes in his article. Instead, he and the Shan also ran, and that was a mistake. Seeing this, the Kachins regained their courage, and intercepted them again. This time Snow, using the Shan as a translator, tried to impress the Kachins with the serious consequences of killing a foreigner, and he again threatened them with his automatic. The Ka-

11. Snow, transcript of diary 6: 28–33.

chins laughed and advanced warily. Then Snow drew a line on the ground and had the Shan warn the Kachins that Snow would shoot to kill if they crossed the line. One of the Kachins spoke at length to the Shan and, by his words, reduced the latter to hysterical fear. Snow could not persuade the Shan to translate, but he suspected the Kachin had told the Shan in detail what would happen to him even though they would not harm the foreigner.

When the Kachins moved closer to the line, he fired near the feet of one of them. This time they did not flee, but did jump back, recognizing something fearful and unknown in his weapon. Just as Snow began to wonder if he would have to shoot to kill, two soldiers came running in response to the sound of gunshots. The Kachins fled at their approach and had disappeared by the time the rest of the escort caught up. Snow did not wander far from the caravan again.[12]

On the last day of his journey, Snow was given a sharp reminder that he was "once more in contact with White Civilization" when he sighted a female apparition dressed in a smart riding habit and mounted on a spirited English horse. This apparition turned out to be the wife of the Bhamo British deputy-commissioner, Mrs. Clerk. After a brief chat, she invited Snow to stay at the circuit house and have meals with her husband. She was on her way to visit Wyatt-Smith in Tengyueh.

Snow's account of the final portion of his caravan trip, described in his last article below, matches his diary account, except for his description of having tea at Bhamo. After arriving at the circuit house, rather than tea with an attractive lady and her husband, Snow had a more prosaic tiffin alone. Afterward he met the obliging, elderly Mr. Clerk, who approved his wife's invitation to Snow to stay at the circuit house, and invited Snow to drop in on his club. To round off the story for his readers at home, however, Snow moved his sense of surprise at returning to Western civilization from his meeting with Mrs. Clerk to an imaginary tea with her and her husband at Bhamo. The "softest, darkest eyes," however, probably belonged to a young Burmese woman named Malami. They are later attributed to another young woman, Batalá, in *Journey to the Beginning*.[13] Both Snow's diary and his articles reveal that this later story, in *Journey to the Beginning*, of being knocked unconscious by a mule's kick and waking to the tender, loving care of

12. Ibid., 46–49.
13. Ibid., 55–56; *Journey*, 63.

Batalá, is fiction. But more of this in the introduction to the next section, concerning Snow's stay in Burma and his travels in India.

Chronology 1931

February 1	Leaves Laoyakuan, 6:30 A.M.; Arrives Lufeng, 4 P.M.
February 2	Rock decides to return to Yunnanfu; Changes mind
February 3	Leaves for Shanhsuehkuan (Fragrant Water Pass), 8 A.M.; Arrives Shetze, 5 P.M.
February 4	Leaves Shetze, 6 A.M.; Arrives Kuantung, 3:30 P.M.
February 5	Leaves Kuantung, 7 A.M.; Arrives Chuhsung, sunset; Stays at Morgan's Mission two nights
February 7	Leaves Chu Hsung, 7 A.M.; Arrives Lu Ho Kai, 2 P.M.
February 8	Leaves Lu Ho Kai, 7 A.M.; Arrives unnamed village
February 9	Leaves before caravan in predawn darkness; Arrives Pu Peng, 3:45 P.M.
February 10	Leaves Pu Peng, 7 A.M.; Arrives Yunnan-yi, P.M.
February 11	Leaves Yunnan-yi, 7 A.M.; Arrives Hung Hai, 4 P.M.
February 12	Leaves Hungai, 7 A.M.; Stops at T'au Kui Tze Miao (Tranquility Country Temple); Stops in Hsia Kuan (Small Pass)
February 13	Arrives Tali
February 14	Moves to Kuhns's
February 15	Attends Sunday church service
February 18	Leaves Tali, 9 A.M.; Arrives Ho Kiang Pu, 6 P.M.
February 19	Leaves Ho Kiang Pu, 8 A.M.; Arrives Yangpi 2:30 P.M.
February 20	Leaves Yangpi, A.M.; Arrives T'ou Ping Pu, P.M.
February 21	Leaves T'ou Ping Pu, A.M.; Arrives Ba Too Pa, P.M.
February 22	Leaves Ba Too Pa, 7:45 A.M.; Arrives Yungping, P.M.
February 23	Leaves Yungping, 6:30 A.M.; Arrives Sha Yang, 3 P.M.
February 24	Leaves Sha Yang, 7:30 A.M.; Crosses Mekong; Arrives Hsui Chai, P.M.
February 25	Leaves Hsui Chai, 6:30 A.M.; Arrives Yungchang, 3:30 P.M.
February 26	Stops in Yungchang
February 27	Leaves Yungchang, 8 A.M.; Arrives Pu P'iao, P.M.

February 28	Leaves Pu P'aio, 8 A.M.; Arrives Lao Chai, "almost dark"
March 1	Leaves Lao Chai, 8 A.M.; Arrives Kan Lai Chai, 4 P.M.
March 2	Leaves Kan Lai Chai, 10:30 A.M.; Arrives Tengyueh, 4 P.M.
March 3	Stays over at British consul's; Hires new mules and crew
March 4	Stays an extra day
March 5	Leaves Tengyueh, 10 A.M.; Arrives Nantien, 4 P.M.
March 6	Leaves Nantien, 6 A.M.; Arrives Kanai, P.M.
March 7	Leaves Kanai, A.M.; Arrives Hsiao Hsing Kai, 5:30 P.M.
March 8	Leaves Hsiao Hsing Kai, 8 A.M.; Arrives Wan Hsien, P.M.
March 9	Leaves Wan Hsien, 8 A.M.; Crosses into Burma; Arrives Wan Phia Yang, 4 P.M.
March 10	Leaves Wan Phia Yang, 9 A.M.; Arrives Khua Lang Kha, 2 P.M.
March 11	Leaves Khua Lang Kha, A.M.; Arrives at waiting bus, 11 A.M.; Arrives Bhamo; Stays at circuit house

Start of a Trek over the Age-Old Trail of Commerce across the Mountains
of Yunnan Territory toward Tibet and Burma

Caravans, you know, do not run on schedules. You cannot send your man round to a place where he goes up to a cage and says, aloofly conscious of his importance as the servant of a foreigner: "We are leaving tomorrow with the 5:43 caravan for Tali; a first-class ticket for the trip, and, mind you, a stout riding animal for the Master!"

Ah, no, it is neither so simple nor so certain as that. Yunnan caravans are perhaps the most dilatory, most whimsical, most procrastinating means of transportation surviving in this efficient century. They remind you that the word *travail* was born of travel, and you understand why. So many things may delay them: bandits, failure to procure escort, the scarcity of cargo, extended haggling over the price of loads, sick mules, drunken muleteers, or heavy rains. They are all legitimate excuses for lingering near the comparative comforts of the capital.

But there are seasons, of course, when caravans leave almost daily. During the harvesting of the opium crop and the bean crop, and when the big imports of rice arrive, the *Ma Ko To* (honorable owner-manager of horses, the head muleteer) cannot afford to humor his temperamentalisms. There is heavy traffic on the roads from late February till June, when the rainy season begins. From June till August caravans are few. Then they begin briskly in September and carry on busily till the middle of December, when they slack off till after the Chinese New Year holidays.

I arrived in Yunnanfu, the pivot of most caravan trails in Yunnan, in midwinter. The caravans were getting smaller and leaving less frequently. I had to get together my equipment—my cot and bedding, cooking and eating utensils, some staple foreign foods, saddle and bridle and various other necessities of the road, none of which I had brought with me. It sounds simple enough, but when you begin to inventory all the things you need for forty-two days away from civilization it is astonishing how large the total grows. By the time I was ready to leave the outlook was not encouraging.

It had, of course, never been encouraging. Before I left Shanghai to come down to this wild corner of China, with the intention of traversing the road to Burma, I was notified that the trip was hazardous, with danger always of being attacked by bandits, robbed, kidnapped or murdered. There was a peculiarly malignant disease known as "relapsing fever," which took its victims in four days and has been regularly decimating the roadside population for months. Moreover, it was essential that the traveler so unreasonable as to wish to take these risks should be well acquainted with the local dialect. I was not. He should at least have a guide and interpreter with him. I had none. And he should certainly bring a full foreign camping outfit and his own servants with him. I could not and would not. Finally, the officials whom I questioned at Nanking tacitly admitted that the province was unsafe for foreign travelers and the representative of our own government most familiar with Yunnan informed me that he did not view my trip as a "sane or salubrious undertaking."

When I reached Yunnanfu I learned that, unlike much of the alarmists' talk that goes on about any part of China outside the treaty ports, there seemed to be some basis for apprehension in Yunnan. Chinese officials (except those in the Bureau of Foreign Affairs, who blandly assured me that the road was always safe) declared that it was a foolhardy adventure and apt to end in disaster. The consensus of foreign opinion seemed to be sane. There were almost daily reports of brigandage and the burning of villages. There was the indisputable fact that several foreigners already had been murdered in the province. While I was in the capital some bandits near Kochlu, not far away, held up a passenger train and kidnapped more than 500 Chinese, carrying them all into the hills for ransom.

The effect of these bits of news was depressing. But my plans had gone too far to be abandoned. I proceeded to try for a caravan, but the season was not right, and the few muleteers in the city were contenting themselves with short stages near the capital. It looked as if I might have to wait till after the Chinese New Year to get away. I could, of course, have hired my own mules and ventured it alone. But it would have been more expensive, and I should have got little of the big caravan life, which was the experience I wished.

I had no men except a Szechuenese cook whom I could not trust much because of the unpleasant reputation he had left behind him. I believe the story was that he had threatened to murder his last employer, a missionary lady who had sacked him on the excellent counts of thievery, lying and inebriety, conduct which she felt ill became him as a convert to The Word, for he had long professed Christianity. The idea of starting on a long trip with nothing but Ho Shih-fu, as the culprit was called, did not intrigue me. But I was considering it as the only way out of my dilemma when a more satisfactory solution appeared.

Dr. Joseph F. Rock, an American botanist and explorer, had preceded me to Yunnanfu by several weeks, with the intention of organizing an expedition to Likiang, deep in the Yunnan snow mountains. Originally I had hoped that we might be able to travel together as far as Talifu, which was about a third of the some 700 miles I had to do to the head waters of the Irrawaddy River, in upper Burma. But when I arrived in Yunnanfu, Rock's plans were uncertain. Conditions of the road, bandit troubles and Communist disturbances had discouraged him as they had me, and there were other more important considerations that had caused him indefinitely to postpone his departure.

Then one morning I had a note from him telling me, in his unexpected way, that he had organized his caravan, was leaving at once and would like me to go with him. I was surprised and naturally delighted.

Dr. Rock was representing the Harvard Arboretum and the United States Department of Agriculture. Well financed, he was able to hire most of a caravan for his own use; the difficulties of linking up with local talent were not his, as he was bringing in his own muleteers from the west. Rock also had ten Nashi tribesmen with him. They knew every bend in the precarious mountain trails ahead and they were devoted to him. With his official status he was in the eyes of the Chinese an important figure and one worth providing with a much larger escort than they could have been induced to send along for the carcass of a roving newspaper man whose "expedition" had no more sensible an aspiration than the attainment of Burma.

Used to life in the outlands, Rock had with him all those tricky contrivances which help a lone wanderer to forget that he is far from home, the loved ones and the flesh pots. He had such ingenious items as folding chairs, folding tables, collapsible bathtubs, vacuum bottles, and so on. It was no wonder that he was regarded as a kind of foreign prince by the awestruck natives in the far places he traveled. I felt myself fortunate to be in his retinue.

He had been many years in Asia and had met numerous strange and interesting people. He was full of rich anecdote, genial and with a fine sense of humor. Knowing the country so well, he was instructive, not in a heavy way, but pleasantly communicative, with none of the cold hauteur that is common to world forsakers. It was agreeable to contemplate a trip with such a companion, and I regarded it as unfortunate only that his trail left me at Talifu, to turn northward to Likiang, six days further on, while mine led down to the Burma frontier, almost a month further south.

The arrival of our caravan, like that of all caravans, was delayed; and like all caravans its departure was also delayed. The Ma Ko To kept us waiting while he found his extra mules. Then Rock got down with a fever and was in bed for four days. When finally we moved away from the capital January was nearly over and though the nights were still bitterly cold the sun at midday was ardent.

The ancient caravan trail to Talifu has now been superseded, for the first thirty-five miles beyond Yunnanfu, by a provincial motor road. After collecting taxes for road construction for the last twenty years the Government has, to the astonishment of all, actually progressed this far on its program. Of course there is really no reason for motor roads in Yunnan yet, since there are but five cars, three of them broken down pre-war models, and all owned by the Government. But nevertheless these buses now conduct a service between Yunnanfu and Aningchow, about twenty miles. We were the first, however, to induce a driver to try out the remaining fifteen miles of the dirt highway, which reaches almost to Lao Ya Kuan, and the real beginning of mountain climbing.

One of the officials gave us his car for the afternoon, though he was a bit dubious about our traveling over the last stretch, which had not been formally opened. He eventually consented, thereby saving us a whole day of caravan travel. We covered the distance in about three hours, and the men, who had started two days before us, had only just reached the agreed meeting place when we got there. None of the muleteers had ever been in a motor car, or seen one, so that much to the chauffeur's annoyance, they took turns in bouncing up and down on the dirty plush upholstery, and having discovered the horn, kept it going till we marched down the winding road to Lao Ya Kuan.

Not far from the village we met about forty Tibetans, tall dark fellows, wrapped in sheepskins and long bo-lo cloth coats of homespun. They had with them about sixty mules, heavily loaded and looking woefully weary and caked with dust. The men were all armed, some of them with ancient muskets and others with long swords slung in crudely worked scabbards of silver filigree. They were virile fellows, with great shoulders and they walked with the long easy grace of the mountaineer.

One of our men stopped to question them about the road and he came back to us with an amusing story. The Tibetans, it appeared, were emissaries of the Dalai Lama, and they had come down clear from Lhasa bearing presents to Lung Yuen, the Governor. They had entered China at Batang and had followed the wild trails through the great heights of western Yunnan, taking about sixty days to reach the lower plain that spreads toward Yunnanfu. During their trip they had not been attacked by brigands, so that yesterday, within fifty miles of the capital, they had not bothered to request the military escort to which their mission entitled them. Toward the end of the day, when they were almost in sight of Lao Ya Kuan, they were suddenly attacked by a band of fifty or sixty Chinese, who descended upon them as they were entering the notorious Old Duck Pass.

The Tibetans, brave men, did not flee. They were furious. Although outnumbered, they held the pass, guarding their mules and returning the bandits' fire with the accuracy of Tibetan marksmanship. Not expecting such resistance, the attackers were surprised and became confused; about half of them scattered and fled. Unsatisfied with this, the Tibetans took the offensive and succeeded in driving the bandits back into the hills, killed one of them and wounded and captured four others. They then marched their captives into the village and up to the local garrison commander. Indignant, they protested that it was a strange country into which gift bearers had to fight their way in order to pay tribute to its rulers.

That same garrison officer met us outside the walls and escorted us into Lao Ya Kuan. He was distressed by the incident, complaining that if the Tibetans reported it to the governor he would most certainly be removed. It was only his abominable luck, for this was the first appearance the bandits had made for two weeks. He felt it was their fault, anyway, for not having brought an escort with them, and assured us that no such evil would fall upon us, as he intended to send 30 soldiers with us the next day.

The officer led us up through the archaic stone streets of the town, made of slabs thrown together like rocks in a quarry. We mounted a hill and in a few minutes arrived at his headquarters, a fine old temple, where he asked us to spend the night. Walking through the courtyard, we were greeted by a squad of twenty buglers, blowing, I suppose, the Chinese equivalent of "Colors." They blew very hard, so that their faces were flushed beneath their rough tan, and their eyes looked unusually wide for Orientals.

Rock quartered himself in what had been the chamber of an abbot before the soldiers had driven him and his monks into the brutal world of realism. I chose the main hall of the temple, filled with dusty wood blocks of the Classics and shadowed with grotesque Taoist idols and tablets to the disciples. The gods were old friends, whom I had met in temples all over China, and I saluted them with respect before digging into my blankets. I think I may have remarked to them that I had seen them in better garments, and lamented that the evil day of the unbeliever had crept so far into China. Old Kuan Ti was looking morose in a silken headdress that was faded and torn and the demonic red gleam in his eyes had dimmed so that he seemed to be suffering from myopia. And the God of Wealth and Fecundity, a massive fellow towering almost to the beams of the lofty tiled roof, was holding in one hand a large sycee from which age had effaced the symbolic gilt, and in the other a naked little boy baby badly in need of repair. The usual benignity of his godly gaze had been badly rainstreaked so that he looked pathetic and dejected.

Along one side of the hall rose great doors, heavily carved and once richly lacquered with gilt and vermilion, but now nearly bare. There was a white sharp moon and its shafts bore in through the lattices so that the light lay in argent arabesque on the dim floor. Some of the Nashi tribesmen were singing in subdued falsetto voices—a music that may have been a story from the legends of their kings. I liked the exotic strangeness in it, and an elusive rhythm that I tried to commit [to memory], but failed. While I listened they ceased abruptly; it puzzled me. It was a while before I realized the cause and then I heard it, a nightingale, its throaty song spilling down the night with a fluid lightness and grace. It filled the air with a spacious ecstasy. Indeed, it lulled me to sleep. But it was a sleep troubled with dreams of tomorrow's bandits and exquisite Chinese tortures. Some iniquitous force must have crept into the temple before dawn. Or perhaps those Taoist gods, old friends though we are, were angered at my presumption in sleeping with them.

"Step Ladder Going" on the Age-Old Caravan Trail from Yunnanfu

toward Tali, China, and a Little Bandit History

There is an old Chinese proverb which says that a road is good for ten years, bad for ten thousand. The sage who first made the remark must have been thinking of Yunnan; no other corner of the empire could have offered better testimony to the accuracy of his wit.

Yunnan's caravan roads have been in use for many centuries. From time to time they must have been repaired and reconstructed, but their routes were seldom altered. Today there are few efforts at improvements. Old and broken stones are occasionally removed, and new ones put in their place, but that is all. Year after year the trails bite deeper and deeper into the flesh of the mountains.

Now, legend has it that the once Imperial Highway from Yunnanfu to Tali, a distance of about 250 miles, follows a path marked down by an Indian Buddhist monk who entered the province a thousand years ago, on his way to Canton. If that is so, he must have been a stout saint, and in a noble hurry, for he traveled like a giant, giving no quarter to the mountains.

It is on this tortuous pathway, over the imprint of millions of iron-shod hoofs and straw-sandaled feet, that I have been walking, creeping, slipping, and now and then riding, for the past ten days. We have come sharply up to six, seven, eight thousand feet and higher, only to drop at once into brief valleys half a mile, sometimes a full mile below the narrow peak passes. We have spent whole days gaining altitude, and every foot of it stiff climbing, and then we have lost it all in an hour of breathless descent. We have marched up and down and ever straight across knife-edged ridges, row upon row of them. Yet always, much further than the eye can reach, these same barriers rise like a great troubled brow between us and the faraway inland civilization. We are deep in the blue-hearted sierras of Central Asia.

The Yunnanese, it appears, believe in the short line road wherever possible. No snaky gradual or winding ascents ease the traveler's climb; they are all frontal attacks, right up the face of the rocky, soaring peaks, sometimes at a 45-degree angle. The wonder of it is, since roads become the beds of rushing mountain torrents in the rainy season, that

181

Hats were a matter of great style along Snow's caravan route (above and opposite page).

there is anything left of them when the caravans start over them in the autumn.

Today, for the greater distance you move across broken stones, usually with their sharp edges upturned and every step affording the possibility of a sprained or broken ankle. Where the crude paving has disappeared completely, the road is pitted with holes, often a foot deep, caused by the mules stepping always in the same place; such a road is called L'i-tzu lu by the Yunnanese—literally, "step-ladder going," and the phrase is apt.

Some idea of what this kind of travel is like may perhaps be conveyed to you through the following experiment. Go to a New York skyscraper and pour a trainload of lime and rocks down its towering flights of stairs, so that each step is well covered. Over this turn a fire hose for two days, and then let the mixture dry. Somehow set up a cold, terrific wind through the upper stories, while on the lower floors the steam jets are left wide open. Now bundle yourself into sheepskins and walk up and down (or ride a horse if you prefer) for eight hours. In such a way you may soon understand the joys of mountain climbing over the Imperial Highway of Yunnan. But no, not quite. For you will have no wondrous horizon of cloud-dimmed peaks, nor wild roses rioting down the roadside, nor the glamour of caravan bells tinkling and mountain men singing as they march. And you will, of course, have nothing so wicked and exciting as a Yunnan bandit in a Manhattan tower.

There have been brigands in this province for as long as men remember. At times they have been powerful enough to hold many towns and villages; at times an energetic magistrate has put aside his opium long enough to disperse them, so that for a while caravan travel was safer than residence in Illinois. About four years ago their numbers began to increase rapidly.

It seems odd, but the road grows safer as you draw further away from the capital, where the largest body of Yunnanese troops is stationed. Between Lufeng and Shetze, only three days from the capital, the Fragrant Water Pass is harassed by the disciples of the notorious Tieh Ko Piao, or Iron Watch Mantel, who is said to have murdered more than 400 people before he was shot, not long ago, by a rival brigand who fancied one of his mistresses. During the fourth day, on toward Kuantung, the menace is Pu Tai Tai, a woman bandit, who leads 200 men, known as the fiercest and most ruthless on the road. The fifth stage is disputed by two outlaw chiefs, formerly subalterns in the provincial army, who some months ago deserted and with their

Government rifles and ammunition began collecting from the luckless caravans the wages which they said should have been paid to them. Several other minor bandit zones have to be crossed before you breathe more easily in Tali.

Tali itself is now comparatively safe, although only within late months. For four years the city and a district within a radius of fifty miles were controlled by Chang Chi-bah, whose exploits have joined the classics in Yunnan's long saga of banditry. Among his crimes were the kidnapping of three French priests and the murder of four magistrates. He was small, they say, and he stuttered, but once a day he ate a human heart, which gave him the strength and courage of many men. He could drink you under a table, and he was fond of the ladies, pastimes which ultimately led to his ruin, for he was betrayed into the hands of his enemies, while inebriated, by one of his concubines.

Many of the villages along the road show signs of these bandit depredations. At Shetze the walls have fallen, and half the houses stand demolished, with only here and there a charred beam or post remaining gaunt and desolate. The magistrate returned only a short time ago, after an absence of two years, and many of the population are still refugees in neighboring hamlets. Although Shetze is less than eighty miles from the capital, the brigands held it for eighteen months with little or no opposition.

Ya Tsang, Kuan Tung, Lu Ho Kai and other towns we have passed are only beginning to recover from the scourge of the outlaws. Many of the male inhabitants have been murdered and scores of the young women carried off. There is no wealth. All are wretchedly poor. The meager supplies available in the markets are only such as meet the urgent necessities of life.

But though we have constantly expected them, no bandits have troubled our caravan. Now and then, through the field glasses, we have sighted armed men, standing high on the pine clad slopes and gazing down at us, but they have made no movement of attack. It is a little disappointing, because we are all well armed, and ready for them. Dr. Rock, my companion, and I both carry automatics. Rock's ten Nashi tribesmen have rifles and the dozen muleteers carry muskets, swords or long knives. In addition, through the more perilous passes, we have been given large escorts, sometimes thirty soldiers. Our forty mules would make a rich prize, but we have felt we could put up a good fight for them, with the ghost of Chang Chi-bah himself.

But the escort has to be paid, of course. You take your card to the magistrate and ask if the road is safe and he replies: "Yes, we have no bandits in my district," but all the same there will be twenty soldiers sent along to guard you tomorrow. It is expected that you will buy their food and pay for their *pu-kai,* the flee-bitten quilt furnished them at the inns. It is not much. You give every man two paper dollars, worth about four American cents each, and they are quite satisfied. There is something left to buy enough opium for a dozen smokes from the pipes they all carry with them.

Indeed, you can hire five soldiers for less than a mule or a pony costs you per day. The labor of animals is better paid than that of men. Only the Szechuenese bearers of *hwa-gons* (the primitive mountain chairs used in parts of Yunnan) get approximately the same as the beasts of burden. Values seem oddly distorted. You can buy the services of a strong man for two years, cheaper than you can buy a good mule. And near the capital four girl slaves can be purchased for the price of one well-bred pony.

But in Hungai, where we are stopping for a day before entering Tali, there are few surplus females to be bartered in this way. Wives are in demand and the women walk abroad with an air of self-assurance, as though well aware of their indispensability. Some of them are of mixed blood, Chinese and Lolo, for there has been much intermarriage here. Occasionally you see one, healthy and buxom, and in an Asian way handsome. She looks at you; a long-nosed foreigner, with a dark curiosity, but since you return her gaze with a steady amusement of your own, she is frightened and turns suddenly away.

Hungai is embraced by tall splendid peaks of admirable symmetry, some of them snow-capped, and the Chinese call this "Vale of the Mists," for it rains nearly always. The city was once the capital of the Nan-Chao Kingdom, which flourished a thousand years ago, and there are ancient tombs, some worthless ruins of the palace, and many celebrated temples. We are staying in one of the latter, an old Buddhist shrine, cresting an eminence at the edge of town.

In the afternoon the rain is blown slanting across spaces incredibly green with paddy and set here and there with brown thatched huts. Through the latticed windows I can see peasants in shapeless raincoats of palm fiber and wearing great mushroom hats dripping like flowers, working knee deep in the flooded fields. Nearing the city gate are some Lolo tribesmen, bareheaded and dressed only in uncured skins clinging like hair to their bodies. They come in from somewhere in the mystery of the mountains and on their naked shoulders bear huge logs, taller and fatter than a Dutchman. The scene reminds me of something, and then I remember: it is like one of Yamata's landscapes of old Japan.

While I am standing thus, immersed in the melancholy of mid-afternoon, someone coughs, and I turn round to see one of the monks, his hands clasped before him, bowing like a reed and as if he were saying *Ah Mi To Fu!* before the great Lord Buddha. Behind him is a Chinese, an old man with a gray straggling beard, watery eyes, a gaunt figure clad in a silken robe. He has a small boy with him, and at my gesture they both come inside, the boy with his mouth wide open, as though seeing a dragon, but the old gentleman smiling with that odd sweet smile cultivated by the rural Chinese of a past generation.

"*Ching tso, ching tso!*" I invite. "*Ni yao cha!*"

We sit down and presently the monk returns with some tea, palest amber, but fragrant and delicious. My guest asks my name, age, nationality, whether I am married and why not, where I come from, where I am going, why I am traveling, and if they are still fighting in the north. He makes other inquiries which I do not understand, but answer in the affirmative or negative, as the mood strikes me. All the time I am wondering who he is and what he wants, feeling only that his visit will somehow cost me money.

But before I can find out about him, he rises and prepares to leave. Perhaps I was mistaken. Perhaps he merely wished to have a look at my preposterous foreign eating implements. He expresses his admiration for my magnificent country and deplores the barrenness of his own. Then he bows low, shakes his own hands, and leaves me, still puzzled as to the generous impulse which prompted his call.

When the monk returns for the tea cups, I ask him where the fellow came from and what he wanted.

"Ah, he is a venerable Buddhist from the village of Ming Shih, not far away. He has come to Hungai for the New Year festival. Hearing that you were in town he decided to pay you a visit. He is old and he thinks he will not live much longer. He thought he ought to see one foreigner before he dies, so that he will not be unduly astonished if he should meet one in Paradise."

I remark that I will be damned, but the monk hurries off chuckling to himself, saying that he cannot understand that kind of talk.

Chinese New Year's Eve Celebration in Talifu in the High Hills of Yunnan
under "the Eves of Roof of the World"

They are more dazzling, I suppose because you come upon them all at once, from behind the quietude of purple hills. A moment before it was a world patterned in shadowed valleys and dark slopes that you seem to have been crossing all your life. Then suddenly it is this nearness to a god, this opaque veil torn from your eyes and leaving you, as in a clear dream, staring into a wild shower of white light. Majestic and terrible in their grandeur, taller than the sacred Fujiyama, and wearing a mantle of snow iridescent in a tropic sun; not one peak, but a dozen, each higher than the next, until in a furious ecstasy they culminate on a windswept summit nearly three miles high. The Tsang Shan, Snow Mountains of Tali!

Here ends the Imperial Road to Tali, and here begins the Golden Road to Burma. And here, by the grace of God, my Szechuenese cook gets the sack. But that is another story.

Tali is an olden city, a thousand years or more, men say. It does not look a thousand years old, for there are few living Chinese cities that do; but it looks much as it might have been a thousand years ago. That is not a paradox. The truth is that very little is built in China to survive more than a hundred years. A few temples perhaps, or some imperial tombs, but even they are often reconstructed once a century. What happens is that crumbling houses and shops and walls and gates are rebuilt about as they stood in the beginning, so that while you have few ancient structures you have the same thing reborn again and again, and on the same terrain. That is Tali. Destroyed many times by earthquakes, wars and floods, it nevertheless remains a city untouched by the changes of time.

One of the proofs of Tali's antiquity, and of its turbulent history, are the thousands of upraised graves laid on the slant of the Tsang Shan. Among them, if you are a Sinologue, you find epitaphs carved in Tali marble long before the Son of Heaven had made his power felt in Yunnan; which was a great while ago indeed. Among these aisles of the dead there are tombs to the Myriad Heroes, those Chinese and Mongol warriors who died proudly here for Kubilai Khan, when he conquered the city in 1272. And not far from it there is another, erected some years ago by the Manchus. It honors the memory of the unknown soldiers killed during the Panthay rebellion which centered round Tali, then held by the Moslem Sultan Suleiman, who made war for the glory of the Prophet.

The city lies in a shallow plain, girdled on one side by the Tsang Shan snow peaks and on the other by a great inland basin of night-blue water, which frequently beats into such angry waves that the Chinese do not call it a lake, but "Ehr Hai," the Secondary Sea. There is an old wall, crenellated and pierced by four gates, of which the southern is rather fine, though badly damaged by the last earthquake. Two main streets, at right angles, join the four gates, but the north-south way is the important one. Here are gathered the rice merchants, fur buyers, opium dealers, provisioners of all kinds. On market days it also attracts the principal rogues and charlatans of the neighborhood, who squat with their baskets full of everything from excellent Yunnan walnuts and oranges to musk and ginseng guaranteed to restore the full powers of youth to a middle-aged man of 80.

It was the day before the Chinese New Year when I entered Tali, and the city was filled with a crowd in carnival mood. True, according to the Nanking Government the Chinese calendar is now obsolete and has been for the two years since the Kuomintang ordered the national adoption of foreign reckoning. But "the voice of the capital is often weak"; at this distant place it can scarcely be heard at all. Men do as their fathers did before them, and they heed the calculations of the old astrologers who tell them, according to the equinoxes, when the dragon has put on his new coat.

It was a good time to visit Tali, for the population was heterogeneous and full of color. There were long lank Tibetans, dressed in sheepskins, smelling of tsamba and rancid butter, who rode through the crowds on highland ponies that were shaggy, saddled with prayer rugs, and clamorous with jingling bells. Min Chia women, in tight fitting jackets and blue trousers bordered in red and tucked into bright leggings, came into town bearing huge bundles of fir branches tied to their backs. Lolos, male and female, gaping with wondrous eyes at the peddler's wares, bargained for the cloth of their yearly garment. A few Nashis, wearing swords and costumes half furs and the rest bits of gay rags, were noticeable for their skin, dark as an Indian's, and their long handsome stride. And the monks, in their dirty gowns and with shaved heads, shouting the classics above the noise, and collecting alms for it;

Hair styles were also matters of individual taste and vanity.

and the mangy dogs, snarling viciously and getting a kick in the ribs for it; and the caravan animals, stumbling in under their last loads of the year; and small boys naked in the chilling air; and Mohammedans, a few here and there in white turbans, most of them owners of shops; and above all the Chinese, talking endlessly, haggling over their miserable wares, coughing, spitting, laughing, quarreling, hurling deadly insults at each other, at the tribesmen, at their children; and nearly everybody apparently enjoying himself hugely as is the custom in holiday season. It was magnificent.

Wandering through the bazaars I gathered the usual following of inquisitive youngsters, shameless and not to be shaken by threat or evil glare, their eyes staring wide at what they considered my fantastic dress and their ears alert for my undoubtedly fantastic Chinese. But I had grown used to them; they no longer bothered me; they had become a part of life, just as the funny solemn faces of rude gapers become a matter-of-fact business to the monkey behind the bars. Only at night, when the dragon was brought forth to chase the demons from the streets, did I lose my side-show popularity with the younger generation.

That dragon was a wonderful fellow and took a chief part in the New Year festivals. I trailed him through the town, fascinated by his weird antics, and joining in the roaring mirth he provoked. He looked quite real. His body, about 20 feet long, was made of strips of bamboo bent into serpent shape, covered with green, transparent lacquered cloth and had a great wicked head with eyes that were tongues of flame. A dozen monks, hidden from the spectator, walked under him, carrying the torches that illumined his sinuous body and putting him through the steps of the grotesque dance. He was led by a band of musicians wildly beating gongs and drums, clashing cymbals, playing flutes and fiddles. And after these bedlam-makers came devil-dispellers; a group of monks busily lighting off strings of firecrackers and now and then chanting charms and superstitious phrases.

Up and down every street they went, stopping here where an elderly merchant was sticking up his doorway gods for the thirtieth year of the republic or lingering before an inn whose proprietor brought forth small bowls of steaming rice tea for the monks. They pranced in front of the Confucian temple where a very old man sat quietly and smiled, as though wondering if next year's dragon would not take him through the vermilion mists to the jade paradise. They paused before a lantern-lit doorway [through] which drifted the heavy, voluptuous odor of opium and where stood three pretty painted girls who seemed to be speculating upon the gentlemen with whom they would spend the night. Beating a fearful din, describing strange circles, and the mystic symbol of jen, the parade wound on and on, followed by an army of boys and a laughing, pushing throng of young men and women bent on evicting the evil spirits of the old year from the thresholds of all those who paid tribute to the dancing dragon of the new.

I suppose I had grown accustomed to hearing nothing but Chinese, and it certainly did not sound to me, as a young lady in a treaty port once put it, "like a bunch of chop suey and chow mein." Chinese is perhaps not a beautiful language, but it is admirably suited to facial expression, well fitted to convey the exact meaning of one's thoughts. It seemed natural to me that no one around me should speak anything else, so that I could not, like one of the writers of our successful travel narratives, "thrill to the sinister mystery of the Chinese tongue." There was nothing sinister about it and nothing mysterious. So I cannot submit to you any of the "creepy feelings" that are said to run up one's spine while surrounded by the "treachery of an Oriental night." But when a casual voice, speaking in what was unmistakably American, reached me from out of the crowd I was startled as if its owner had come from another planet.

"When did you blow in?" it asked.

He was a tall young man, blond and good-looking, with broad shoulders and eyes that were the clearest blue. He wore a Chinese gown and Chinese shoes, and when he smiled he showed white teeth. He was the first white man, except my traveling companion, whom I had seen for many days, but I controlled my excitement and answered him with a nonchalance to match his own:

"Just arrived this morning. I came in with Dr. Rock, but he has gone on to Likiang and I am going to Burma as soon as I get a new caravan. My name is Snow. Who are you?"

"My name is Kuhn. I run the foreign mission here, the C.I.M."

We shook hands.

"Where are you staying?" he inquired.

"Over at the Ritz-Carlton by the South Gate. I have the Chinese suite. You know, the one with the Oriental rats, spiders, fleas and a broken roof. Charming."

"Well, you'd better come over to our place," he invited. "Mrs. Kuhn and I can give you a clean room and some wholesome food. We're plain, you understand, but I think you'll like it better than your inn."

I rather thought so, too. But it was incautious of him, I concluded, to ask me before he knew whether I smoked, drank, lay in bed on Sundays or played cards. So I advised him that I was guilty of all, but could give up everything but cigarettes. Did he still want me?

"Smoking is a vice," he said. "But come on over at once. We'll put up with you." He grinned. He was a nice guy. I asked him only one more question. It was rude, but to me this was no time for the tedium of etiquette.

"Have you, by any chance, got a bath? I haven't bathed for years!"

"We have a tin tub and plenty of hot water, if you call that a bath," he said.

"Lead me to it!"

And he did. I removed several layers of Yunnan dust from my tender epidermis and an hour later stood, warm and with a pleasant glow through my body, leaning on the casement of my loft room in the Kuhns' Chinese house. I lit a cigarette.

It was quiet, except for the burst of an occasional cracker put off by some late celebrator. There were stars out, steady white points in a deep somber sky. The night, so still, seemed like something carved in a dark stone. Beyond the curving roof, aloof and tremendous, rose the peaks of the Tsang Shan, glittering like royal treasure. They held in them the intrigue of the unknown, through them lay my trail, and behind them, Burma.

From Tali to Yungping, China
by Caravan with an Occasional Stop
at Some Buddhist or Mohammedan Monastery
High in the Mountains

Caravan. It is a glamorous word. In it there is mystery and the urge of the unknown. But my caravan, which I organized in Tali, was so small it hardly deserved the name at all. Three mules, three ponies, a Min Chia tribesman for a head muleteer and another Min Chia for his assistant. They were both little men, but with strong, sturdy legs, like nearly all tribesmen. They wore turbans of red and black toweling over shaven heads that were rarely uncovered; short coats of lambu; long cotton sashes around their waists, and trousers that ended just below the knee. They went barefooted most of the way, but over the sharper peaks they sometimes wore straw sandals.

The Ma Ko To was well pleased with himself; he had fleeced me in bargaining for the thirteen-day trip to Tengyueh. He had got me to agree to pay him $40 silver, double the ordinary rate, a mule. That amounted to about $1, American money, a mule day, and it was a price unequaled in these parts since the Roosevelt expedition came through two years ago. But the New Year's holidays were on in Tali and no Chinese muleteers would move out at any inducement. I felt fortunate at getting the tribesmen and I was content with our bargain.

Besides my equipment and provisions we carried some loads of salt, grayish stuff molded into huge cones weighing thirty catties each, and a batch of needles, both items that are as good as legal tender in this part of Asia. We were not a prepossessing caravan, as I said, but we had a lead mule dressed in all his finery of plush tomtoms, crashing bells, and with a mirror in his forehead; a noble little animal, prideful and conscious of his responsibility. We moved through the dumpy little villages with an attitude of style.

I also had two Chinese, young fellows whom I had picked up in Tali to replace the Szechuenese cook, Ho Shih-fu. The latter's crimes were numerous. He had a habit of "losing" things, particularly articles that could be sold along the road. He was lazy, he was impertinent, he was a drunkard, a liar and had a hypocritical manner about him that was irritating. Like all Szechuenese, he spoke so rapidly that I could not understand him, and he knew this and made the most of it when inventing excuses for his offenses. He was a good cook, but undoubtedly a bad egg. In the end I had to take him by the seat of the pants and the scruff of the neck and escort him to the street. When I heard, a few weeks later, that the Seventh Day Adventists had taken him on as an evangelist I was glad that I had not weakened. I had always felt that his eloquence was wasted in the humble duties of cook.

Shou-chu and Ching-ming, the two boys I hired in Ho Shih-fu's place, were also Christians. I got them both for what my Szechuenese had been costing me, and though inexperienced, they were not versed in the arts of corruption and they were anxious to learn more about the strange ways of foreigners. Ching-ming, whom I christened "Jimmie," had done some cooking for a Westernized Chinese in the Salt Gabelle, so I put him in charge of the food.

We got away from Tali on the second day of the Chinese New Year. The streets of the town were deserted. Every one was off feasting himself or the gods and the clatter of our caravan seemed to break irreligiously over the quiet stones. For a morning we followed the level road beside the Tali lake, which lay tranquil as a cloudless sky and unmarked even by a fisherman's sail. Two hours out, I stopped for a visit at the celebrated Kuan Yin in Tang Miaotze, an old temple which seemed to grow out of the sides of the hoary Tsang Shan Mountains.

Some monks, dressed in gray quilted kimonos, and wearing long rosaries carved from peach stones, greeted me and served me New Year's tea, with small cakes and confections. They were gracious and hospitable, as Buddhist monks nearly always are to travelers; they invited me to stay with them for several days, feeling reasonably sure, of course, that I would not accept. Then the abbot opened an inner shrine and showed me the famous life-size statue, carved in teak, of the soldier-statesman Tang, who governed this district after the Panthay rebellion, which he was largely responsible for suppressing.

The chief attraction of the Kuan Yin Tang is a white marble pagoda, set in a pool fed by mineral springs, in the main courtyard. Beneath it is a huge stone of granite, alleged to have been brought from heaven more than 2,000 years ago by the Goddess of Mercy. In a nook inside the pagoda, reached by a marble bridge and stairway, there is a finely carved idol of Kuan Yin, which appears to be covered with pure gold. This temple is probably the oldest in the province. It dates back to the time of the Nan-Chao Kingdom, about 1,000 years ago, and has been an object of pilgrimage for pious Buddhists for centuries. Tibetans come to it, and Chinese from the highest officials to the least pretentious peasants. While I was here a magistrate arrived, with his concubines and bodyguard, to perform the New Year duty.

I burned some joss before the male deities in a farther shrine, thanked the abbot and gave him a few dollars toward his reconstruction fund; the recent earthquake had knocked down a few of the gods and several of them had suffered serious concussion of the brain. Then I rode on, but could not catch up with my caravan till it had nearly reached Hsia Kuan, where we made the noon halt.

Hsia Kuan is built on the left bank of a river by the same name which flows out of the lower end of Ehr Hai, the Tali lake. It is a tributary of the Yang Pi, which one crosses two days further on. Hsia Kuan is an uncouth place, and the inhabitants are said to be notorious for their incivility. Yet I had a pleasant Chinese meal in a tea house over a gate, where the cordial proprietor gave me some baked duck from his own banquet table.

And as I went from the town I saw, through an open doorway, four priests clad in crimson and yellow robes and wearing regal miters on their heads. They knelt before an ancestral altar laden with offerings of fruit and flowers and lit by an amber candle that looked sensuous against heavy silken embroideries, hung everywhere. In low voices they intoned the classics. I stopped to listen to them. They were an unexpected splendor amidst the crudities of Hsia Kuan and an impressive testament to the strength of a great faith. But when I said something like that to Shou-chu, my Chinese Christian, he looked sad and said it was false worship, sinful and superstitious.

South of Hsia Kuan the country is sparsely populated, and sometimes we rode for a morning without passing a village. The altitude rose. As we crossed the Tsang Shan range the air was better on the high precipitous slopes. Deep forests, many of them still untouched by men, surrounded us when we descended to follow the ravine through which swept the river. There were pines and fir balsaam and occasionally banyans or wild tamarinds. Often, flanking the road for miles, there were tea roses, or some of the innumerable species of rhododendrons, with their profusion of pale lavender or white flowers. There were many wild plum trees in blossom, and they lay on the hills in patches like strips of gossamer silk, or when there was no wind, like delicate pink clouds put there to do nothing but look lovely.

At the end of the second day we reached Yangpi, a Mohammedan town. The people are said to be backsliding Moslems; however, they do not observe the fast days, they do not answer the morning and evening call to prayer, they drink wine and offer it on the family shrine to the departed ancestors. I spent the night before one such altar in a Mohammedan inn.

The Yangpi River flows swiftly and with a rush and song as it passes through the town. We crossed it, before dawn, over a Yunnan bridge, made of a series of great iron chains strung between two stone towers, with pretty gates. The chains are about 200 yards long and suspended parallel, at intervals of ten inches; over them is a wooden planking, and their ends are imbedded, under the towers, in concrete of native mixture. Nearly all large bridges of Yunnan are of this type. Most of them were erected during the Ming Dynasty, between five and six hundred years ago. They are still solid and quite safe, though now and then the chains have to be replaced.

This neighborhood was part of the bandit Chang Chi-bah's territory and it is only a few months since his successors were driven from Yangpi itself. The magistrate there thought that I should take along an escort. He sent four of the local militia, mere boys with belts of cartridges wrapped over both shoulders, and with businesslike German rifles of a fairly recent date. They said that a caravan had been attacked two days before, about ten li outside Yangpi.

No more deceptive measure of distance exists than the Chinese li. According to some it is roughly a third of a mile. But if it is over mountainous country the li may be no more than 400 yards; if it is an exhausting struggle up a steep, difficult trial, it may be only 300 yards; while a li downhill, or over the level stretches that occasionally happen even in Yunnan, is often half a mile or more. So that when you start out for what the muleteers call a 100-li stage you have no notion whether you are going to travel fifteen miles or thirty. You ask your caravan chief how far it is between this village and that and he replies: "If you are going north it is 95 li, while if you go south it is only 75." No amount of argument can make him admit that the distance is bound to be the same either way you travel. "Distance," he tells you, "is a relative word. It is a matter of time and effort rather than of here to there." And, accordingly, he collects more for his mules from you on an uphill trip than he does on the return.

T'ai-p'ing Pu, at the end of the stage, was a bedraggled cluster of huts leaning sadly against a lonely pass high in the mountains. It had only one inn, the filthiest I had seen; there was no temple and no school, so I had to stay in it, my pony being quartered with the pigs in a kind of sub-cellar also occupied by the owner, his wife and their two young children.

Two days more of wilderness and a night spent in a canyon where wolves howled; then, in late afternoon, we rode upon the edge of a bowl of high mountains and below was a great spacious plain. I saw patches of marigold and rice fields again, mirrored in thousands of little squares of placid water. In the midst of them, set like the motif in some mosaic pattern, lay Yungping.

Coming into a city by caravan is quite different from arriving by train. On a train you see a few scattered houses, and quickly they thicken; the tracks multiply and suddenly you are in the station. In a caravan you often look upon a city three or four hours before you finally ride up to its massive gates.

Yungping was like that. It drew near so gradually that each little story I amused myself by inventing about it had ample leisure in which to expand itself plausibly, flower into a satisfactory climax and perish with agreeable dignity. Thus, by the time we had reached the suburbs I felt well acquainted with both the city and its inhabitants, for we had struck up a certain intimacy while I was using them in my pleasant and useless fictions.

A Night in a Mohammedan Mosque by Virtue of an Almost Forgotten
Persian Phrase and an Opium-Addict Magistrate in Yungping

I entered Yungping toward sunset, at the end of a hard stage. I was dusty, hot and weary. All I desired were four walls, some quiet and a chance to go to sleep on my cot. But I could not have that. Yungping, although a town of 10,000 families, had only three inns for travelers, and I found these filled with Moslems, Buddhists and filial sons who had come in from afar to pay their annual respects to the gods and their venerable ancestors. There was no chance of getting a loft to myself; if I had stayed in one of the inns I should have had to endure opium smoking all night and the talk and expectorations that go with it. At times I suffered that, and enjoyed it; but I did not feel like undergoing the experience again. So I searched for a temple. Eventually, I came upon the Ching Tseng-tze, a Mohammedan mosque.

Looking in through the gate, I saw that it was clean and in the courtyard had a garden of mauve and creamy white poppies. There were fifty or sixty people congregated in the pavilion beyond the prayer tower, many of them wearing the low-crowned fez of the Chinese Moslems. They were darker than most Chinese, and some of them had Mongol or perhaps Tartar profiles, with strong sharp delineations of the nose, and firm markings on the chin. I stepped inside unnoticed and stood in the shadow of the gate.

Presently there was a stilling of voices and men looked upward. Following their gaze I saw a man in a white robe standing on the balcony of what I suppose should be called the minaret. It was not in Turkish or Persian architecture, but like a Chinese pagoda, except that it had long rectangular roofs that rose slowly to culminate in a point crested by a golden ball. The priest lifted his hands toward the flaming heavens where the sun was disappearing in the direction of Mecca. Then in a high melodious voice, he cried out the prayer to Allah. Three times he repeated it, while those in the courtyard bowed low to the poppy-scented earth and made the responses.

I noticed that on one side a building, long and with a full loft, had been newly erected. Going into it, I found that the upper story was clean and the walls were whitewashed. They were pieced by little shuttered windows and inside it was cool. None of the rooms was occupied. I turned to Shou-chu.

"Here is where we stay," I said. "Go down and tell the elders that they have some guests for the night." But he hesitated. He assumed I was a Christian and he thought it irregular for me to stay in a Mohammedan mosque. Anyway, he believed I ought to go with him to explain; they would not like it if he went alone. So I did.

"Good evening, gentlemen," I addressed the old Moslems. "I have just come in from the road and I am tired and want a clean place to sleep. There is no room in the inns. I think I will stay here. Do you mind?"

They were astonished at seeing a foreigner and more so at my unusual request. It was quite obvious that they did mind very much. They murmured among themselves and I fancied they were speaking of the cheek of this dog of an infidel.

"No," said one of them finally. "It is impossible. We have no charcoal here for your fire, no wood, no water. Besides, this is not an inn. Only Moslems come here."

"I know that. But I will get the charcoal and water. I will pay your caretakers, of course. Surely you will not send a stranger away when you have so much room in that loft?"

But it looked as though they certainly would. They said that it was entirely contrary to their custom; no foreigner had ever slept here before.

"It is not like a Buddhist temple, where the lying monks are only too glad to get your money. No, we are honest men and we do not need your alms. We do not know you. Perhaps, if you go to the magistrate and he says for us to receive you, why that may alter matters."

I was angry. It was the first time I had met with such obstinacy and independence. Most Yunnanese had regarded me, as a foreigner, with some deference; none of them had ever refused to accommodate me provided I was willing to pay for it. But then the humor of the situation came to me. I imagined a parallel case in America. Suppose I were a Chinese traveling through, let us say, Kansas. Suppose I had my own men, serving me Chinese food, and I was dressed in Chinese clothes. Going into a town I disdained the hotels because they were crowded and filthy, but I went up to the Catholic Church and announced that I was going to spend the night sleeping before the altar. Would I get such a tolerant reception as I was receiving, here in Yungping? I believed not.

I forgot my wrath, and looking at the worried old guardians of the temple, I chuckled. And because a Chinese always prefers to smile rather than look gloomy, these men laughed, too, though they could not have told me why. Then, happily, a remembered phrase from my Persian studies came to me. Still smiling I turned to them, and said rapidly:

"La Ilaha illa la, Mohammed rasul Illah!"

"Ah, indeed," replied one of them, "and Mohammed was His Prophet!" They were surprised and pleased and wanted to know where I had learned the salutation. Their attitude changed. They became more friendly.

"You see I am not ignorant of Moslem ways," I lied. "And I will, of course, respect your beliefs while I am in your mosque. Moreover, I am no Christian missionary but merely a traveler on his way to Burma."

They were all obviously relieved; their last trace of hostility disappeared. One of them called to a caretaker and ordered him to fetch some water and charcoal at once. He told another to sweep the loft and sprinkle it with water. Then Shou-chu, looking morose, went off to get the muleteers to bring my loads, though it was clear that he considered the whole proceedings fishy and unorthodox.

"And remember," I shouted after him for the benefit of the Islamites around me, "no pig for dinner tonight!" The elders laughed, hypocritically I thought, for I rather imagined they ate pig themselves.

Shou-chu's distaste for the adventure was not unnatural. There is a strong prejudice against the Mohammedans, particularly in Yunnan, where people still remember the Panthay Rebellion of the middle nineteenth century. The followers of the Prophet live more or less to themselves, seclusive and aloof. They distrust the unbelievers as heartily as they are in turn disliked by them. Riots and small wars over religious issues are frequent.

After dinner I took Shou-chu with me and went around to call on the magistrate. It was quite dark and I kept my flashlight on constantly as we wound through the narrow, ill-paved streets, scarcely wide enough for four men to walk abreast. After a while I became aware that we were being followed by two men and a young girl. I flashed my light on them and they shrank back. They were peasants, simple people with no malice in their eyes and certainly not dangerous; we went on, saying nothing. But when they persisted in trailing us down every byway and through every gate, I became irritated.

"Ask them what they want!" I said to Shou-chu. He did, and reported that they wanted nothing.

"Well, tell them to quit following us." They agreed, turned to leave, one of them lagging reluctantly. I focused the sharp beam on him; he stopped, and with a timid smile, came back. He said something quickly, and Shou-chu began to laugh.

"What is it?"

"Oh," said Shou-chu, "he wants to know where you keep the oil in your lamp, and how you avoid spilling it!"

I had no time to explain electrons, positives and negatives, and I am not sure that I could have done so anyway. So I told this curious man that "oil" was powdered like coal, and was wrapped up in a cell. It could not "leak." He looked at me and he was too polite to call me a liar, but with an expression of superb skepticism in his face, he turned and with dignity strode off through the night.

As we neared the yamen we were met by two runners who said they had been sent to escort me to the magistrate. They carried huge Chinese lanterns, faced with lacquered silk, and they wore long quilted army coats, several sizes too large for them. They led me up to the outer gate of the yamen, where I was saluted by two military sentries. Then we passed through a moon gate, and then another. We came into a garden that had just been watered, and the air was streaked with pleasing scents of hyacinth and roses. At the end of it Magistrate Leng Peiching met me, smirked and bowed slightly.

My Chinese was not up to conversation with magistrates. After a few honorifics I turned to Shou-chu and asked him to carry on for me. Shou-chu was something of a scholar, unusually learned for a servant; he had got through all the classics besides knowing the Bible much better, I am sure, than I did. I had previously told him what I wanted to know, so I felt safe in leaving the talk to him. He launched into it heartily and he and the magistrate were soon deeply involved, so that I could understand very little of what was said. Occasionally I interjected a question, or a pat remark, but for the most part I had the prudence to appear to be listening.

Presently he coughed informatively, and Shou-chu and I rose to go. I suspected that he was anxious to return to his opium pipe, the odor of which clung to his garments like a dark, evil perfume. He walked out to the gate with us, and to my surprise took me by the arm in a very friendly manner. He smiled and he showed white teeth; in his eyes, too, I saw that there was a smile. I had a curious feeling that he was amused by me and by my learned servant.

"My country," he said as I was about to leave, "is very poor. We have no roads, no motor cars and none of the fine things so abundant in your prosperous land. We are barren and we are all slaves of the cursed opium. It is very sad." But he did not look as though he, personally, was at all depressed by it. The feeling that he was laughing at me was emphasized as I said good night to him, and walked off hurriedly.

"Well," I inquired of Shou-chu, "did he answer your questions?"

"You mean your questions?"

"Yes. About schools and land taxes and so forth."

"No, he did not. He talked irrelevantly. I think he had been smoking too much opium. When I asked him how many jails there were in his district, he recited one of his poems to me. Ai-ya! I think he was a bad magistrate—an opium smoker!"

"On the contrary he must have been an entertaining fellow. I wish I had listened more carefully to him."

Shou-chu's disapproval of opium was not affected. He had been preaching against it to all he met, ever since we had left Tali. It did not disturb him because his reform talk met with a phalanx of indifference. He was something of a zealot and he enjoyed the sensation of crusading.

"Ai-ya!" he repeated as we entered the great gate of our Moslem mosque, "an opium smoker for a magistrate and a *Hwei-hwei miaotze* (Mohammedan mosque) for an inn! I shall be glad if we leave Yungping early tomorrow!"

We did. We crept out of the city, with the night trailing us. But in a little while there was a flush in the sky and then a swift dawn. Another day lay before us, and mountains, and the mighty Mekong River, striding through the grandeur of its gorges.

A Dangerous Stage on the "Golden Road to Burma"

Where One of China's Most Turbulent Streams Must Be Crossed on Flimsy Bamboo Rafts

The Mekong is one of the great rivers fed from the melting snows off the mountains of central Tibet. It flows for several hundred miles quite close to the Yangtze-kiang on the north, and the Salween on the south. Then, in western Yunnan, each turns slowly toward its mouth; the Yangtze-kiang, mighty and majestic, to water the great fertile basin of the Middle Kingdom and empty into the Yellow Sea below Shanghai; the Salween to proceed in a straightforward way through Southern Yunnan, in the Shan States, and out at Moulmein, Burma; while the Mekong, full of changes of mind and whimsical convolutions in every direction, ambles through Yunnan, the Shan States, Siam, Indo-China and eventually, still undetermined, breaks into a dozen mouths as it lowers into the sea through Cochin-China.

But where we passed it the Mekong moves with a steady sobriety on its southward voyage. It is sure of itself here; it does not waver. It has made its bed and it is lying in it; deep, very deep in it. It has cut its way through mountains over 8,000 feet high and now it flows, a mile below the summits, serene in its victory and with a grace and tranquility almost incongruous in the face of the sheer, terrible cliffs.

It took us five hours to cross the defiles. We struggled up the ridge of mountains that forms the north bank, and when we reached the top of what seemed to be its highest crag (but was not), we looked down over a breathless drop of almost 4,000 feet, and saw the Mekong. The downward path was onerous and very steep. All pretense at a road was swept away here, and the trail became a trench, then a veritable crevice that shut out everything but the soaring crags. The mules and the horses slipped and the pack thongs of rawhide creaked, but the animals kept their balance and did not lose a load.

We did not see the gorge again for an hour. Then gradually the walls of our trench lowered and we came out upon a shelf of rock that warily followed the base of the mountains. Below us rolled the Mekong, wide, silent and imperturbable. Where it was narrowest, pressed between two towering shoulders of the mountains on either side, an ancient chain bridge spanned it. But the boards had been removed and some workmen were forging new links for the heavy chains. We had to cross on a bridge made of bamboo rafts and only one man and one animal could pass over it at a time.

Before going over, I went up to the stone gate of the old bridge and looked on at the sixty or seventy men making the new chains. They used crude anvils and worked over fires of charcoal. In their mud-walled huts, built under a protrusion of rock, it was hot, smoky and oppressive. The men worked stark naked and rivulets of sweat streamed down their bent figures.

"How much do they get?" I asked an old gentleman who was smoking a water pipe and apparently was in charge of the work.

"Sixty cents a day, *tach'ien,*" he said. Sixty cents *tach'ien,* or "big money," in Yunnan means three small silver pieces, the equivalent of about fifteen American cents.

On the opposite shore we started at once up the Hsueh Shih Kuan (Water Rock Pass). It was three hours more of toilsome climbing to gain the height we had lost in the crossing. A narrow river rushed down beside the trail and the roar of its innumerable rapids filled the canyon with a rumble like the great guns of war. It is a brief stream, but while it lasts it has a wild, joyous career, so that it somewhat reminds you of those young people who start off with such brilliance, but live themselves to death before they have had time to get anywhere. It has its beginning in the nearby mountains and its end in a dazzle of foam, where it joins the Mekong. Over one stretch, the Chinese declare, it drops 5,000 feet in less than half an hour. But, alas! I am afraid I cannot even tell you the name of it. My muleteers called it Kuai-ti Hsueh, or "Hurrying Waters."

At the head of the pass we entered a scant but fertile valley, well cultivated. A few rice terraces climbed haphazardly up the gentle slopes, but most of the land was planted in poppy. It was a good crop and stood on vigorous stems, three or four feet tall. The blossoms were nearly all a stainless white, with here and there a shy lavender and, very rarely, a daring red that seemed to make the others blush and shrink away. Peasant girls, sunburned and robust, walked among the flowers and pierced the pregnant pods with their little four-bladed harvesting knives. Before dawn tomorrow they would be up to collect the sticky, creamy pollen that drips from the wounds overnight.

Poppies are the second or third crop in most parts of Yunnan, but here they seemed to be the first. For many days now, when the land was arable at all, I had seen little else in plant, except occasional patches of vegetables to care for the family's needs. Peasants often complain that they do not like to grow poppies, but are forced to do so by the government. Local authorities everywhere collect "fines" for acreage planted in poppy; but if the farmer does not devote a certain percentage of his land to the cultivation of the illicit flower he is obliged to pay "taxes" to the equivalent of the amount of fine! Naturally, he prefers to take his profit. Thus ingeniously does the Yunnan government maintain the appearance of enforcement of the national anti-opium law, while at the same time it derives a huge revenue from it. Yet everyone takes it for granted, and after all it may be a saner system of scofflawing than we have devised for evading the Volstead Act.

Coming into villages, the first thing you see are the opium stalls. Generally they are placed just outside the gates, and on market days they do a brisk trade. Local refining methods are cruder than those employed by the British in India; the poppy juice is just alternately boiled and dried in the sun, but the product is the best in China. When prepared it is poured into great earthenware jars and from these ladled into smaller jars which hold two ounces, enough for many satisfying dreams. It is very cheap, of course; something like ten American cents an ounce.

Nearly all Yunnan Chinese smoke opium, though the habit has not got far among the tribes, where tobacco and fiery rice brandy apparently are sufficient to arouse the more exquisite lusts and passions. It is not uncommon to see a lad of 5 or 6 with a well-developed habit for opium. This is not hard to understand when you see how early the palate is inured to it. The children are practically weaned on it. Several times I noticed Chinese mothers spread a streak of the dark brown fluid on a piece of sugar cane and feed it to an infant to stop his bawling.

The Mekong stage brought us to a mountain village called Hsueh Chai and there we found an inn, blessedly uncluttered with other caravans. It was run by a jolly old Chinese who had long white hair, excessively long fingernails and on his chin a few straggling hairs to which he extravagantly referred as his beard. He gave me a loft where family gods were ranged and ancestral tablets hung against the walls. Then he brought me a jar of wine, some little cakes and New Year's tea. He remarked that I was the first foreigner he had seen for two years, but his enthusiasm was not so great that he neglected to charge me double the ordinary rate for his shelter.

While I was eating the inn master's young son came up to put some food on the altar. There were bowls of steaming rice, vegetables, some chopped pork floating in shoya sauce and other delicacies. He put his offerings between some sticks of incense, clapped his hands three times and performed the kowtow. Then he went away, but in less than a minute he returned, collected the food and started off with it.

"Here," I said, incredulous, "you don't imagine your ancestors have had time to appease their hunger already! Why not give them time?"

He smirked at me. "It is the custom," he replied. "And anyway if I left it here all night my honorable forebears would not eat it, but assuredly the rats would. Moreover, we below are hungry." And he hurried off to make his meal, with a parting look of superiority, as if to say, "How little you know, untutored one, about the etiquette of fulfilling one's filial obligations." I survived the snub, however, finished my meal and offered up the remnant vegetables and pudding to the gods. In the morning it was gone, but I could not recollect having heard a single rat.

The road to Yungchang next day was through wild, heavily wooded country, too rugged for any cultivation. The mountains stretched high, blue and endless under a warming sky. Toward noon we passed the first big caravan we had seen since leaving Tali; the New Year holidays were about over and from now on we saw more travelers. This caravan was a string of sixty Tengyueh mules and sturdy ponies. They carried cotton, opium, and two or three loads of jade and amber. Evidently some official must have been interested in the cargo, for they had an escort of twenty soldiers. It was a prosperous outfit and the Ma Ko To was mounted, which is unusual. He had a spirited little pony, jet black and with a circlet of bells jingling happily. He sat on a beautiful Tibetan saddle blanket and he rode with his elbows wide, Yunnan style. Over his shoulders there was a yellow silk scarf and a long chain of silver beads, while around his waist was buckled a silver sword. But on his head—good heavens! there was a soft felt hat with a pheasant feather stuck in its slanting brim and he wore it with an air of derring-do! When he passed me he saluted, laughed and showed white teeth. He was handsome and splendid, and he knew it. He quite took my breath away. He looked like Robin Hood.

Yungchang lies in a great plain between the two mountain ranges that form the divides of the Mekong and the Salween. Although it is now fully cultivated and deforested, it was until comparatively recently covered with a thick semitropical vegetation. Burmese warriors once brought their elephants as far as this city and vanquished the inhabitants in one of those battles of gore and carnage from which the ancients used to get such pleasure.

My hostel was known by the fanciful Sign of the Red Dragon. It was built around the usual courtyard, and it had two loft rooms which must once have been rather pretty with their carved wooden shutters under a green tiled roof. But that was many years ago; one look at the present interior caused me to shrink in alarm, and I demanded that the place be cleaned and scoured. The young inn master was reluctant to believe that I was in earnest; apparently nobody had ever made such an outrageous request before. He remarked that the sleeping mats were in good order and he could not understand what else a man could want; surely I did not mind a little dirt.

But eventually he was persuaded that I was serious and he went to work with a decrepit broom. In five minutes he emerged with a large basketful of trash, wornout sandals, broken bottles, bits of tile, broken glass, pieces of dirty rags and a great quantity of extraordinarily dirty dirt. Shou-chu, my servant, then gave the room a second cleaning and came out with a second basket almost as full. I made a reconnaissance at this point and managed to find more dirt in the corners, a woman's small shoe, a broken opium lamp and a pair of spectacles without lenses, which I gingerly handed over to the proprietor. To his chagrin I then had all the sleeping mats thrown out the windows and practically exhausted his water supply by having the floors scrubbed. Such a spectacle had never been witnessed before, and probably never will be again. The water dripped down on the tea sippers below and they rushed out, wishing to know what the devil was up to.

After the ablutions were completed the room seemed more habitable. Even the inn master, coming in to have a look at the results, was impressed. He brought up his brother, who was staying with him at the moment, and had him see what had happened. I was apparently regarded in the light of a phenomenon; quite a number of Chinese had gathered in the courtyard where they were told the story of the Great Cleansing.

I was rather pleased with myself. I knew that I had been a considerable nuisance and I derived from it a deep satisfaction. I felt somewhat like the princess who could not sleep because of the pea under her twenty mattresses.

At the same time I did not flatter myself to think that the exhibition would have any permanent influence on the ancient customs of the Sign of the Red Dragon. The loft was clean when we left it in the morning for Tengyueh, but I dare say the next meticulous traveler who happens into it will be shocked to discover therein a number of worn-out sandals, broken bottles, bits of tile, broken glass, dirty rags and a great quantity of extraordinarily dirty dirt!

The Sulphur Springs of Remote
and Inaccessible Western Yunnan, China

Where the Old Chinese Custom of Bargaining
for a Wife Still Exists

Near Pu P'iao, a day south of Yungchang on the Golden Road to Burma, there are some celebrated sulphur springs feeding into a large marble pool said to have been built for the officers of the Great Khan's army more than 600 years ago. They are very popular still, and at the holiday season draw festive crowds. The natives come down from the wilderness and up from the valleys to bathe here in the curative waters once regarded as sacred.

Grass huts are laced together, encircling the pool, and in the neighborhood temporary shelters are put up. There are little tea houses and restaurants, gambling and opium parlors, toy bazaars, candy stalls, old women selling chestnuts and colored rice balls, and sometimes a troupe of vagabond actors. And there are more pretentious places, made of thatched pine branches where silk-clad singing girls, all scented and amorous, entice the unwary stranger with their dark wanton eyes and the tremulous music of their lutes.

It is rude and somewhat uncouth, and yet there is this about it a robust hardiness and vitality that impart to it a kind of primitive grandeur. The scene has the romance of a circus and the vigor of a soldier's leave. It reminds you, when at night it is splendid with huge yellow torches, of an old Chinese woodcut of an ancient night of carnival.

The salt tax inspector, at whose office I camped for the night at Pu P'iao, took me to the springs. When we arrived at the pool I was dismayed to find it already dotted with scores of Orientals, men and women, stewing blissfully in the hot, murky water. Fortunately, the salt inspector was a man of resource. He darted into one of the mat sheds and in a moment returned with two huge earthen jars. He then led me to the source of the pool, where the springs bubbled in gracious darkness. There I had a satisfactory scrub in esoteric isolation, and it quite refreshed me. Then I wandered back up the bazaar street, marveled at the crowds and bought a red and white rice ball, which I threw at a pretty child, swimming like a water cherub in the pond. Presently my friend rejoined me, and together we felt our way back through the labyrinthine paddy and over a dim bridge into Pu P'iao.

In the morning, earlier than usual, we started down toward the valley of the Salween. It is a stretch at all times thick with an endemic fever, and caravan men do not consider this crossing lightly, and often start off three or four hours before dawn in order to clear the most dangerous part of the trip before the sweltering heat of mid-afternoon.

Unlike the Mekong, the Salween swings into view an hour or two before you reach its edge. The chain bridge is a fine old structure, dating from the fifteenth century. It has a main span and a lighter secondary one to take care of the flood flow: they are divided by a staunchly built and fortified pier and mounted with the usual graceful gate.

The Salween here sweeps by pale and slender, a river headed eagerly for the south. It has a bed of huge boulders, worn smooth by centuries of turbulent flow, and if you look up the sides of its rocky channel you see the high marks of previous floods and how they are being cut forever deeper. Far up the valley, but clear in the unclouded sky, there are the snow peaks that nourish this stream; they glisten, lovely and imperious as white-haired dowagers. Some of their majesty seems to ride down with the Salween as it moves so swiftly, impatient to fold into the distant embrace of the sea.

Just over the bridge there are some horse inns, and beyond them, under mat-shed stalls, a large fair is run by the Shans, who hold the Salween Valley as their domain. It is fertile land and tempting, but the Chinese dare not venture into it; with their physical resistance constantly drained by opium, they are easy prey for the fever. It does not much bother the Shans, whose worst vice appears to be betel chewing among the old ladies. They live here quite content, except during the rains; then, having planted their crops, they retire for two or three months in the hills.

The market was gay. Nobody seemed to mind the heat but myself. There were many tea houses run by Shan women, and most of the stalls were also run by them. I saw displays of tribal homespun in geometrical patterns, reds, blues, and yellows; I saw arrowheads for sale and pieces of flint with bits of steel, and blue cotton cloth, wildcat and leopard skins, cheap soap, unwashed rice, brick tea, tawny colored sugar, grayish salt, pins, needles, hunks of white taffy and walnut brittle, ornaments of jade and silver, strings of tobacco, and one woman with boxes of imported rouge and lipstick.

The Shans wore a black or orange or white skirt caught in a bow at the waist, and above this a little jacket with colored collar, quite snug and charming. They had strips of bright cloth wrapped round their legs, and they went barefoot or wore wooden sandals like geta [Japanese wooden clogs]. Older women, with their hair done in tall regal coiffure, had small sweet faces and, unlike the Chinese, they did not stare at you incredulously, but with candor and amusement in their merry eyes. Two young girls walked gracefully on dainty feet and had small, delicate hands. Artfully they put flowers in their hair, a red rose or a dark camellia or a spray of peach blossom. They were winsome and attractive, and they looked as if they would be delighted to hear you tell them about it.

That evening I stopped at the pretty little inn of a Shan village perched high on the side of a windy gorge. It was a clean place, comely and neat, like the Shan mother and her daughters who ran it.

When I had dined the matriarch, who called herself Mme. Loi, came into my room, apologizing, and leading a young girl who kept her face hidden in her hands. She was a woman of some education, apparently, for she spoke elegant Chinese, full of the old-fashioned "courtesy talk" that foreigners hear less frequently nowadays. But she looked at me squarely, and there was humor and laughter in her eyes that once must have been rather roguish. Alas! all her fine conceits and allegories and allusions were wasted upon me, and she soon discovered that she must restrict herself to my limited vocabulary. She asked my name, my occupation, my nationality and my destination. Then:

"How old are you?" she inquired.

"I am 25."

"You are married, of course?"

"No."

She did not believe me. No man can reach the age of 25 without having at least one wife. But she continued:

"And you have no children?"

"No."

She paused, and the young girl for the first time lifted her hands from her face and stole a shy glance at me. I saw that she had soft skin, lighter than almond, and full red lips and very dark shining hair. She had been weeping.

"How would you like to have her for a wife?" Mme. Loi suddenly demanded.

I was not sure that I had understood.

"Excuse me?"

"How would you like to have Me Le, this daughter of mine, for a wife?"

The situation was new to me; no one had offered me a wife before and I did not know what to say. One could not simply refuse without a reason, and I had already told her I was a single man. But the moment was dramatic and I did not wish it to end too soon.

"What would I do with a wife?" I asked, finally. "I am not a wealthy man. I cannot afford such nonsense."

"But this daughter is an extraordinary girl. She can read and write. She plays the zither. She is only 16 and still young enough to be taught many handsome things about the world." She enumerated her virtues in flowery terms so that poor Me Le flushed and giggled hysterically. "Moreover," she concluded, "she will not cost you much. I have six daughters and one more or less does not matter."

I was curious. "How much?" I asked bluntly. After some graceful irrelevancies the matriarch intimated a price of 300 silver dollars.

"But that is manifestly absurd!" I exclaimed. "No wife is worth three hundred dollars."

Mme. Loi, however, was not unreasonable. She thought that an agreement might be reached if I would suggest a price. I had no intention of doing so; no matter how low the figure I named, there was always the possibility that she might meet it. Indeed, I began to fear that she might give me the girl. And though it was perhaps lack of imagination on my part, I could not that instant quite fancy myself honeymooning with a Shan wife over the caravan trails of Yunnan. When the old mother had brought her price down to $100 I thought the daughter's humiliation had become too painful. I said that a man must have a few hours in which to consider matrimony and that she must give me till morning to decide. Mme. Loi thought the request was not unnatural, so she bowed low, smiled and left the room. But not Me Le.

She apparently decided that she would find out something about her prospective husband. She sat down on her heels and surveyed me gravely. Then she took off her turban and shook her head so that her hair tumbled down over her shoulders. Slowly a wan smile crept over her face and then gradually her eyes grew radiant. She was very pretty, I decided, and like a flower. It gratified me to believe that perhaps the prospect of our marriage was not altogether revolting to her. Suddenly, she smiled broadly, walked over to my cot, kicked off her sandals and without a word began to untie the knot of her skirt.

I was alarmed.

Snow identified this girl as Me Le, the child-bride for whom he was invited to barter.

"Ai-ya!" I shouted, took her by the arm and led her swiftly to the door. "Tsai wei," I said. "Sweet dreams." Yet there was something so disturbing and provocative about the impudent little smile she gave me as she shrugged her shoulders and walked away that I decided to leave earlier next morning than I had planned. I called Shou-chu, my Christian brave, and told him that we would tie on the loads at 5 o'clock. He said yes, but he looked so gloomy that I asked what was wrong. He said he understood that I intended to take along Me Le! I was touched with his concern.

"What do you make of it, Watson?" I asked. But, of course, he did not understand, so I added in Chinese: "Why does she want to give me her daughter?"

He explained. It was all very simple. Me Le, it appeared, had secretly accepted the inn ma-fu, a Chinese, as her lover. They had been having a ravishing time till the matriarch finally discovered them only that morning. She was so angry that at once she made a vow by Buddha's image that as punishment she would marry her daughter to the first traveler who stopped at her inn. And I, out of 400,000,000 Chinese, happened to be that traveler. Shou-chu's exposé settled the matter. I would have no ma-fu's mistress for my bride.

I rode all that day and the next. Many caravans, coming from Tengyueh, passed me on the road, with their loads of cotton, tinned-milk, opium, and now and then a well-guarded mule or two with jade or silver. The sun grew warmer and the vegetation more tropical, with increasing forests of dense bamboo and occasionally a few palms. But always there were the rolling mountains, stretching infinite and invincible, like the eternal waves of the sea.

At last I rode down into Tengyueh. On the slopes of the mountains rising up from the wide plain some monasteries lay like white handkerchiefs put out to dry. Below, advancing far, were paddy fields with their heads, now green, now brown, leaning delicately from the wind. I came into the suburbs of the city and was surprised to find many shops and stalls and even the main market outside the massive time-stained walls.

Tengyueh. I remember the bazaar street with its hundreds of brown little men sitting under huge umbrellas, yellow ones, like those you see over the carts of itinerant fruit vendors in America. I remember entering the great South Gate and walking along wide streets that seemed empty, but the cleanest in Yunnan. There were some thickets of bamboo, I think, and their sobbing reminded me of Hangchow and of a clear summer day under the Thunder Peak Pagoda of West Lake. I saw some Chinese women, dressed in blue and white silk, and one of them wore a sprig of jasmine, while another had her glossy hair stuck with dozens of little bits of jade and gleaming gold ornaments and bangles.

Suddenly, as the sun sank beyond those cerulean peaks, a young Chinese lady came riding through a gate. She had tiny bound feet fitted into red embroidered slippers and she wore blue satin trousers and above them a little waistcoat of padded red silk. She rode like a man, straddling a bright red dragon rug on a white and black pony. When she came near my dusty mount she lifted her eyes and smiled and bowed low over the pommel of her saddle. I raised my hat and made a flourish with it as she rode past with all the splendor of a young empress. That is what I remember about Tengyueh.

The "Lao-lu," Old Road to Bhamo
Just across the Burma Border from Kanai
in the Yunnan Province of China

Two main pack trails from northern Burma converge at Tengyueh. I looked longingly at the "short road" to Myitkina. It would take me to the Burma border in four days and to the upper waters of the Irrawaddy in six. Over that route I would climb gnarled snow peaks at 12,000 feet and pass through primitive tribal territory of the Zis, the Marus, the Kachins and Tingra Nungs. I searched for muleteers to take the trip. But it was the wrong season for incoming cargo from Myitkina; no caravan master was willing to risk returning with empty mules. I could have paid double rates, of course, but my funds were too low for that. I abandoned the scheme and took the alternative.

That was the lao-lu, the "old road" to Bhamo, which I had planned to follow when I began my journey. By this way it is five stages to the frontier and about eight days to the first outpost, where British officials were stationed and steam navigation ends on the Irrawaddy. The road traverses tribal districts equally as unknown as those toward Myitkina, with Kachins, Shans, Zis, Lisus and a few Marus scattered here and there. My objection to it was that it was through low country, for it drops sharply beyond the Tengyueh; Bhamo is only 361 feet above the sea. After so many weeks in them, my affection for the mountains had grown deeply. I did not like the idea of slipping away from them so quickly into the shallow febrile hills and jungles. But there was no help for it.

The Min Chia muleteers, who had brought me from Tali, could not, with any bribe, have been induced to go down to Bhamo. They were mountain men, used to the hard winds and snows and they had a superstitious fear of hot climates. They had heard that men cooked their food simply by putting it in the sunset Shing-kai (Bhamo), and they believed it as firmly as they did the legend that the Ak'as, in southern Yunnan, had long tails like apes.

I also lost Shou-chu in Tengyueh; he would venture no further. He had been more of a companion than a servant, it is true; but for that reason I missed him a great deal. We had grown intimate in the long days on the road; he had enriched the hours with little anecdotes of his people, and (which was vastly more important) he had listened cheerfully to tales of some of my own experiences. We shared a genuine regret in parting.

But Ching-ming (Jimmie), my "sort of cook," stayed on. He had to surrender the high estate of his office, however, and became first assistant to a master of wayside cookery whom I managed, by good fortune, to pick up in Tengyueh. His name was Wang, and he had for several years served as the head man in the expeditions of a Scotch botanist, who had trained him as only a Scotchman with a high sense of what constitutes "dooty and efficiency" can. In fifteen minutes he could produce a five-course meal in the heart of the jungle, climaxing it with century pudding such as is the despair of young Western housewives. There are probably not more than half a dozen such cooks in all China. He was an artist. After a day of the excellent eating provided by Wang I was his abject admirer, mere putty in his hands.

Several caravans were leaving for Bhamo shortly, and I had little difficulty in arranging to join one of them. It was an outfit of sixteen mules and ponies, rather huskier than those of central Yunnan, better fed and obviously better treated. The muleteers were Shans and Chinese. Six of our animals traveled empty. The rest carried salt, skins, orpiment [yellow arsenic used as a pigment], and a small quantity of carved amber, besides my four loads. The Ma Ko To planned to cover his deficit on the down trip by collecting outlaw fees for the return, as there was a brisk traffic moving north from Bhamo. In the season mules fetch $50 (silver) for loads from Bhamo to Tengyueh, the highest rate of any pack trail in Yunnan. It cost me only a third of that, however, for the full eight-day trip in the opposite direction.

The caravan was glad to have me. My presence, as a foreigner, gave bearing to the party and a measure of protection. Ordinarily the "old road" is quite safe, but periodically there is a tribal outbreak and then the caravans move stealthily. A report of such a rising reached Tengyueh just as we were about to leave. It appeared that a party of Kachins had raided and burned a Shan village three days from the Burma border. Two of the savages were caught and at once executed. It happened that they were sons of a Kachin *du-wa* or chief. His tribe at once declared a feud against all "foreigners," meaning Shans and Chinese, as the Kachins regard themselves the only rightful heirs of the land. It was alleged that all caravan travel from Burma had halted and that the Kachins, in their war paint and charms, were attacking, burning and plundering, all along the route.

Such rumors are common in Yunnan. I had met with a variation of this tale at practically every stage. Road conditions were always "precarious" and already I had wasted too much valuable time waiting for them to be pronounced "safe." They never are, and it is doubtful if they ever have been. I scoffed at the muleteers' fears and declined to request an escort from the Tengyueh tupan. Soldiers are not ordinarily granted to expeditions through this part of Yunnan and I foresaw further delays if I officially announced myself and insisted on military protection. My muleteers seemed somewhat disgruntled when we started out, though it may have been the depressing effects of the vast burial grounds through which we began our southward march into the land of the Shans.

In reality the Shans are not to be classed with the indigenous tribes of Yunnan at all. They are far more advanced, culturally, than any of the aborigines, many of whom remain in a state of semibarbarism. Shan civilization is perhaps more ancient than that of the Chinese. Certainly the Shans of Yunnan show superior breeding to the Chinese here, though it must be admitted that the latter are the most densely ignorant and superstitious in China.

The Shans are more numerous, more widely scattered than any other racial group in Yunnan. They are the only ones found in any large numbers in other parts of China. According to Chinese history, they dwelt originally in the valleys of the Yangtze and Yellow rivers, in central and northern China. Gradually they were absorbed, or driven back, by the more aggressive Chinese and Mongols, till at length they reached the southern end of the great Asian peninsula.

The Siamese are Shans, the only self-governing nation of them left today. Likewise, the Laos, the Tonkinese, the Annamites and probably the Nom Khmers, all of French Indo-China, are branches of the Shan family tree. The Talaings of southern Burma are related to them; practically all of Burma was once ruled by Shans. They still constitute about one-fourth of the total Burma population, most of them dwelling in the northern jungle and mountain country known as the Shan States.

That is rather an encyclopedic outburst for me. I hasten to assure you that the information is not original. It is the result of talks with Stanley Wyatt-Smith, an Englishman who has spent much labor in tracing the origin and migration of the Shans of eastern Asia. Some of his researches and deductions are the only data available to illuminate the blank pages in the ancient history of the polyglot and heterogeneous tribes here, of whom so little at present is known.

The Chinese exercise a loose control over the Shans south of Tengyueh. Each district is under a sawbwa, who is nominally responsible to the Chinese authorities. As an institution, the sawbwanate in Yunnan dates from the Ming Dynasty, when the Chinese conquerors subdued "the southern barbarians." Most of the original sawbwas were Chinese soldiers, rewarded for valorous conduct. In time, as generations of sons succeeded fathers, they intermarried with their subjects, until today they are barely distinguishable from them in form or feature. Some of the sawbwas arrogate much pomp and splendor to their office, surrounding themselves with the atmosphere of petty potentates. A few of them are said to be extremely wealthy. They are also hospitable, as I learned while I was the guest of one of them.

A Visit in the Home of a
Cultured, English Speaking Ruler
of 50,000 Chinese and Shans
in Faraway Kanai, China

We reached Kanai at the end of an easy downward stage. I rode up the main street, where Shan women, in net black turbans and white coats and trousers, stood idly behind market stalls of magnificent vegetables and looked at me candidly, appraisingly and speculatively. Under the guidance of Wang, who had visited the town before, we started up a byway lined with clean adobe walls. Through the center of it coursed a clear crystal stream, down a channel laid with white stones and fringed with little clusters of hyacinths and tea roses. And it was then that the two Shan youths, with silver mounted swords slung so gallantly from their wide scarlet sashes, rode up on pretty pinto ponies and addressed us in Chinese. They were from the Sawbwa to present "his respectful good wishes and an invitation to dine from his barren table."

Would I condescend? Would I! I was so pleased and astonished that in my haste to accept I forgot the formality of the three refusals which Oriental etiquette demands. What mystified me (and still does) is how the Sawbwa knew, almost to the minute, when I was arriving in Kanai! His must be a well-ordered dominion, where news of a stranger's coming reaches so far ahead.

Taking along my last bottle of Henessey's Three Star and two plaques of Tali marble as gifts, I trotted after the ruler's bearers. The Sawbwa's residence was at Old Kanai, about two miles to the northwest of the main town. To reach it we had to ford the Taping River. Then we followed a single track across golden fields of mustard and a scattering of poppy, and entered a heavy thicket from which we emerged not far from the village. The Sawbwa himself, mounted on a fine black pony, greeted me outside a stockade made of tall pointed stakes of bamboo, securely lashed with knotted grass rope, a good protection against bandit and beast.

We dismounted and exchanged salutations in Chinese. The Kanai Sawbwa was a man of perhaps thirty-five, though he may have been

221

thirty or fifty. The age of Orientals is an enigma to me still; often the years seem to slip over them unnoticed, leaving shadows but no wrinkles, or sometimes the only sign is a dullness over the fine luster of their eyes. He was slender, but not as tall as I, and barefoot; he moved with a lithe grace that made me suddenly conscious of the restrictions of Western dress.

The earth yields to these people, appears to embrace them; to us, shod in hard nails and leather, it sometimes seems to turn an adamantine heart. The Sawbwa wore loose trousers, Shan *b'aum-bies,* of a pale silk that clung like a caress to his supple thighs. He had on a white tunic and over it a red vest of brocade. Above this was a bronzed face and a generous mouth around which there lingered a smile, as if the world still amused him. He wore no turban and his hair was trimmed close to his small shapely head.

"You have come very far," he said. "You are very tired." Gracious! He spoke English. My astonishment pleased him.

"Ah, yes," he explained, "I was to one of your English schools in Burma. They teach me to read the books, to writing, and to make sums without the abacus. It was agreeable while lasting. Now I am glad to be back for my people. Soon I forget all you Englishmen teach. Ha! Ha!"

I assured him that I was not English, not even British. I was an American and had nothing whatever to do with those who had brought the benefits of education to sawbwas. And then, wholly irrelevantly I am afraid, I gave him to understand that the English and Americans, despite their common language, were as different as two races could be, and that both of us were glad of it.

"I know," he surprised me by answering, "England and America are like Japan and China. You think England is a nuisance; England think you a nuisance. All the same you could not get along without each other." It was rather shrewd, I thought, coming from a back country ruler whose subjects, most of them, had only the haziest ideas about England and as for America, alas! they had never heard of us.

I liked the village. It was all Shan, with huts of bamboo or grass walls and thickly thatched roofs. Here and there I saw a shrine where incense smoldered before an image of the Buddha, of whom the Shans are pious votaries. Everything was clean; it seemed too paradisal to be true; even the infants had scrubbed ears and unsmudged faces.

There were fat palm trees, with necklaces of cocoanuts and before every hut a rose bush or a rhododendron. An old gardener went by, with a basketful of jasmine and blush camellias and both women and men gathered round him and chose fresh buds to twine in their thick glossy hair. Several rivulets, piped down from the mountains in tubes of bamboo, washed through the town, gurgling musically. Along their banks I saw water lilies, and then a lace of violets. Violets! I was swept by a fleeting nostalgia . . . the memory of a shadowed place where I knew other violets grew, quite like these, in a Missouri wood a whole world away.

As we approached the Sawbwa's house we passed a noisy little waterfall that filled a dark pool shaded by classic tamarind trees. Two Shan maidens stood in it half immersed, and languidly splashed each other.

We entered the Sawbwa's spacious garden and through it to his big house, elevated on teak stems. We sat on his mat-covered floor and talked and smoked bad cigarettes, but drank good warm rice spirit. (He did not take Buddhist prohibition seriously; not many of the Shans do.) He told me that he governed 30,000 or 50,000 people. He asked me if Italy and France were at war (a curious rumor which has spread among all the officials of Yunnan), and he wanted to know if it was true that Chiang Kai-shek had killed 5,000 Communists by sinking them in a junk at sea.

After we had eaten, the Sawbwa called in his two wives, both young, and clad in blue b'aum-bies and white shirts. They carried a great weight in silver on them, with several bracelets over each arm, and anklets of thick plate above their naked feet. They bowed to me, smiled and sat down behind their husband. One of them, I thought, was quite lovely. There was a carved delicacy to her features, she had the soft exquisite hands of a child, and slender wrists, like the stem of a flower. Her eyes were very dark, but gay, and she had an abundance of hair massed like a tiara on her small head.

Presently some musicians came in. One had a long drum, made like a huge spindle, which he carried on a cord slung over his shoulder. It impressed me as unique. It certainly was like nothing in China. I asked my host about it.

"Long before," he said, "it was make Shan war drum. Now not wars for many years so we make peace drum. Tonight—we make pleasure drum." He lustily ordered that my wine bowl be refilled.

Pleasure drum? I did not understand. But in a moment two Maru singing girls arrived and I perceived that I was in for a concert. They were strongly built women, but not without grace, though it was evi-

dent enough that they were of an entirely different race from the Sawbwa's wives. They wore silver earrings the size of saucers beneath their
jet bobbed hair, and the puzzling thing was that those cumbersome
ornaments became them and invested their handsome swarthy faces
with character.

When they saw me they were neither embarrassed nor frightened.
They measured me steadily and at the conclusion of their survey looked
at me with cynical eyes. Evidently they decided that I was not too
nauseating for an auditor, at any rate, for finally they smiled deliberately, and began to sing.

I had anticipated the performance with indifference, expecting the
usual tribesman's imitation of Chinese falsetto. Abruptly I realized I
was wrong; this was original music. Here was resonance, vibrant and
rich, that clung to the air and stirred it, now with prime passion, now
with an elemental tenderness. It was always in minors, and the voices
almost muted, but it somehow managed the illusion of volume. It was
remarkably articulate and intelligible, not refined, but not coarse. It
was sincere. I have never heard any other Oriental music remotely like
it. For a long while, forgetful of time, I sat listening to it, enthralled.

At last I rose to go. The Sawbwa walked with me down to the gate of
his village.

"Why must you hurry to Burma?" he asked. "Stay here with me.
Life is easy. You will have no worries. We are a contented people. I
have a young son. He would like you and you could teach him English."

I did not at once reply, and evidently he understood that I was
waiting for persuasion. He added:

"I will give you a house. And—those Maru girls will take care for
you." He gave me a mundane smile, and interrogated me with his
eyebrows.

I smiled also, but for a different reason. The tip of my nose quiv-
ered. I experienced an odd tumbled-up feeling. I was no longer walking
with a Sawbwa in a mountainous mid-Asian state, but up a quiet
brook through the woods of a town in Missouri.

"Thank you," I said. "It is impossible." A moment later I mounted
my pony and rode off through the moon-streaked night. Two of the
Swabwa's bearers went with me, for he had confirmed the report of the
Kachin rising and had sent them along as escort for tomorrow's hill
and jungle.

Arrival of Caravan in Burma, Land of Teak, Elephants and Glittering Pagodas

after a Brush with Kachin Bandits on the Chinese Border

It was my last day in China, though not my last in Kachin country. Tomorrow, when I crossed the Yunnan border beyond Man Hsien Kai, the Kachins I met would be British subjects of Upper Burma. I was elated with the thought of a new land so near, and impatient to be there. The muleteers irked me with their demand for a two-hour halt at noon, so I had gone ahead of them, alone and on foot.

It was hot and only a faint breeze stirred as I walked through the jungle. Fecund walls of ferns and trees, interlaced with long serpentines of verdant vine, pressed up to the edge of the path, that gradually narrowed. There were many wild fig trees, with magnificent leafy arms, and occasionally, breaking its shower of scarlet over the dense green like a deliberate sin, I saw the brilliant Flame Tree that the natives call "Cloud of Blood." There were palms, thrusting their slender stems high above the rest, and with their graceful heads poised like lofty thoughts. Then, for distances growing so thickly that they seemed a curtain for something mysterious and dramatic beyond them, there stood clumps of elegant bamboos, so gregarious and yet so tragic and aloof.

Musing thus, I progressed deeper into the vast spread of greenery. Gradually I realized that I had got off the main road and was following a thin trail that threatened to expire altogether. I had passed no one for over two hours and it occurred to me that it was a delightful spot for a murder.

The knowledge that the Kachins were on the warpath did not serve to comfort me. I recalled the warning of the Kanai Sawbwa, who had declared that the present outbreak promised to be as severe as the last one, which occurred in 1924 and was suppressed only after several hundred people had been massacred. But from the Kachins I had seen thus far I believed they hadn't the courage to attack me. How timid and frightened they had been! The women when they saw me invariably ducked from sight behind the nearest hedge, while the men fled

A Kachin chief poses with his wives.

past the terrifying spectacle with winged haste. Still they all carried those unpleasant looking dahs, curved swords, short but very businesslike. And I remembered that a French father whom I met far back in Yunnan had assured me that once their fanaticism is roused by the tribal sorcerers they are extremely dangerous people. That padre, who proselytized among them many years ago, had also told me of their strange faith. I thought of some of their extraordinary superstitions as I walked down the jungle trail.

The Kachins believe in a spirit world peopled by "Nats" or demons. Around them is shaped the whole social and religious existence of the various tribes. It is their opinion that there are thousands of these little busybody deities, one for nearly every uncomfortable sensation and circumstance in life. It appears that the Nats' chief office is to annoy helpless humans, whom they bite with the keenest relish. They have enormous appetites and are eternally at their distressing tasks from the moment a man or woman is born until death.

These reflections were interrupted by a sudden crackling of twigs from behind the screen of foliage. I stopped. Four men, clad only in loin skirts, but all carrying dahs, and with daggers strapped to their waists, stepped onto the road and confronted me with stolid faces. They were Kachins. Fantastic tattoos covered their lean, small bodies, and their hair was clipped in Cromwellian fashion. They remained, twenty yards ahead, waiting for me.

I had a small automatic with me, a .25 that looked like a toy, but could give a real and deadly bark at close range. I took it out, released the safety, and walked on toward the men; flight, which I, of course, thought of, would have been silly and perhaps dangerous. The Kachins were lined across the road and they made no sign of giving way for me as I approached. When I was about fifteen feet from them I halted.

"Get out of the way," I ordered. It was a comfort to hear my own voice, even though they could not understand. I supplemented the words with appropriate gestures, and motioned menacingly with my gun. But they grinned and did not budge. They raised their dahs and shook them at me. They looked so funny they made me laugh and it was like something by Zane Grey, or watching a cinema thriller. It did not seem possible that a situation so ludicrous could encompass a serious threat to my life.

Nevertheless, it was all obviously real. When the men moved toward me, with their wicked dahs glittering, I realized that the next move was mine. Picking up a stick, I marked a semi-circle in front of me, an operation which the Kachins observed with studied gravity, no doubt thinking it was foreign magic of some sort. Then I said, "The first one of you who comes beyond that line gets this"—and showing my gun again I made them comprehend, by the universal language of signs, what I meant. They hesitated a moment, and gazed intently at the circle, and at my weapon. After inspecting both of them from a distance, they evidently decided they were innocuous, suddenly laughed and started forward. Very probably they had never seen an automatic before, or they would have kept a more respectful distance.

I moved back a short way and waited. They came up to the line in the dust and paused, while two of them reached down at it gingerly with their dahs, as if they expected it suddenly to coil up and eject venom. When nothing happened they boldly obliterated the mark and spat upon it. Then, with a shrill cry, a most hair-raising cry, they descended upon me at top speed. It was very unsavory, but there was nothing else for me to do—I fired instantly. I did not aim to hit any of them, but shot just in front of their feet four times in rapid succession. The shots cracked out, sharp and clamorous.

Clearly this reception was not at all what the Kachins had expected. It had astonishing effects.

All four of them stopped in their tracks and leaped, like newly decapitated chickens, high in the air. Then they turned and ran madly into the same thicket whence they had come, screaming as if they really had been hit. They were absurdly like naughty children frightened by discovery at a Hallowe'en prank. It was the most amusing spectacle I had seen for many months, and I was consumed with mirth. I sat down in the middle of the jungle and rocked with laughter. The descent so swiftly from possible tragedy to the most farcical comedy was too great a strain on my taut nerves.

Not till I started on did I notice that in his precipitous flight one of the braves had dropped his dah. I picked it up and shouted into the trees, "I appropriate this as a legitimate spoil of war!" It made a unique and pretty trophy, and enabled me to substantiate my story when I reached my caravan, half an hour later, on the main road.

One experience of this kind was enough; after that I religiously clung to the caravan. Toward noon the following day we rode into Burma, and though for three days we passed many Kachin villages, none troubled us. They were quite peaceful, and apparently not in sympathy with the Kachin rising in China.

Finally, we drew near Bhamo. The road wound out the last hills and crawled through the last valley. I realized that my journey was really at an end when I heard a curious sound that at first I seemed only dimly to recall from somewhere in the past. It was a cross between the bellow of a bull and the scream of a wild goose.

"*Che-ko chi-chia! Che-ko chi-chia!*" exclaimed my world-wise cook. "That is a gas cart!" And so it was; or, to be more accurate, it was a motor horn.

A few minutes later we rounded a clump of tamarinds and the crazy, cursed, twisting, cavorting, whimsical, lovable caravan trail that I had followed for so many weeks indulged in its final flourish. Then it meekly lost itself in the wide, well banked, straight and surfaced frontier motor road. And there, at the end of it, stood an American truck, with a sagging bus body and an engine turning under its hood, battered but unbowed. With a regretful sigh I climbed into it and resigned myself to the embrace of civilization. We moved off, and the high slopes of mid-Asia, with their radiant dawns, and the rough kindliness of their wind-bred men, receded into the mist of a blurred, pleasant memory.

Not long afterward I sat sipping fragrant tea with a gentleman and a lady, and the lady was clad in a cloud-pink skirt and she had the softest, darkest eyes that I have ever seen. I was a guest in the land of teak and elephants and ivory white pagodas. I had reached the end of the Golden Road to Burma.

V. Colonial Burma and India

Introduction to Section V

Edgar Snow stayed in Burma for approximately six weeks but wrote only two articles about his experiences there, one set in Mandalay and the other in Rangoon. Using his detailed diary notes, he wrote instead several articles about his caravan trip and sent them to Conso Press. His article on Rangoon was probably written after he left for Calcutta, since he describes a romantic nighttime visit to the Shwe Dagon that, according to his diary, took place on his final night in Burma. His diary entries for Burma are neither as extensive nor as detailed as those he kept during his caravan journey. However, they do reveal a mix of fact and fiction in the different versions of his youthful romance, which were published first in his article for Conso Press and years later in his autobiography.

When he first arrived in Burma, Snow stayed at the circuit house, with Mr. Clerk. According to Snow's diary there was only one other guest at the House, a British foreign service auditor named Badock, who could have stepped directly from the pages of a Somerset Maugham novel. Badock had been a sickly, crippled child whom doctors had not expected to live past the age of fifteen. Instead he had clung determinedly to life, but, as an adult, he insisted that he was resigned to dying at any moment. Because of his physical deformity, he thought himself unattractive to women of his own race. Consequently, in his imagination, they seemed unavailable, but he spoke of the beauty of oriental women "in a voice that trembled and at times broke with the sheer loneliness of his image." Badock had a collection of "quite admirable" photographs of nude Indian and Burmese women that he readily showed to Snow. He described just as readily his practice of carefully distinguishing his "carnal whims" from his photography. After persuading a young woman to pose, he deliberately permitted "the subject to reclothe herself, step out of the room, and start home, before suggesting business of another sort."

The next day, March 12, Badock's Indian boy, Puddin, guided Snow through a variety of business errands before taking him to a Kachin school at the American Baptist compound. However, the man in charge, aware of Badock's reputation, suspected Snow's motives as well, and was decidedly uncordial. They returned to the Circuit House, where Wang prepared his last tiffin for Snow, and the two settled their accounts.

233

About 3 P.M., Puddin appeared with two Burmese ladies, "one of them stout and perspiring, the other tall, slender and with a tragic face." He thought Snow might want to take their photographs. When Snow quickly refused, he said, "If like, Mastah, can photograph with out dress." He was visibly pained when his offer failed to arouse Snow's interest, but he and the women left quietly. Half an hour later he reappeared with another subject. This time Snow was pleasantly surprised by the diminutive beauty and grace of the young woman.

Badock, meanwhile, had also returned. He persuaded the young woman, named Malami, to pose nude on a wildcat robe that Snow had purchased. The photos taken, she slipped into her silk longyi and crepe shirtwaist. Mumbling and giggling confusedly, she started back to her village. Following Badock's "nice etiquette" Snow waited until she was out the door before calling her back and suggesting, "There is something else. . . ."

She came back. Snow records discreet details in his diary of what followed. At 2 A.M., his knee began to swell from a mule kick he had received two days earlier. Malami applied warm compresses to soothe his pain. Snow wrote, "She is like something in burnished copper, only softened, animated by some divine power. There is something infinitely restful, comforting and preciously sweet about Malami." This is the seed that flowers into the story of Batalá, the beautiful nurse-vision Snow sees when he wakes from a malarial fever and the pain of a mule kick to his knee in *Journey to the Beginning*. Batalá, like Malami, enchanted him: "I had been a lonely stranger and she comforted me. I had been sick and weary and she made me whole again."[1] The problem is to distinguish the romantic gold from the dross in which it originated.

The differences between the facts recorded in his diary and his later fiction are instructive. In the diary, Snow's injury seems far less severe than that he described in *Journey,* and there is no indication that he suffered from malaria. Malami, the girl-woman, but eighteen, was not a professional nurse, and he knew her for only the two days and one night he was in Bhamo. He never saw her again after sailing downriver on the *Taping*. In *Journey,* his romance with Batalá begins with her taking solicitous care of him for more than a week. They correspond after he leaves Bhamo for Mandalay and Rangoon, and she later joins him in Rangoon.

The diary makes clear that Malami left at 6 A.M., and Snow was

1. Snow, transcript of diary 2: 4–6; transcript of diary 6: 56–58; *Journey,* 63–66.

grateful that Badock, at breakfast, was "discreetly silent about last night." Malami came back that afternoon when Snow was packing his trunk and provocatively explained that she intended to go with him to Rangoon. He insisted that was impossible, but she stayed and helped him pack. When that was finished, she made up innocent games for them to play until, while playing blind man's bluff, she tripped over his fur robe and "bundled into a laughing, sobbing little heap of silk and flesh." When Badock, carrying his camera, knocked on Snow's door an hour later, both Snow and Malami were exhausted. She posed for more pictures.

After dinner, Malami went along to the boat to see Snow off. He wrote that, in a last moment of weakness, he might have taken her with him. He savored the prospect of flaunting British colonial propriety, but he feared the row the other European passengers would have created. "As it was their noses were up at a high slant because Malami walked to the gangplank and kissed me."[2] This impulse was satisfied by later experiences he had in Rangoon with a second young woman, named Ma So, who like Malami was young, beautiful, and sexually available. He fictionally fused Malami and Ma So into the Malayin of the Conso Press article in which he flaunts British colonial propriety during the raucous celebration of the Burmese New Year.

There is no indication in the diary that Ma So was from Bhamo or that she had a brother whom Snow befriended. She was a seventeen-year-old Talaing girl whom he met at a friend's house soon after arriving in Rangoon. The attraction was mutual. She went home with him that night and visited him on several other occasions. The brother mentioned in the article is a convenient fiction linking two separate women. There is, however, another factual link. Ma So, like Malami, posed nude on Snow's wildcat fur, but this time for his camera rather than Badock's.[3] Two photographs of a nude woman on the wildcat fur, marked "Batalá" in Snow's writing, survive. It is not clear whether the photos are of Malami or Ma So.

The romantic nocturnal visit to the Shwe Dagon that he describes as taking place with Malayin, in the article, and with Batalá, in his autobiography, actually occurred with Ma So, on his last night in Burma. His diary records it as almost as poignant a leave-taking as that with Malami.

2. Snow, transcript of diary 6: 59–60.
3. Ibid.

But with these background events in mind, the lyric tribute he pays to the bejeweled splendor of the "phallic spire" in his article seems more than a little self-indulgent. His surprise encounter with Malayin, during the celebration of the Burmese New Year, and their subsequent visit to a café and movie that so disturbed British propriety are not recorded in the diary. The independence of both Malami and Ma So deeply impressed Snow. That impression and his observation of how much of the work and business of Burma was done by women resulted in his tribute to their "caste-free independence and comparatively high degree of social freedom." The significance of these romantic fictions in Snow's development as a journalist is more fully discussed in the Introduction.

One of the Americans on board the *Taping* at the dock in Bhamo engaged Snow in conversation. He was Douglas Parmentier, former New York banker and president of Harper Publishing Company, who took credit for discovering the writers John Dos Passos and Glenway Wescott. As Snow understood it, Parmentier had chucked everything, divorcing his wife a year or two before, to "see the world before it was completely spoilt." He had come up the Irrawaddy intending to join a caravan through western China. He had heard of Dr. Joseph Rock and hoped to join up with him. Instead, he met Snow just emerging from the jungle.

Parmentier had already traveled extensively, but still seemed to be searching for some illusive romance, adventure, or new spiritualism. Snow's description of Parmentier is haunting and carries the disturbing suggestion that he saw in the older man an image of his own romantic questing, only at a more advanced age and with more privileged world-weariness:

> Parmentier reveals in his face more clearly than I have ever seen the soul of a supremely selfish man. There is a hardness to the jaw; something that suggests he has callously helped others to suffering and pain rather than experienced it himself. He is strikingly handsome. . . . Everything about him suggests the man of sensation; an individual who has starved his soul for the realization of all appetites of the body. I do not suggest lewdness; that would not suit him. He would wish his pleasures refined, artistic, richly emotional, like music or graceful movement.

Snow and Parmentier left the *Taping* at Mandalay. They toured Mandalay together before Parmentier insisted on loaning Snow thirty rupees for his train ticket to Rangoon and then left himself for the

British hill station at Maymio. Guarding his short supply of cash, Snow traveled third class to Rangoon and delighted in the company of a husband-wife acting team who gave him a quick, rich lesson in Burmese theater.[4]

The transcript of book 7 of Snow's diaries begins in the middle of a discussion about a romantic figure yearning for companionship, who "blunders in every attempt at intimacy; and his youth, in the Orient, will not compensate the victims of his ignorance as sometimes it does in western countries." Snow had just received a letter from Al Batson with news of his book, *Vagabond's Paradise,* and John Marshall's "emetic" *Vagabond de Luxe.* The romantic figure referred to probably is the protagonist of one of these books.[5] Snow had met Batson late in 1928 on the railway trip arranged by the Chinese Railway Minister, Sun Fo, to test Japanese claims that they were not interfering with Chinese rail traffic.[6]

Snow's first editorial for the *China Weekly Review* was severely critical of American vagabonds who selfishly took advantage of others' good will in their irresponsible quest for adventure.[7] Yet, he himself chose to be a vagabond and frequently reveled in the role. How then was he to be a responsible vagabond? His primary answer, for much of the rest of his life, was to travel the world championing the cause of the oppressed. But sometimes this question posed itself in terms that were not so clearly defined. Concepts of the pleasures and responsibilities of sexual relations between men and women were budding in his still youthful consciousness with curious consequences.

Batson's letter complained that Marshall's book "contained one chapter after another of thinly veiled seduction of native princesses and daughters of merchant princes." This reference occurs in Snow's diary just prior to his description of the refined sensual selfishness he finds in Parmentier's face. Parmentier probably had witnessed Snow's ambivalent parting from Malami, or Ma Le as she is also named in the diary, particularly her farewell kiss. Her provocative effort to persuade Snow to take her with him must have made Snow understand that she hoped for more from their relationship than he was willing to give.

Thus the fictional story he wrote soon after, of Mme. Loi's effort to

4. Snow, transcript of diary 7: 1–2, 7–8.
5. Ibid., 1.
6. "Why the Rolling Stock Isn't Rolling Out of Tsinanfu," *China Weekly Review* (January 12, 1929): 274–75.
7. "The American College Boy Vagabond in the Far East," *China Weekly Review* (July 27, 1929): 279–81.

sell him her sixteen-year-old daughter, Me Le, as a bride, seems most likely an effort to quiet some of his own internal questioning of the responsibility of his behavior. He gave Mme. Loi's daughter a name nearly identical with Ma Le. Also, Me Le is described as provocatively persistent, like Ma Le, even after her mother has left the room. But the O. Henry twist Snow gives the story in the next morning's conversation with his sulking Ma Ko To serves a double purpose. By suggesting that he was only a pawn in Mme. Loi's effort to punish her daughter for her imprudent passion for the inn ma-fu, Snow disarmingly mocks any inflation of his ego resulting from the attentions of the mother and daughter. At the same time, he probably was reassuring himself that he knew little or nothing of Ma Le's sexual history and, therefore, was in some sense justified in not taking her with him to Rangoon. He would have no inn ma-fu's mistress for his bride. In any case, his personal experience almost certainly provoked him to a journalistic vignette that charmed his readers.

When Snow reached Rangoon on March 18, a letter was waiting for him from his new sister-in-law, Dorothy. He answered on March 20, and the tone of his letter indicates that he felt an instant rapport with her. His letter also reveals that his brother's marriage made him think about his own future home and his interest in women:

Dear Dorothy:

Etiquette, I believe, decrees that I should have written you long ago to tell you how joyous I am that you are Mrs. Howard John Snow. But etiquette is a tedious thing. It is nearly always insincere. It conspires to reduce to formula emotions that ought to be spontaneous.

The truth is that I did not write to you because I was not glad that you were Mrs. Snow. There was of course no personal malice in this. Never having known you, how could I disapprove? But I regarded you as something which had upset the regular flow of my plans. Momentarily, you became obnoxious. The news that Howard had actually got married startled me, shocked me. I was suddenly depressed and for a great many days I felt much older than I am.

You see this was a natural, a selfish reaction. For as long as I can remember I have always thought of Howard as an entity which figured more or less constantly, directly, in my life. He was all important to me in the way that an older brother, I suppose, always is. I had never tried to imagine anything vital enough to divide the loyalty that had grown up between us.

Always I had thought that when I got back to New York it would be for a life with Howard. We would know girls, of course, after the careless way; but nothing disturbing for longer than necessary experience, nothing that would outlast its own first rapture. . . . And then abruptly you broke in on the scene and it seemed to me that the whole future had to be reconstructed.[8]

About the time he was writing this letter to Dorothy, he must also have written the fictional article of his refusal of the Sawbwa's invitation to stay in Kanai tutoring the Sawbwa's son and enjoying the pleasures of the Maru dancing girls. The obvious moral of the story probably had particular personal reference. His relations with Malami and with Ma So were memorably gratifying and reassuring. He lingered in Burma for more than six weeks. But like Herman Melville, who eventually had to choose between home and the Edenic charms of Fayaway and the Typees almost a century earlier, Edgar Snow compulsively, if ambivalently, moved on to India, thus resuming his journey homeward.

In *Journey to the Beginning,* Snow recalls the Burmese peasant revolt led by Saya San early in 1930: "As I was there when the uprising began I stayed on for a month, to write the only detailed reports of it published in America."[9] The only report I have found by Snow was published in the *New York Sun,* July 10, 1931, with a dateline of June 2, 1931, Rangoon. In early June, Snow was somewhere in western or northern India, a continent away from Rangoon. He was in Simla at least until May 29, and a letter to his father was sent from Bombay, dated June 13. In *Journey* he also claims that he followed Gandhi from Simla to Bombay. Nothing in Snow's diary entries of his days in Burma indicates that he was aware of Saya San's revolt or of the gathering of future nationalist leaders that he describes in *Journey* as then taking place at Rangoon University.

Snow probably got the story of Saya San's rebellion from Indian nationalists, with whom he came into close contact, and filed the story from Bombay. Who was responsible for originally indicating the story was filed from Rangoon—Snow, Conso Press, or the *New York Sun* editors—is not clear. But, in his autobiography, Snow represents himself as being better informed and more concerned with the Burmese nationalist movement than either his diary or anything that he published during his stay in Burma indicates.

He also exaggerates the time he spent in India in his autobiography: "I was in India more than four months on this initial visit."[10] In fact,

8. Letter to Dorothy, March 20, 1931.
9. *Journey,* 68.
10. *Journey,* 71.

he was there less than three months. He arrived in Calcutta on April 25 and left Madurai for Colombo, Ceylon, on July 11. The diary of his India stay is even more helter-skelter than that for Burma, but it leaves no doubt about his entry and exit dates.[11]

In addition to the travel articles that Snow wrote about Calcutta, Benares, Delhi, and Agra, this section includes the article about the trial of Communists in Meerut and a feature piece he wrote on "The Revolt of India's Women." Snow was still both a journalist and a travel writer, interested in India's national revolution as well as in the aesthetic wonder of the Taj Mahal. His six weeks in Burma, following six weeks on the caravan trail, may well have been something of a vacation from the intensity of Asian nationalist politics. But he arrived in Calcutta in the midst of significant public political ferment over the efforts of Mahatma Gandhi to lead a broad-based national revolution. The situation must have seemed familiar to Snow. Almost three years earlier, he had arrived in Shanghai not long after Chiang Kai-shek had destroyed much of the rival Red leadership in the Kuomintang and was moving swiftly to consolidate and enlarge his own leadership of the revolutionary Chinese nationalist movement.

Gandhi was, however, a very different nationalist leader from Chiang Kai-shek. On April 5, 1930, while Snow was still in Shanghai, Gandhi had reached Dandi, the small community by the sea that was the goal of his famous "Salt March." The next day, in a deliberate act of civil disobedience, he challenged the world's sense of justice concerning the British tax on the Indians' use of salt. Gandhi was arrested in May; boycotts and strikes followed. Other leaders of the Congress party were jailed. Gandhi's imprisonment proved more of a threat to British rule than his other activities. In February 1931, as Snow began his caravan trek from Yunnan, Lord Irwin began a series of negotiations with Gandhi that led to the Irwin-Gandhi Pact. A national Congress meeting at the end of March, dominated by Gandhi, ratified the agreement. It was a limited truce in Gandhi's campaign of civil disobedience about which many on both sides had serious misgivings. But Gandhi was authorized to represent the Congress at the Round Table Conference to be held in London in the fall of 1931.

Snow arrived in Calcutta between the March meeting of Congress and the Round Table Conference in London. He spent his first few days in the steamy port city as a typical tourist, but on the fourth day

11. Snow, transcript of diary 7: 13; transcript of diary 8: 5.

he called on Ramananda Chatterjee, the seventy-year-old editor of *Modern Review,* who quickly asked after the health of Agnes Smedley. Snow records in his diary a lengthy discussion with Chatterjee over the state of affairs in India and particularly over the significance of the Irwin-Gandhi Pact. He then quickly visited the editors of *Liberty* and *Advance,* two Hindu nationalist newspapers, and *The Mussulmen,* "a sectarian, conservative paper with a kind of half-suppressed communalistic tone to it." He was impressed with Subhas Bose, leader of the left wing of Congress, whom he compared to "the liberals of China, the so-called 'reorganizationists' of Wang Ching-Wei."[12]

His diary's list of books to read is eclectic, including Mayo's *Mother India,* Durant's *The Case of India,* Lenin's *The Proletarian Revolution, The Essentials of Marx, The Bhagavad Gita, The Amanya Ranga* and *The Kama Sutra,* Rolland's *Mahatma Gandhi,* Buck's *The Good Earth,* Maugham's *Of Human Bondage,* and Conrad's *Youth and Other Stories.*[13] Snow diligently read, wrote, and talked to editors and political leaders as he tried to understand the significance of political events in India. He also made time for a visit to "The Line," an extensive red-light district in Calcutta that catered to Westerners. While he was at first curious about the coarsely public sexuality and drunkenness, it quickly repulsed him. It did not compare to his treasured memories of Ma So and Malami.[14]

By May 12, Snow was ready to leave Calcutta. He hired a boy to travel with him on the train. He apparently planned brief sightseeing stops in Benares and Agra and then to travel on to the summer capital at Simla, where he might find the political leaders who were shaping the fate of India. The dirt and poverty of Benares seemed to him a fitting commentary on its significance as a sacred religious site.[15] Hinduism, like Confucianism, seemed to Snow the enemy of needed modern reforms. His bantering conversation with his guide reported in the article below accurately reflected the distaste he recorded in his diary. There is no indication in his diary of a stay at The Swiss Hotel in Delhi or of his meeting a Rajput named Asham Din. There was no time for such a visit between his departure from Benares and his arrival in Agra. It is possible that he later visited Delhi between longer, recorded stays in Simla and Bombay. Except for references to the hotel and

12. Snow, transcript of diary 7: 18–21, 23.
13. Ibid., 20.
14. Ibid., 24–25.
15. Ibid., 26–31.

Asham Din, the account of his Delhi visit could be drawn from a guide book. In complete contrast are his articles on the Red Fort and the Taj Mahal in Agra. The fort serves as a historical and geographical setting for the architectural wonder that makes Snow question how wretched and imperfect men could achieve such exquisite perfection and then fall back to "the level of our own prosaic civilizations." Such reflections echo the astonishment and enthusiasm he recorded in his diary.[16] The comparisons he drew between the Mogul Mumtaz and the Burmese Supiyalat and between the Taj and the Shwe Dagon suggest that his romantic Burmese memories may well have contributed to his enthusiasm.

In *Journey to the Beginning* Snow indicates that he went to Simla to be present while Gandhi negotiated a truce with Lord Irwin.[17] In fact, as I noted earlier, Gandhi had negotiated his pact with Irwin, and the national Congress had ratified it before Snow arrived in India. He took the train to Simla after only one day in Agra, arriving in summer shorts amid a hail storm. He caught a cold that put him in bed for days. His diary records a lengthy, cordial interview with Madan Mohan Malaviya, elderly Congress leader, scholar, and journalist. He wondered how Malaviya could believe so fervently in capitalism yet call himself a socialist, and how he could be so sophisticated and open yet abide by his Brahman caste rules and dine only with other male Brahmans.[18]

Snow also met another young Western journalist in Simla who would eventually write his way to considerable fame, William Shirer. In 1979, Shirer would publish a memoir of Gandhi in which he would recall first meeting Snow, in India in 1931. Both were foreign correspondents during World War II, and their paths occasionally crossed again. Shirer remembers Snow remaining staunchly "out of sympathy for the man I revered," Mahatma Gandhi, until the latter's assasination in 1948. Snow was at Birla House, where Gandhi was slain, in New Delhi during this tragic event. He wrote a tribute to Gandhi for the *Saturday Evening Post* that Shirer described as "one of the classics of American journalism."[19] By 1948, after years of witnessing and reporting man's inhumanity to man, not only in China, but across the

16. Ibid., 31–32.
17. *Journey,* 74.
18. Snow, transcript of diary 7: 33–37.
19. "The Message of Gandhi," *Saturday Evening Post* (March 27, 1948): 24–25; William Shirer, *Gandhi: A Memoir* (New York: Simon & Schuster, 1979), 231–32.

globe in World War II, Snow had become much more appreciative of Gandhi's religious idealism.

Snow filed a story from Bombay that appeared in the *New York Sun*, describing an interview that he conducted on a walk with Gandhi in the hills of Simla. The lead was Gandhi's desire to visit the United States, but Snow concluded the story by suggesting that Gandhi's "power lies in his supreme justice, sincerity and purity as a man, and his exceptional shrewdness as a politician." Because this combination has heretofore been considered impossible, he also notes that many find Gandhi an enigma.[20] His diary suggests that, in 1931, he was one who did.

The diary does not make clear when Snow left Simla, when he arrived in Bombay, or by what route he traveled. He wrote his sister, Mildred, on May 29 from Simla, indicating that he might go to Kashmir that day and then on to Peshawar, if he could get a check cashed. At this point, Snow seems to have been very uncertain of which way he wanted to or could go. A letter from Horace Epes, dated June 23, arrived in response to a letter from Snow, dated May 26. Snow's letter apparently contained a proposal to Conso Press about his travel plans from India to home. Unfortunately his letter has not survived. The same day Epes wrote his letter, he cabled Snow to eliminate Persia and Arabia from his travel plans and head for New York. Snow's letter to his sister indicates that he already was wondering whether home meant China or the United States. But Epes sent both the letter and the cable to Snow at Bombay, so apparently Bombay was already in Snow's plans regardless of whether he returned to China or to the United States.[21]

References in Snow's diary, supplemented by those in his articles and his autobiography, suggest that Snow traveled by train from Simla to Delhi via Meerut and from Delhi to Bombay via Agra and Udaipur. However, there are surprisingly no substantial, detailed entries in the diary that definitely establish visits to any of these cities on this trip between Simla and Bombay. In his diary, Snow does sketch a story of Sundaram Shastri, a small merchant of Meerut, who is belatedly recognized as the rightful English Lord Gardener. It is not clear how much of this story is fiction. It begins, however, "One evening I was in a little

20. "Gandhi Asserts American Visit Impossible," *New York Sun*, datelined June 24, 1931, Snow's scrapbook.

21. Letter to Mildred, May 29, 1931; letter from Horace Epes, June 23, 1931.

village near Meerut. . . ."[22] There are no notes in his diary that indicate that he personally observed the trial of Communists in Meerut, which he describes in the article below. It is possible that it was on this trip that he stopped at The Swiss Hotel in Delhi, met Asham Din, and then visited Delhi's Red Fort, as described in his article below. But again there are no diary entries describing Delhi. Udaipur appears only in a list of extraordinary travel sites in his diary, and he refers to the city in his article on the status of Indian women, below. In *Journey to the Beginning,* Snow tells of traveling with an Indian CID agent who suspects him of subversive activities but who leaves the train in Agra convinced of his innocence.[23] There is no hint of this encounter in the diary, but this would have been the most likely occasion for it to have happened. The dates recorded in the diary allow for the possibility, without definitely establishing, that Snow could have spent several days traveling from Simla to Bombay. However, his diary details his visits to Calcutta, Benares, Agra (on a previous trip), Simla, Bombay, Madras, Madurai, and Colombo.

A story on India's boycott of foreign goods appeared in the *New York Sun* July 3, but was datelined June 10 from Bombay. Snow wrote his father a long, revealing letter June 13 from the Taj Mahal Hotel, Bombay:

> I am seriously considering going back to China, to remain there till next spring. I have not enough money to come home now; living in China is much cheaper than anywhere I know; and I am sure I can work better there (on articles and my book) with fewer interrupting influences, than in New York. However, it's not yet decided; I am waiting for a reply to a proposition I made to the Consolidated Press. If they accept, I may go on with my trip through Persia, and home, as planned originally. That should see me in New York by—but no more dates. I've broken enough already.

While he might relax under a eucalyptus tree in the mountains of southwest China, congratulating himself on all the romantic experiences he had had instead of selling advertising, when writing to his father he reluctantly admitted that he also wanted to have more tangible evidence of success:

> It seems to me important that I have something—damn that phrase— something to console you and all of us, for this endless road I've run away

22. Snow, transcript of diary 7: 43–44.
23. *Journey,* 78.

from you. . . . This matter of a choice as to returning to China or to America has troubled my sleep for weeks. I wish I knew whether you would find it in the largeness of your heart to believe that I should be doing what I am convinced is to my best interest—and ultimately yours—regardless of what decision I make.

He advised his father to address his letters in care of the American Consulate, Bombay, "I can give you no better address now." He presumably received Epes's cable, advising him that Conso Press could not support the slow pace of his travels through Persia and Arabia, about ten days after writing his father. That would have convinced him to head for Shanghai, not New York. In Snow's memories of his childhood, his father's is the voice of skepticism, his mother's, the voice of religious faith. He wrote his father about the Indians he had come to know: "What particularly shocks me about them is no matter how cultured, educated and intelligent they are in mundane matters they cling to the feeblest and most childish religious beliefs that are in contradiction to all they know, through scientific knowledge, to be the facts of life. The one exception to this whom I have met is Jawaharlal Nehru—president of the Indian National Congress."

Snow saw Nehru twice at the palatial home of Nehru's wealthy friend, J. U. D. Naroji in Bombay. According to his diary, he began by asking if Nehru's beliefs were "along the lines of English socialism" rather than Communism. Nehru said yes, but added, "I do not call myself a socialist, however, in the sense of Fabianism. I am essentially a man of action and I advocate straight-forward policies aimed at the realization of certain principles." Under Snow's continued probing he went on, "The state should control certain public utilities and vital industries. It would manage and operate them. Wealth of the individual should be limited and all exploitation by industrialists should be eliminated. I would like to attain the same thing as the communists of Russia with regard to an industrial policy, but through different methods."

Nehru insisted on a clean break with the British government. India could not remain within the British Empire. Relations between India and Britain should be those of friendly sovereign nations. To Snow's question about the influence of the Communist party of India, Nehru replied:

The Communist Party of India, as such, scarcely exists. I doubt if it holds more than a hundred members. But communist ideas are largely

Snow admired Jawaharlal Nehru's social vision, but also noted that Nehru was a class-conscious aristocrat.

supported by many leaders of the Nationalist movement. The thing that has kept large numbers from joining bolshevism in India is its advocacy of destruction of autocratic and imperialist government by means of violence. We are opposed to that, naturally, as all Nationalists are now convinced that it will not work in India. We are also opposed to the idea of accepting directions or instructions from Moscow, or of being under Russian influence or tutelage.

Snow pressed him on the role of the Trade Union Congress. Nehru responded that the strength of the Congress had split into many weak factions the previous year, over cooperation with the Gandhi Satyagraha Campaign. He thought the most interesting leader of the Trade Union Congress was Deshpandi, who had organized the first strike by mill-hands and textile workers in 1928, but who had lost most of his influence with the national Congress party and with the masses because of the failure of a strike he organized in 1930.

Mindful of Nehru's own Brahman caste, Snow asked what he thought of the caste system. "I think it is thoroughly rotten and corrupt to the core. It ought to be completely abolished: it is medieval and undemocratic. I like nothing about it." When asked to compare his views of Hinduism with Gandhi's, Nehru gave a deprecating smile and noted that Mr. Gandhi was a very religious man. But Nehru believed the evils of Hinduism far outweighed its good points. "The sooner people are given education and knowledge in place of quotations from the Gita the better off India will be." While Nehru was persuaded that Gandhi's policy of Ahimsa (the doctrine of refraining from taking life, non-violence) was suited to the Indian temperament, he would have had the government abolish temples, idols, and the priesthood and replace them with schools, books, and teachers. This was Snow's kind of man and one that he could comfortably praise to his father.

Nevertheless, he summarized in his diary, Nehru was no genius as a politician: "Fundamentally an aristocrat, secretly he is shocked or frightened by the thought of power suddenly being wrenched from the present controlling elements and administered by Indian peasants and laborers. You sense this in him at once, though he doesn't say it. This inner loyalty to the preservation of [the] bourgeoisie accounts for his renunciation of Communism, and his gradually waning influence among the proletariat."[24]

24. Snow, transcript of diary 7: 38–42.

Snow's diary records that on June 29 he visited workers' housing in the Bombay mill districts with Yusef Meherally, president of the All-India Students' Association and secretary of the Bombay Youth League, and another correspondent, Eugenie Peterson. There is no indication in the diary that Suhasini Chattopadhyaya or Adi Adhikari accompanied Snow on this visit as he indicated in *Journey*.[25] An open sewer ran down a five-foot lane dividing two rows of two-story tenement houses. Each tenement had thirty rooms on each floor. Emaciated children ran naked through the sewer drain, splashing themselves with its contents. They carried that filth, on their feet, into the hovels, both during the night and during the day when the heavy rains forced them inside. There was a single water tap for each tenement of sixty rooms, housing approximately five hundred people. This tap was the only source of water for drinking, washing, and bathing. Early in the morning the people swarmed like "caged cattle, ready for the slaughterer's knife."

Through Meherally, Snow questioned a worker with hollow cheeks and bright feverish eyes, who lived in one room with his father, mother, sister, wife, and four children. He had been married nine years, and his wife had borne nine children, but five had died.[26] It was a scene to remind Snow of the cruel poverty and hunger he had seen in the famine at Saratsi or the deadly child labor workshops of Shanghai.

The next day he went to a fashionable wedding of two professors, Chandra Bhal Yohri and Rishalakshi. Many film people were there, and Sarojini Naidu, who was of considerable interest to Snow, gave a polished little talk that impressed him with its mix of saucy wit and original philosophy. Besides her effective cameo performance at the wedding, Snow had watched her "manage" Gandhi's talk, from her seat beside him, before the Bombay Dinner Club. She advised Gandhi what to speak about and when to speak louder, and he seemed to welcome and accede to her guidance. This seems to be the meeting that Snow describes in *Journey* as being organized by a radical group called the "Young Europeans."[27] Sarojini Naidu was the best known member of the very talented Chattopadhyaya family. Snow uses them to illustrate the progressive achievements of Indian women in his article below.

He records a vivid description of Sarojini as well as a lengthy interview in his diary:

She is not beautiful, but her eyes are remarkable, and their soft lustre,

25. *Journey*, 79–80.
26. Snow, transcript of diary 8: 8–9.
27. *Journey*, 81; transcript of diary 8: 2–6.

with hidden lights changing now to fire quick-lit, now to dark wistfulness rather strange in her somewhat matter-of-fact face. She is opinionated, strongly willed, strongly sexed. . . . At deep she is emotional. . . . Yet she can at times appear cunning, shrewd, calculating. She is not a great woman; but she is witty with an acute, well-balanced sense of humor, and conversational brilliance. She is highly intelligent, but not intellectual.

Snow found her strongly class-conscious while paradoxically completely without color, race, or religious prejudice. "She might eat with a member of the depressed class and forget that the hereditary caste barrier existed between them. But I do not think she would eat with a person whose intelligence, wealth, family, and material position were all obviously much inferior to her own." Culture for her is something separate and more important than education. "The women of Hyderabad are in fact more advanced along the cultural planes of life than are the women of America, most of whom are literate." America is too young to have a great culture.

Snow wrote that one of her sisters—probably Suhasini—said rather critically, "She has no political or economic logic. Her greatest service to India has been as a hostess." The student leader Meherally was, however, more generous, "She has strong influence for good. She is temperamentally incapable of doing anyone harm, but if she were to attempt it she would, I think, fail." When Snow asked him about Sarojini's political influence, he responded with an even more eloquent summary tribute: "She has a strong emotional appeal around which campaigns can be made to revolve. Through her charm on the platform, her endearment as a poet, her grace as a woman, she is a personality—and in the long run a personality can wield far more influence than a politician."

Snow recorded in his diary that before he left Bombay, ironically on the morning of July 4, "Ex-colonel" Jimmie Parker stopped him in the lounge of the Taj Mahal Hotel for a private word. They went upstairs, and Parker explained, "A high official in the Government asked me the other evening if I knew a fellow named Snow. I said yes, I did. He warned me I had better keep away from you. He simply said, 'That man travels with three passports' and raised his eyebrows significantly." This meeting is more fully developed in *Journey to the Beginning*.[28]

Snow's diary indicates that he arrived in Madras on July 8 after a long train ride that was made even more tiresome by a Eurasian with an indefatigable penchant for platitudes who shared his compartment.

28. Snow, transcript of diary 8: 34; *Journey*, 80–81.

Snow recorded a visit to the aquarium and to the ocean beach in some detail, along with other historic and tourist information, as if he anticipated sending a piece on Madras for "The World Today." But his diary indicates that he had moved on to Madura (Madurai) by train by July 9. He hired a seventy-five-year-old guide, Pagas Ram, for two days of sightseeing and again wrote notes sufficient to suggest that he was thinking of yet another travel piece. His diary does not explain how he traveled from Madurai to Colombo, but it indicates a two-day stay in Colombo, July 11–12, before he boarded the *Chichibu Maru* for Shanghai.[29]

The leisurely trip that he had planned to make through the remaining half of the world to return home was now turned around. His brother's bachelor apartment in New York was no longer available to him. He had stayed away too long to claim the advertising job once promised to him when he returned, and a major economic depression made job prospects grim in the United States. But Snow had won some credence in America as an experienced writer on China and more recently on India. He knew he could live comfortably in Shanghai. His caravan trip from Yunnan to Burma stirred in his imagination as the subject of a salable book. If he was turning back from his original plan to travel around the world, the prospect of writing such a book was another step in the fulfillment of his original dream. And it might be that tangible something he could bring back to his father, brother, and sister to justify his long meandering journey.

Chronology 1931

April 22–25	Takes ship from Rangoon to Calcutta
May 12	Leaves Calcutta, 8:15 P.M., by overnight train
May 13	Takes overnight train Benares-Agra; Arrives 10 A.M.
May 16	Arrives by train at Simla
July 8	Arrives in Madras by train from Bombay
July 9–10	Arrives Madurai
July 11–12	Arrives Colombo

29. Snow, transcript of diary 8: 12–19.

Down the Irrawaddy River to Mandalay
Glamorous Chief City of Central Burma
Site of the Glittering Palace of Supiyalat

There is a fullness to the word, an evenness and roundness of tone, and a subtle message in the euphony. It is perhaps because you love the East that this name disturbs your heart and quickens in you a languorous desire. Mandalay. Pathetic King Theebaw and the cruel lovely Supiyalat.

I came down on the wide, yellow scarf of the Irrawaddy, in the river boat *Taping.* For three days we followed the impatient lowering stream, dropping from the wooded hills in the Shan States to the vast, parched flatness of middle Burma.

Along the uncertain banks I saw brown monasteries with iron roofs and pretty fluted towers where golden bells tinkled ceaselessly. Frequently there were white inclosures, serene to the eye, and in them vase-like pagodas, banded with gold, that thrust up chaste spires traced like embodied sonnets against a cloudless sky. We passed Burmese villages, somnolent in the hot noons and mysterious with laughter and shadowed movement in the moon-bathed night.

Sometimes, when we lingered at one of these, I walked through their lanes, dusty, but shaded with palms, and lined with clean huts, mat-spread, straw-roofed and perched on slender stems of teak.

This bi-weekly visit of one of the Irrawaddy flotilla is an eventful hour in the placid routine of village life. Young and old turn out for the occasion, so that from a distance you see them, clinging in bright clusters to the sandy shore and waiting to greet you with candid smiles and fluttering kerchiefs. Standing aloof on the bridge, the British skipper observes with satisfaction that these merry, silly people are all dependent upon him, for how else would they get their chutneys and cotton and silk and the meaningless news of the world that arrives in the Imperial malls? And as the anchor drops with an ostentatious clatter the squat steamer, with its fat bourgeois bottom, reminds you of a Tammany politician about to dispense free ice to the East Side poor.

Burmese girls, their thighs marked provokingly in brilliant silk tam-eyins, look like blossomed things plucked from the sun-drenched corners of some remote garden. Little groups come down to the stream with great earthen water jars poised on their high-piled lustrous hair, and you marvel again at the effortless grace of Eastern women. And Burmese men, in their striped or checked lungyis (skirts as gay or gayer than a woman's), sit restfully on their heels and watch their wives shoulder the burdens delivered from the Taping. Below them, shouting and laughing, children dive in and out of the water.

Now and then I waved at a Burmese junk, floating contentedly with the slow current. Its crew drowsed, seeming to put great trust in the huge dragon eyes painted on the bow of their craft. Occasionally we passed a long teak raft, on the two months' journey from the forest to Rangoon, and sometimes with five or six families dwelling on it in igloo-shaped huts of grass. Often, above the jungle that was never far away, the sky was fogged with heavy layers of lazily moving smoke, where peasants burned away last year's tropic growth and annealed the soil for a paddy crop, soon to be nourished by the rains.

So I drifted into the south, and up to the gates of that city which the Burmese kings once charmingly called the Center of the Universe, after the modest way of Kubilai Kahn.

An amiable rover whom I met in Bhamo went with me through the Mandalay bazaar. There were hundreds of stalls, and they had a great variety of articles—perhaps the best display of Burmese goods in the country. You were offered bowls and goblets and many ornaments of hammered gold and silver, moderately good things in jade and amber, Burma rubies, amethysts and opals; black and red lacquer were patterned in gold leaf, Indian, Chinese and Burmese silks and brocades and embroideries, objects carved from teak and ivory and sandalwood, provisions, the delicacies of Europe and the hot, spicy sauces dear to the Burmese palate—and all of it in the dirt and disorder of an Eastern market.

Most of the shopkeepers were girls and women, as in other parts of the country. It appears to be an old Burmese custom for the wife to earn her share of the rice and her husband's as well. That probably explains the caste-free independence and the comparatively high degree of social freedom enjoyed by Burmese women. They move about where and when they choose on a nearly equal status with men. Yet, unlike the "emancipated" women of the West, the Burmese woman's charm remains in her intense femininity, in the suppleness of her reedlike body, the sudden submissiveness of her dark eyes so quick with humor, the small shapeliness of her hands and feet and in the classic instinct of movement that makes her gesture a piece of living art.

A flower market held sprays of jasmine, white camellias and large, rich chrysanthemums, swaying on their stems. Behind them stood Shan and Burmese maidens, so elegant themselves that you thought again how aptly King Mindoon had called his harem "Those of the Fragrant Lotus."

The streets of what was once called Kala Town, where the King permitted his foreign traders to dwell, are wide, dusty and flat, only the rise of the hill breaking the line of sky. I moved down toward the "Gem City" built by the good King Mindoon and lost to the British empire-builders by the weak and dissolute Theebaw. From a distance I saw the first peaked tower, with its radically upturned eaves, and then another and another came into view above the saffron flush of the long crenellated walls. Presently my carriage drove up the moat and through the great gate, open now to anyone. I followed a dusty road leading up to the Palace.

When Mindoon conceived this royal town, less than a hundred years ago, he strove to rival the splendor of the Forbidden City of Peking and he drew the best craftsmen of the Middle East into the task. But his ambition was realized only in breadth of perception and luxury of space. How could men who had never seen it copy the breath-taking and finished magnificence of the Celestial City? Art in Burma was only beginning, and the centuries of culture reflected in the glorious lines of the Golden Palace was to the young Burmese mind exotic and incomprehensible. Perhaps, given another century in which to develop, Burma might have created forms of beauty truly original and great. But they started too late. The British came along and sold them corrugated iron.

The discovery was at first a shock; those harsh metallic roofs, such as are used on our tank factories or to "beautify model workmen's settlements"; those hideous roofs on Supiyalat's Palace. Yet King Mindoon selected this material as well fitted to his purpose. He admitted he would have preferred gold or silver, but his kingdom did not hold enough; when he saw the galvanized iron its glitter pleased him, and he gave his order.

Glitter. That was the motif of it all. To shine splendidly, to gleam with a steady fire and so to reflect the brilliance of the ruler, the Arbiter of Existence. Jewels clung to the *hti* that topped the seven-tiered tower which rose over the immense Audience Hall; the tall magnificent columns of teak were everywhere stamped with patterns of gold; the walls of the Middle Queen's Chamber were studded with crimson and yellow glass, the numerous wide mirrors were edged with gilt; the Lily Throne and the Bee Throne were drenched in satiny gold; and the King's Pagoda, faced with an intricate mosaic of colored glass, glittered blindingly in the glaring sun. The power of this beauty was perhaps primitive, but it was vigorous and it expressed a fine, candid passion for dazzle.

It is tarnished now. The gold leaf is gone, cruelly exposing the crudity of the carving; the lacquer has cracked and lost its luster; broken and colorless, the leaded glass glitters no more. All the rich furnishings, all the fabulous wealth in jewels were plundered when the British invaded the Palace, less than half a century ago. It is a Gem City no longer. Over it hangs the tragic empty melancholy that descends upon places of spent glory.

I walked over the green lawns once splashed with the color of royal Burmese maids at play, and past the faded magnificence of the Queen's Golden Monastery, out into the cool gardens. They are still lush and beautiful as in the days when Supiyalat made love here to her make-believe king. Then I went through the Chamber of the Sacred White Elephant and saw, nearby, his feeding pavilion.

Walking timidly around the Palace were a few Burmese men and women and I noticed that when they passed in and out of the lacquer throne halls, they removed their velvet shoes, and talked in whispers. Was it possible that some old reverence stayed in them yet for the wicked Queen, and the half-mad King who gutted his own dominions?

"No, not for Supiyalat and Theebaw," a Burmese scholar told me later. "We have small love for them. It is our lost freedom that we mourn. When we see the Palace we think of the Golden Era when Mindoon ruled and we were rich and happy and free men. The British are not tyrants, but they are invaders and we are their subjects."

It was nearly dusk when I turned to leave the Palace, but a last ray of the sun clung to the blade-like spires, so that they burned like sacrificial fires. Seen closely the Center of the Universe had been an edifice of pseudo-art, curious and interesting, but in the way that a child's dreams are. It lacked reality; it entertained rather than thrilled the heart. But as I drew back into the distance, and surveyed it as you flatter a painting, I felt for the first time the strange ruthless grace of it, massive, shadowy and splendid.

I understood then what the artist hoped for it and with his inadequate skill did not quite achieve. Now in the half light it seemed a fitting court for the last of the red monarchs, the last to exercise the awful power of life and death over men, the last to soothe his most savage and extravagant lusts. Here I could believe how Theebaw's players laughed and sang with tragic eyes while behind the palace eighty young princes and princesses perished and were trampled into their rude graves by elephants.

Rangoon, the Chief Port of Burma during the Hot, Dry Spell

Which Precedes the Springtime New Year's Celebration—the Shwe Dagon

For a month I lived in a Rangoon cottage not far from the Shwe Dagon pagoda. Behind me there was a dusty garden of pineapples and over them hung withered mangoes on drooping trees. The garden was bordered by a few parched coco palms with tall, bare trunks. Some mohurs, with their foliage fiery gold, were the only virile things left in the landscape. In the evening wild birds came to them and plunged into song. But in the day I never saw them; bird and beast crept into the shade and were silent, while the sun laved the earth in a still deluge of heat.

So, at this season, as the drylipped soil awaits the coming of spring, the Burmese New Year occurs. It is announced by the arrival of Nat Thingyamin, the Reigning Spirit, he who cut off the Brahma's head. This year, according to the astrologers, he comes charging down on a long green serpent, in one hand holding a spear, in the other a gong. With him come scribes carrying two sacred books, one of which is called the Book of Gold, the other the Book of Evil. And the names of those who have not lived virtuously during the year are inscribed in the Book of Evil. Thus are the deeds of men recorded up to the hour of death, and thus rewards and punishments determined.

At this time the monks from "*poungyi-changs*" make known the Seven Flowers that shall be worn with favor, and the girls and women, depending upon the day of the week on which they were born, gravely array new blossoms in their hair. There is feasting and rejoicing and an exchange of gifts. Children honor their parents with relishes and spices and cups of gold; sweethearts and married folk renew avowals over perfumed drinks.

All over Burma little men and women carry armloads of flowers and musk to the feet of the Great Lord Buddha and in the temples light candles and sticks of sandalwood. Into the sacred ponds they toss rice balls and popcorn, thereby acquiring merit by feeding the sacred fish. Then from his mite of savings the Burmese takes some silver and going into the market buys a bird or perhaps a young monkey. Freeing it, he utters a lusty shout so that Nat Thingyamin, riding by may remark his virtue and enter him in the Book of Gold. But the part of the celebration most enthusiastically observed fits in ideally with the muggy weather.

Now, in twelve months the human body collects much pollution, sins leave their subtle stains. It is necessary that the evidence be erased and chastity restored to mind and heart so that all may begin the year with new virtue. This is the rationale behind the gay water festival held by the Burmese during the week of Nat Thingyamin's sojourn among the children of the earth.

From iron balustrades or from roadside ambush mothers and daughters pour scented water on the heads of their husbands and lovers. The benison purifies them. At the same time it insures fidelity during the coming year and intensifies their ardor in the enterprise of love. On the streets children chase each other with squirt-guns and goblets of water, and in front of the temples stand groups of laughing young men, naked to the hips, who thoroughly drench each maid or matron who comes to pay homage to the gods. People in carriages or motor cars are attacked from the roads by shouting men and women armed with ever-flowing water jars. No one escapes. No one except the forbidding Englishman!

It is all done in a spirit of fun and men and women take their wettings with admirable good nature. While the festival lasts most Burmese go about dripping from the top of their well oiled hair to the soles of their sandaled feet. But the Europeans complain. Despite the arid air and the ardent heat, the white masters regard the custom as an affront to their dignity. They consider such liberties unbecoming in a subject race. In the past irascible old English gentlemen even went so far as to haul young celebrants into court for dousing the virginity of their shirt bosoms, charging them with assault and battery. Nowadays Burmese carefully exclude the Britishers from the annual ablutions.

I found myself exempted with the Englishmen; it so happens we look somewhat alike, and to the Burmese there appears no difference whatever. One late afternoon I walked, through waves of yellow heat, toward the river. The sun was only an inflamed silver on the edge of the sky, but it had done an excellent day's work. The air was thoroughly cooked, my skin burned, and in my throat there was a taste like dead incense. Even were not the defilement of a year's pleasurable sin upon my soul I should have welcomed a chastening shower.

It appeared, however, that nobody wished to waste—or risk—his holy water on a non-conformist. I did my best to encourage the crime from those who carried baptismal urns ready on their shoulders, but the only thing I got was a spray of jasmine which a laughing girl light-heartedly tossed in my face. Finally, a young Burmese lad, emboldened by my friendly glance, took a shot at me with his squirt gun, and his accuracy was astonishing. The sensation was somehow humiliating, so I obliterated the smile and substituted for it the supercilious look of an orthodox British colonial. After that no one troubled me.

I reached the river front and followed it, gazing at a row of Burmese sampans. Suddenly with no sound of warning, a niagara engulfed me. My light suit was well soaked and I had the sheepish feeling of being in tights. From behind me I heard a throaty girlish laugh and I turned angrily—my enthusiasm for the water festival had instantly vanished. I saw a slender little figure in a green tameyin and a crisp white shirt. Why didn't she run? She stood quivering with mirth and her small hands clapped tightly on her thighs. "Thakin!" she exclaimed, "you have forgot Bhamo so soon?" Good Heavens! It was Malayin, sister of Meg Ba Win, whom a month before I had left a thousand miles away, in upper Burma.

No one could be irritated very long with Malayin. She seemed hard-ly real, she was so small and fragile and like a child, though she was 17 and in Burma a woman is "getting on" at that age. I cannot remember her face without its smile, a roguish communicative smile with her rather thick but ruddy lips parted over teeth incredibly even and white. She had eyes provocative in their dark merriment and in her mass of inky hair (that gleamed even at night) she had laced a dainty garland of cornflowers, for Malayin was Monday-born. "You—little wretch," I muttered, and promptly forgave her. After all, I argued, her brother had been kind to me, and hospitable; but the truth was I couldn't have been annoyed with Malayin if she had crowned me with her water jar—instead of its contents.

In the quaint English which had been taught her at a mission school in the hills, Malayin explained her sudden appearance in Rangoon. She had come all the way from Bhamo for her first pilgrimage to the Shwe Dagon and to celebrate the New Year with her Rangoon rela-tives. Meg Ba Win had accompanied her, but tonight he was off to a *pwe,* and nobody ever knew when a man would come back from a Burmese theater. Malayin herself had nothing to do but drown pedes-trians for the rest of the night. I persuaded myself that I would be a public benefactor if I entertained her otherwise.

It pleased me to take Malayin to a cafe, where I studiedly ignored the frigid glares and rudely audible comments flung toward our table. It pleased me further to prick local feeling by taking Malayin to a movie. By these two simple acts my name automatically was struck from half a dozen party lists. The thought did not disturb me. Malayin was having a grand time, and I too. Her eyes shone as we came out of the theater. "Thakin," she said, "I want to ride in a gharry." So, I discovered, did I. We hailed a carriage and climbed into it behind a whiskery Indian driver who, with an admirably balanced salvo of invectives, strengthened by a crack of his long whip, induced his rheumy old horse to trot off into the moon-drenched night.

A little river breeze had come up, and the earth stirred and threw off its torrid blanket. It was cool riding. We passed through flanks of palms and mohurs that flung great arabesques of shadow and silver across the pathway. Thickly, stars clustered and bejeweled the velvet sky; softly, like a mantle, glamour dropped over tropic Burma. We drove for miles, for hours; the driver chose the way.

When at last we turned back, the Shwe Dagon rose ahead, dimly diffused in gold. It seemed natural, though no one spoke, that we should drive up to the foot of pagoda hill and stop. Above us the glowing shaft loomed omnipresent, majestic and terrible as truth. It gave off a subtle aura that seemed to impel you, powerless, into its web even as the disciple of the divine Gautama is enthralled by the Eightfold Path. There is little mysticism in my nature, the covert rites of corrupt religions leave me cold; but the immense beauty of the Shwe Dagon at magic midnight would perplex the most pragmatic heart.

"Come along, Molly," I invited, and together we climbed the terrace that leads to the flower-strewn base of the phallic spire. We came from the little used western approach, and over broken flights of steps, past stalls that in the day sell sweets and perfume and flowers to the pilgrims. Now they were dark; we saw no one, Malayin, as we neared the top, slipped off her sandals. She gestured, amused, at my shoes. Off they came, and we stepped onto the marble platform.

The Shwe Dagon, as everybody knows, is the tallest pagoda in the world. From its base to the tip of its jewel-studded tip, it is 417 feet, all covered with gold.

The hill it stands on further augments its height, so that from far down the Rangoon River, long after the city itself is folded under the horizon, you still see the blazing crest of the Dagon parting the sky. It is a massive thing yet it tapers with a Grecian grace, superbly simple. The effect of its erotic symbolism is classic.

The Shwe Dagon is supposed to have been contemporaneous with the inception of Buddhism. Burmese legend gives the date of its construction as the fifth century, B.C. It has been growing taller and wealthier ever since. Its lavish richness (the uncalculated fortune in gold that cloaks its turgid flanks, and the treasure of rubies, emeralds and diamonds embedded in its polished spire) represents the accumulated tribute from centuries of worshippers. Five million people visit the Dagon every year, pilgrims from Burma, India, Siam, Malaysia, China, Japan—all the Buddhist countries. It is divinely sacred to almost a third of the human race. Besides eight hairs from the head of Gautama Buddha, it enshrines the drinking cup of Kankathan Buddha, the robe of Gaunagohn Buddha and the staff of Kathapa Buddha.

We walked down aisles of lighted temples, hundreds of them, clustered like votive offerings round the towering pagoda. Before some of the images candles burned, or electric torches. Flowers spilled down the glossy pavilions, and from them drifted an odor dark, heavy and sensuous that narcotized the night.

Now and then, as we passed an attractive god, Malayin left my side to perform the kow-tow. I noticed that she preferred the ones that glittered most; cut and stained glass appealed to her. When she knelt motionless, with closed hands, her little figure, pliant and supple, seemed to merge with the shrine. Except for the yard of fluttering gossamer silk at her throat she might have been an image herself, full of still omniscience.

"My dear," I warned her when finally the gharry, creaking, drove us back to the city, "your yearning for nirvana is going to end you up with corns on your knees."

She laughed and reproved me with a sidelong glance. "You are silly," she replied. "It was for you I prayed something."

"Oh?" It was amusing, yet somehow vaguely comforting to know that. I fancy that if Heaven heeds any one, it will lend attentive ear to the demands of Malayin.

Involuntarily I looked back at the Shwe Dagon. A shower of light, like a nimbus, clung around it, emphasizing its aloof and secret splendor. I remembered an old Burmese legend how supplications to the Dagon rise up through its golden column and are released in the sparkle of its jewels.

Calcutta, India, City of Contrasting Beauty and Squalor

the Hindu Rituals on the Banks of the Sacred Ganges River

A still, tall figure seated high upon a still, tall horse. Beneath the animal's iron legs a granite pedestal on which, inscribed in bronze, is a pretty story about the exalted equestrian above it. The statue is of Clive, the conqueror of Bengal and boys' hero of Britain, the tea clerk who founded the British empire in the East.

Around him, scattered over strips of parkway that separate Calcutta's Bund from the busy thoroughfares, sit other British heroes, mounted in bronze. Hastings, Cornwallis, Dalhousie, Curzon, Hardinge, Butler, Minto, aloof and huge, magnificently immutable. They gaze from under kingly brows out over the empire which they have built. Austere, haughty men, giants in metal, with their height augmented by the giants of horses on which they sit. One has a perverse desire to stick a pin into one of their parts.

Facing them are long rows of business buildings, hotels, restaurants, theaters, mosques and temples. Late models of American and British motor cars glide past, their cushioned seats occupied by British business men or Anglicized Indians. Trams rumble through the park and on toward Dalhousie Square to thread beside great banking houses, rising like feudal fortresses, high above the River Ganges.

Beside these modern conveyances move ox-carts, Victorias, gharries, rickshas and various make-shift vehicles. Occasionally, swinging through a back street, you see a shuttered palanquin, carrying a lady in purdah on a visit to her relatives. Herds of cows amble up and down the busiest streets. Standing on a sidewalk in front of the Great Eastern or the Grand, Calcutta's newest hotels, are other bovines, sacred, and with little silver ornaments tucked neatly under an ear.

This is Calcutta before the rains come. It is the hottest time of the year. Now the temperature reaches 112, sometimes higher, and with the air steamy from the river the days are torpid and enervating. If you walk a mile you are wet through. If you go on a real errand or mission into some desolate spot of the city where the Hindus live amidst filth

261

and flies you return a sodden, weary lump, feverish, irritable. You take four baths a day and long for the relief of sundown.

Under such a climate one might hope that the Europeans would discard their Western rainment for garments more suitable. They do not. They appear to enjoy the inquisition of boiled shirts and heavy stiff dinner jackets. Regularly, even as ritualistic as the Hindus' purification ceremonies, they go home not to shoeless, collarless comfort, but to pour themselves into starched dress. Certain of the clubs and the hotels will not dine a man who is not wearing his formal armor. It is a matter of social prestige. The assumption is that if you don't wear a dinner jacket it is because you don't own one. This insufficiency definitely places you on the lower rung of the social ladder. You are not a sahib.

But Indians undress for the weather. They wear loose-flowing garments of coarse cotton cloth—the drapery of a dhoti. Some of them wear less than that. For the workers, the army of burden bearers who labor for the white rulers and brown, a strip of khaki suffices.

The reason for this ultimate simplicity in dress is, of course, not fashion but economics. They are not trying to pose as sadhus or fakirs. The truth is that 50,000,000 Indians own nothing but that loin cloth. Yet without property they certainly are more comfortable than their English dinner-jacketed superiors. I do not wish to be misunderstood. This is no advocacy for a nudist movement among the Europeans, though admittedly in a country so devoid of humor it would be a diverting innovation.

I did the usual round of tourism in Calcutta. I saw a museum, the library, the markets, the bazaars, Chinatown, the "Black Hole," mosques, temples and various monuments erected for loyal British subjects who handled machine guns well. I saw the Queen Victoria Memorial, what they called Calcutta's Taj Mahal. It cost, I forget how many lakhs of rupees, and it was built largely by contributions from Indian princes who reimbursed themselves by levying additional taxes on the impoverished peasantry.

Then I went to Khali Ghat, one of the most sacred Hindu bathing places. It stands on the left bank of a branch of the Ganges estuary and it is not far from the Victoria Memorial. Thousands of Indians come to it for their daily ablutions. Thousands from adjacent villages once or more a year journey on pilgrimage here to wash themselves of sin and pollution.

The water is muddy and over it hangs an unhealthy odor. Debris, cholera germs, malaria germs float down with it to the sea. Yet when I suggested to the Brahmin priest (who had volunteered his services as guide) that the river must spread disease he was indignant. He rebuked me. He clipped his words, so that every sentence sounded like an endless hyphenation. He said: "How-is-it-possible-for-the-Ganges-to-be-contaminated? It-is-a-sacred-river. It-is-life-restoring-and-springs-from-the-big-toe-of-Vishnu. It-is-the-purest-stream-and-it-gives-cure-for-all-known-sickness-and-disease." His speech was like the endless cascade of a brook; no hesitation, no interval, no inflection.

I next went to the burning ghats, which are a few feet from the sacred bathing area. Here, nearly always, you can find the flames devouring a corpse or two. Beside these funeral pyres you sometimes see a wailing woman who beats and claws her breasts, or a thoughtful male with his chin in his hands, squatting and silent. They wait, retrieve the ashes and dump them into the river, so returning the soul to God. A smell, sickening and repugnant, clings to the air.

Close by the crematory are lanes flanked with stalls offering nuts, fruits, souvenirs and candy of bilious hues. Miniature lingam stones and copies of temple images are sold by toothless old ladies and shirtless, chattering old men. There are little balloons and carved figures, Brahmin dolls and other toys for the pilgrims' children. Flowers, mostly jasmine and tattered roses with sickly yellow pistils, are purchased and laid at the feet of idols by young brides desiring the responsibility of motherhood or by older ones seeking to avoid it.

The priest took me to a pavilion in which were collected a number of meat sellers, who sat behind carcasses of goats and tender young kids, sacrificed that morning. Hindus (except Brahmins, who eat no meat or the substance of anything that has once held life) haggled with the butchers, and as they selected a joint for roast or stew it was hacked off on the spot. The display was beside a large and gaudy temple to Siva.

Calcutta is celebrated for its beggars. They are not a pleasant subject, nor a new one for wanderer's tales, but where they are so ubiquitous an account would lack verity that omitted them. The memory that I have of Calcutta is of those groveling, naked figures, smeared with ashes and dirt, following me, whining, uttering hypocritical praises. They are well distributed over Calcutta's principal streets and new recruits arrive daily. The municipality provides no shelter for them, no food. No one interferes with their operations and now and then they follow you into the shops.

The economic slump has had disastrous effects. Foreign trade has declined to a little more than half what it was a year ago, a third of the figure for two years before that. Numerous European firms have closed; others are bankrupt. A large percentage of those in the Eurasian community are without jobs and have appealed to the municipality for some form of dole.

Jute, Calcutta's principal industry, has been severely struck by the condition of world markets; it has declined 40 per cent in price. Peasants find it no longer pays to harvest the crops in their fields at the present buying rate. Staffs in some of the huge jute mills have been reduced by half and the depression in other industries is almost equally serious. Over a third of the adult male population is permanently or temporarily unemployed.

Yet there is much wealth in the city. Out in the Europeanized suburbs, where many rich Indians live also, are some homes with more rooms than a rajah's palace, and as many servants. Europeans and Anglicized Indians spend lavishly at the hotels, in front of which at night hundreds of Indian paupers stretch themselves on the street and sidewalk for sleep. Nine-tenths of the population lives wretchedly and seldom with enough to eat; one-tenth lives comfortably or in wanton luxury.

Calcutta is a city of sharp inequalities, shocking contrasts, bourgeois snobbery and abysmal poverty and ignorance. Around it hovers a revolting, mercenary stench. You have a feeling of release when at last your train moves from the malodorous platform out into the clean air of the thirsting Bengal plain. Beyond, in the gathering twilight, lies a new vista, unexplored. Gradually, the lure of unknown spaces returns and in you is revived the ancient hope that spurs the searching spirit.

Beside the Ganges River: Benares, India Where Filth and Ignorance Abound

and Where the Great Faith of the Hindu in His Gods Is Demonstrated Daily

The vast plain that stretches from Calcutta to Peshawar and holds the bulk of India's 250 million is a dun-colored expanse, arid and dusty and sprayed by a merciless sun. There are few flowers, and fewer trees; and for miles the earth is rock-strewn and untillable.

I spent the first night out of Calcutta crossing Bengal, followed by a weary morning of travel over windswept desert-like spaces, to arrive toward noon, at Benares, which seems almost to crackle under the consuming fire from the sky. Dust covers everything and every one around, rolling in thick billowy clouds behind the two-wheeled India carts, and curling in little puffs underfoot wherever you walk.

Up comes an undersized man wearing a soiled duck suit and a pair of heavy horn-rimmed spectacles. His face is very dark, and above it he wears a light blue turban; he is bow-legged and his feet are bare. He announces that he is a guide, seems to take it for granted that you have engaged him, and into his eyes comes a hurt look when you ask what his services will cost you. But after you have agreed to pay half what was demanded then he quite happily leads you off to a waiting cart. Climbing into the back of it, you presently find yourself being bumped over cobbled streets into the holiest of holies, Benares, a city so sacred that merely dying in it automatically exempts a Hindu from the penalty of rebirth on this iniquitous terra.

And so we arrive upon the hallowed soil of Kashi, the oldest spot on earth, founded by Siva, highlord of all that is. Reverently your cart halts and dumps you at an entrance to the narrow odorous lanes, damp with spilled holy water and crowded with thousands of men of color. You pass a hypnotist playing his Eastern flute and for a moment pause to watch the charmed serpent rock back and forth on his spring-like coils, his forked tongue darting in and out, in time with the music.

You shudder and move on. To your blue-turbaned guide you re-mark that he is a brave man who would expose himself to the fickle-ness of a jungle snake's moods. But he answers you, wagging his head from side to side, after the approved manner of a Brahmin bestowing information:

"That is not remarkable feat, sir. Indeed, it is no achievement at all, but only trickery. Each morning, sir, this man takes out serpent and holds before him one piece of cotton cloth. Now at this cloth angry serpent strikes again and again, four, five, six times. Then when all poison drained from fangs this man wraps up his harmless snake in bag and brings him to market place for edification of simple peasants in from plains."

You turn down a flagged walk where beggars and holy men sprawl in the filth and reach out leprous hands, blessing you in a whining voice and, after you pass on without heeding, cursing you with more decision. There are shrines and temples at every turn.

An endless human tide swells back and forth between the myriad temples, and to and from the great yellow flow of the nearby Ganges; here a petty rajah, dressed in tailored dhoti and with a jeweled turban to give him an air, striding in advance of his ministers who walk closely behind and are silent and haughty; old men, sore and crippled, creeping on toward the sacred river; women in purdah, led by healthy, barefoot servant girls; grave young Bengalese, Punjabis, Peshawaris, Madrasese, each with his different coloring, each with his daub of paint to mark his caste; pretty girls from beside the Shalimar, with soft, dark skin and deep, shining eyes looking like Eastern madonnas, with their saris folded gracefully over robust shoulders; usurers with crafty eyes and merchants who have eaten too often and too well; black, naked laborers who steal a moment from their toil to grind a lingam stone; and through them all, like streaks of sunlight, move the monks in their rustling robes of saffron.

This is no holiday scene; the players here are in earnest. About them there is none of the gay insouciance that makes Burmese Buddhists seem to possess some secret of living; none of the humorous half-belief you see in the eyes of a Chinese when he bargains with his gods in the spacious beauty of some hillside temple. In the faces of these weaving figures, with their pathetic, little tins of holy water and their miserable flowers for Siva, there is little light, little joy. They reflect neither hope nor despair. They are the immutable faces of blind, stupid, unquestioning faith. For these worshipers there is a genuine significance in the holy cavernous halls, moldy, dim-lit and oozing with mud. It is hard to comprehend, but for them these hideous idols represent a power which they imagine in some way controls their lives. And to them the phallic lingam stones before which they kneel in prayer are things of utmost reality.

It all seemed to me silly, absurd and tragic. It was squalid and nauseating. I could find no beauty in any of the religious buildings; they were crudely proportioned, gaudy, ornate, and revealed an utter lack of balance and harmony which profoundly shocked me. I had been told that in Benares I would be thrilled by the splendor of Hindu architecture, but even the celebrated Golden Temple of Visweswara appeared to me (except for its noble spires) crudely done, and its dark interior was gloomy and undistinguished. The foul air stifled me and the throng was depressing. I was perplexed and sickened and I urged my guide to lead me out of it. I was surprised when he agreed readily, and added that temples disgusted him.

"Sahib," he said, "I do not believe in these things. They mean no more to me than to you. I am an educated man."

"Indeed! Then why not revolt? Why not begin now by rubbing off that paint smeared on your face that shows you worship the lingam?"

"Ah, sahib, what use to talk like this? What is easy for you to say would for me mean ruin. If I oppose the faith then soon I lose my home, friend, even the wife. Then my sons grow up to curse me."

I said no more, but followed him as he threaded his way down to the Ganges. At a landing we got into a small skiff, manned by four thin Hindus. They took the oars and rowed me close to the river bank, under huge masses of red sandstone, cement, marble and brick that tower up to great heights in the shape of holy edifices, rajahs' palaces, schools, burning ghats, caravanserais and pilgrims' hostels. Flags fly from those tenanted by royal or distinguished folk; some have Hindu domes of burnished copper or gilt; some are intricately carved and others have facades decorated with inlays of semi-precious stones. But there is little form or symmetry in any of it; the structures are crowded bewilderingly, and without plan; several of the palaces slant dangerously and one or two already have slipped half into the river. Among these heaps of masonry there are pieces of superb art, but in the fearful, hopeless scramble they are enveloped and lost. In ensemble the spectacle is only slightly less grotesque than Coney Island.

Along this curative stretch of the Ganges thousands of Indians are bathing in places so densely thronged that they stand almost shoulder to shoulder. Behind them are little mat-sheds where women undress and wash their garments, and scattered along the water front are mushroom-like canopies under which squat holy men. The whole population of Benares bathes here at least once a day; it is an essential part of the religion. And my guide, for all his professed iconoclasm, was no exception. Toward noon he remarked:

"It is time to think of food, sahib. I have not broken fast today."

"Very well; come with me and I will provide for you."

"But first I must bathe in the Ganges. I cannot touch a grain of rice till I have done this."

I waited for him. It was a simple process. He merely took off his coat and trousers and waded in; when he was immersed up to his shirt he discarded it. He seemed to be refreshed greatly and, caked with dust myself, I envied him. But when he swallowed three or four mouthfuls of the water which appeared to me polluted with every vile bacterium, I was alarmed. He reassured me:

"I have been living in Benares all my life, sir. Every day I drink water from the Ganges. Never have I been ill. How would you account for it, then?"

I would not attempt it. After all, who am I to dispute the authentic miracles of a river sacred for longer than history knows?

Seventh City of Delhi: the Modern and Prosaic British Capital of India Today

with Its Beautiful Architectural Reminders of Gay, Brave Days Long Past

Delhi is really a "city of seven cities." That many capitals have risen and decayed here since Hindu tribal chieftains, earlier than the Christian era, began to arrogate to themselves the estate and title of princes and kings of the land. But of those early citadels little remains but tattered legends and a few fragments of stone.

The British have dominated the city for more than a century, but the capital of their government was moved here only two decades ago.

It is a strategic point and it is rather surprising that the British managed so many years without making its advantages available. It is almost equidistant from the great coastal cities Calcutta, Bombay, Madras and Karachi, and it is only two days from the Afghan frontiers and Baluchistan. Principal trunk line railways from all directions converge here.

Delhi now has paved streets, a sewage system, light and power, motor cars, traffic patrolmen, bathtubs of galvanized iron, moving picture houses, radios, American soaps, a Buy-British-Goods Association, a Boycott-British-Goods Association, street cars and legislative councilors.

I also found a comfortable hotel here. It was clean and cool and inexpensive. It was called The Swiss and was run by one. He appeared to be the only man in India who had discovered that it is possible to cook food without boiling it. He also apparently was alone among hotel managers in the belief that the taste of food can be improved by judicious seasoning. I settled down in his place quite happily.

In The Swiss I met a traveled Hindu who worshipped neither cows nor monkeys and agreed that there is nothing in the world more devastating than the food served in the hotels of English colonies. This furnished the basis for a solid understanding and we became good friends. He was an architect and was intensely absorbed with the study of the old Delhi fort and other buildings left by the Moguls. Under his tutelage I went to visit those lovely old courts and shadowed gardens and learned many interesting things about them.

But Delhi itself is a great, sprawling city. Humayun's tomb, unique and splendid yet, is five miles or more from your hotel, and the famous Kutab Minar, off in an opposite direction, is eleven miles away. Safdar Jung's tomb, Nizam-ud-din's tomb and the Indrapat Shah Tuglakabad are interesting despite their unpronounceable names, and though distant also are worth toiling through desert heat and Indian dust to attain.

But it was to the Delhi fort that my Rajput friend, Asham Din, led me and at which he would have kept me indefinitely. Asham Din approached his subject with a fervor; he was an architect and he had spent months studying the buildings of the fort.

The Delhi fort was begun by Emperor Shah Jahan in 1639, after he had reigned at Agra for eleven years. Agra was uncomfortably torrid in the summer months and Delhi also recommended itself as a capital because of its strategic location and the importance attributed to it by Indian history. It took nine years and three months to complete the first gardens and buildings and the huge ramparted inclosure; but for nearly two centuries additions were erected by subsequent rulers.

Today, you enter the fort, still stoutly intact, through the Lahore Gate, a three-story edifice, solid and imposing, yet conveying an impression of grace and a tapered lightness of line derived from white marble minarets that crown domes set over delicately wrought screens of redstone. There is an ancient drawbridge spanning the moat that surrounds the red walls, built to a height of 110 feet and wide enough to accommodate a dozen horsemen riding abreast. Beyond the gate is a long roofed street, where the tradesmen of the royal household dwelt and displayed their goods, and at the end of it is the courtyard, terraced and bordered with marble, where the superintendent of the fort transacted routine business.

Now the scene opens out upon the Diwan-i-Amm, the central feature of the whole arrangement. Although it has now lost its original covering of shell plaster and gold and from paneling once heavily inlaid many of the precious stones have disappeared, the facade of white Jaipur marble is still a thing of wonder and breath-taking beauty. Open on three sides, this throne hall is supported by a series of columns joining the roof with engrailed arches, and all finished with an exactness and feeling for symmetry such as you sense in the ruins of the Parthenon and the old Gothic structures of France.

Back of the Diwan-i-Amm the maze of courts and gardens and dwellings of the royal family begins. You walk down stretches of beautifully patterned pathways, some of them inlaid with semiprecious stones, some intersticed with alternated black and white marble. They lead up to the entrances of buildings with open facades, all joined by lovely white marble doorways, arched in the Moslem tradition.

Erected around the rim of the mile-long inclosure are the Asad Burj, the Mumtaz Mahal, the Rang Mahal, the Diwan-i-Kass, the Hamman and half a dozen other cool, expansive buildings, each fitted to a special purpose or made for the use of members of the royal family. Through all of them run marble lined canals, some inlaid with colored stones carved to resemble flowers or birds. There are many baths and fountains are everywhere.

Marble divans beside streams were for reclining or for sleep, and outside the constantly watered gardens were cool always, and in them shady retreats and grottoes offered refuge to the harem women during the long sultry afternoons. Above, between the lofty alabaster minarets, the roofs hold other divans still, and pavilions of marble where the Emperor retired on moonlit nights or was entertained by dancers.

I spent hours rambling in and out of the myriad rooms, and I left each reluctantly. The workmanship, though not in some ways as accomplished as that in the Taj Mahal, is amazingly precise and consistent so that you have the feeling often that it was not done by a thousand artisans working under one command, but by a single individual of mysteriously unlimited facility and capacity.

I understood, when finally we left the fort, why Asham Din and others return here again and again, each time to linger as if in fresh discovery. In the subtle pattern of a wall, or the carved intricacy of a panel, or the rich vignette bordering of a gilded cistern you find material for rapture that lures you back repeatedly. The quality of this art and beauty is that it stimulates in you a chain of reflective thought and stirs a sense of imagery so strong that you feel yourself magically transported for a brief moment into a place of illusion and romance.

That will never be said, two hundred years from today, of the capital recently completed by the British—New Delhi—which lies out beyond the Fort of Shah Jehan, and where Asham Din and I later visited. New Delhi, or Raisina, as it has been named by the Indians, was built for comfort and utility and as the result of a prosaic act of Indian legislature. Its buildings are solid but passionless and dull in a British sort of way, though in their immensity not wholly unimpressive. They have none of the lavish grandeur amid a vast stillness and the feeling of history surcharged with glamour that are intrinsic in the white beauty and brilliance of the Mogul's edifices. I think this difference is somehow symbolic. Since the arrival of the British, Delhi has lost much of its color. Life under their regime seems to lack spark or flame; it is matter of fact, like the government buildings out on the expansive plain where, emulating the past, the British have founded their Raisina—this last and "seventh city of Delhi."

Monuments to a Ruler: Agra, Where the Taj Mahal and Other Temples Testify

to the Power and Artistic Taste
of a Powerful Ruler, Centuries Dead

There is a bazaar near the dingy brick station of Agra and through it run crooked, narrow streets. Adobe buildings, baked black and hard by the dry hot winds, are filled with Indians in all stages of dress, from small naked infants to tall dark bearded men wrapped in voluminous folds of coarse cotton dhotis. Stalls spill their wares onto the pavements, and tailors, bootmakers, weavers and carvers work in shops that are without fronts and into which floods the brilliant sunshine. Women with squinting eyes stroll gravely under enormous burdens nicely balanced on their heads; bewhiskered goats meditatively chew upon scraps in the road; a few bullocks lunge heavily and leer at the world, and occasionally a horseman, with a certain arrogance about him, rides in from the dusty plains.

I took a horse drawn phaeton and with my Bengal bearer drove out upon a wide straight road that led past a fine mosque and then into the open country. Ahead, the crenellated walls of the stout Agra Fort looked drably like great mounds of red earth heaped over an immense tomb. Not till we drew nearer did they emerge sharply from the base of dust filled air; not till I was approaching the ancient drawbridge did I note how skillful was this masonry in sandstone the color of coagulated blood. Then suddenly the whole structure seemed to expand and became an enormous buttress between me and the sky; then above the high, battlemented gates, minarets looked down on me as if they were shining helmets and under them were the heads of giant sentries.

I entered the tower and came out into a wide courtyard, that led up to an inner gate of ponderous design, built of red sandstone and inlaid with white marble. Beyond this stretched the gardens and palaces laid out by those ingenious Moguls who, calling down the dream of sun and moon, worked them into a marvelous pattern of red and white. Here I stood in the presence of a magnificence that flowered three hundred years ago; here stirred the spirit of Antar and over it blew the hot breath of the barbaric Tamerlane and his tribesmen; here I viewed what a Tartar conqueror once molded from the elements into an earthly paradise, fashioning it from the blood and terror of unlimited power. In these aisles lingered glories of a race that equally loved beauty and war, and put as much value upon a bas-relief of exquisite symbolism as upon the conquest of a new princedom.

Agra is a city 5,000 years old, according to legend; according to credible history it began at least 200 years before Christ. But had not Babar, sixth in line of descent from Tamerlane, who once ruled all Asia but China, come to this bank of the holy Jumna and built this citadel, Agra might now be no more illustrious than those hundreds of other mud villages that squat beside this stream, and where men have dwelt as long, but left nothing for the eye of the traveler.

After Babar came Humayin, and then, in 1556, Akbar, who rendered unto God the things that were God's and unto Akbar the things that were Akbar's, a reckoning in which God came out second best. His religion died with him, but the great Agra Fort, and the palatial testimonials in marble which he left after him, remain almost as intact as in days when he ordered them built to suit his inerrant taste.

Akbar's son Jahangir, who fought no battles, but styled himself "Conqueror of the World," was a sensual sybarite, and in his harem were 6,000 women. Among them was Jodh Bai, mother of Prince Khurrum, who when he became Emperor was called Shahjahan. And it is he who is most celebrated in India and in the West, for he outdistanced all his royal predecessors and successors in the breadth and scope of his creations. Shahjahan built the noblest structure of all Mogul art, the most perfect monument that the world has yet produced, which is the Taj Mahal at Agra. More than that, he poured into its chaste marble flanks a romance and a loyalty that enriched it with a tradition exalting it above even the argent stone of which it is built.

In the Taj now lies the dust of Shahjahan and his immortal love, Mumtaz Mahal. But it was in the Agra Fort, in the expanse inclosed by forbidding walls of Indian sandstone, that Shahjahan ruled the universe. Of this Fort they say that Akbar began it, Jahangir defiled it, and Shahjahan restored it so that it would last forever. And as you walk through palace after palace and down marble pavilions beside the continuous baths through which once ran clear rose water, cold in the morning and at night hot, you are persuaded that it was built, indeed, to endure. It seems hardly to have been disturbed by these three centuries; it appears to wait for the return of another Mogul who will repossess it and people it and fill it again with all the rich accoutrements of empire.

There is the Pearl Mosque, where Shahjahan, Viceregent of Allah on Earth, went for communion, and knelt on a strip of ebon marble, while behind him his family prayed also. It is an extraordinary building, its intricate mosaics worked out with superb craftsmanship, its symmetric lines developed by hands and brains of genius and excelled only by other works here in this city of architectural treasures. Every square of the Jaipur marble is polished like a gem; every bit of inlay is a perfect fitting; every piece of calligraphy a mark of untrammeled grace. On one side there is a delicately wrought latticework, executed from a single slab of marble, which alone must have required years of toil from many men; behind it knelt women of the palace in purdah. And in the foreground is a large forum of waxy marble, where gathered the ministers, and the entire palace retinue, for devotions to Allah.

Then you enter the Anguri Bach, or Grape Garden, laced with a cunning arrangement of hidden sprays that water its four squares of rich earth, brought clear from Kashmir. Dividing it are wide marble walks, in the center a huge white cistern, out of which water once rose for the edification of the royal women who amused themselves here. Beyond it is the Khas Mahal, built by Shahjahan and used by him as a drawing room, where occasionally he met his ladies of the "*zanana.*" It had a roof of pure gold, but that was plundered by the Jat vandals who finally destroyed the power of the Moguls. In it still there is much treasure in semiprecious stones, inlaid in the exquisitely traced arabesques that cover its walls.

You go through the main palace, and the palace of the Empress, where some of the fourteen esoteric children of Mumtaz Mahal were born; another of gold and marble where Emperor Shahjahan's daughter, Roshanara Begam, wrote lyrics which are still sung by the courtesans of Agra; another which holds huge marble swimming tanks for the Emperor and Empress; another whose walls are studded with bits of stained glass imbedded in alabaster. There is the great Audience Hall, where you pause to reflect upon the extent of one man's power, how it summoned artistry that in the space of less than a lifetime turned out products of warmth and beauty such as to cause men ever since to speak in their presence with voices that are hushed.

Finally, you go to a corner of this high-built paradise, and from a parapet hard on the top of the blood-red walls you look down upon a spreading valley and across the shimmering waters of the Jumna, which amble through it. From this spot, which is the Throne Terrace, where the ruler used to recline in voluptuous ease while he watched nude slave girls dance, you turn next to the Jasmine Tower. There, in coolness, you rest and direct your gaze toward the white radiance of the Taj, in clear view near a bend in the river.

The Jasmine Tower is small, but distinguished among the palaces for its grace and purity of line. Its art is expressed in an ultimate attainment of verity and delicate balance, in a refractory fineness of its marbled walls, and the fragile, almost feminine quality in its *beauté d'ensemble.* Its thin cloudy panels, its fluted columns and their capitals, the architraves, even the gleaming floors, are heavily inlaid. The designs are flower shapes and those of fantastic beasts and birds, formed from pieces of jade, amber, carnelian, rose quartz and Himalayan stone from afar. Yet so subtly has this inlay been achieved that unless you look closely you mistake it all for a worthy fresco imbued with some unusual texture of color.

The tower was built for the Empress Nurjahan, but later it was given by Shahjahan to his daughter Jahanara Begam. Shahjahan himself came to live with her here when, as an old man, his throne was usurped by his son. Here he lived as a prisoner for seven years, and here, facing his peerless Taj, he died in 1666. It must have been with a certain pride and grandeur of heart, a kind of swollen exultation, that he saw the white flames of those distant minarets languish while the fire in his own eyes dimmed. He died an emperor without a throne, but if it is true that prescience comes with the last breath of life Shahjahan may have had the satisfaction of knowing he had created an immortal testament to beauty.

The Taj Mahal—Than Which Earth Has Not Anything to Show More Fair

This is the story of the Taj Mahal, as told in the annals of India:

Now, in 1592 a son was born at Agra to Jodh Bai, one of the hundred wives of the Emperor Jahangir, and he was named Prince Khurrum. In the same year a daughter arrived in the household of Asaf Khan, illustrious among all the ministers of the Mogul court. Upon this daughter Jahangir conferred the title Mumtaz Mahal, or "Exalted of the Palace."

Mumtaz and Khurrum played together as children; they vowed eternal love for one another. Khurrum, when he became a young man, rejected all marriage offers: he would have only Mumtaz. And so it was that he reached the advanced age of 19 before he was wedded to Mumtaz Mahal.

Now, Jahangir, who had a zanana and a harem which held 4,000 women, had set rather an unhappy example around the palace, so when Mumtaz married Khurrum she extracted from him a promise that while she lived he would wed no other woman. In this she was remindful of the wily Burmese queen, Supiyalat, who prevented Theebaw from enjoying feminine grace other than her own. Khurrum, who was to become the Emperor Shahjahan, was a man of sterner stuff than the dissolute Theebaw. Under the unfaltering love of Mumtaz he flourished as a great leader and able warrior.

Mumtaz Mahal was a woman of keen intelligence as well as of superb physical beauty. When Khurrum began to lead the Mogul armies she accompanied him on most of his campaigns. Together they schemed for a siege against a powerful rebel; together they planned the marble buildings of the splendid palaces they would erect when Khurrum became "Ruler of the Earth."

Mumtaz lived to see many of these dreams realized. Buildings still stand which bear the subtle touch of her designing. She lived nineteen years with her prince, and she bore him fourteen children; eight sons and six daughters. It was following the birth of her fourteenth child that she died, in 1629. Khurrum had been crowned as Shahjahan, Emperor of India, only a year before. Her death occurred while she was journeying with him on an expedition to suppress the rebellion of

277

Khan Jahan Lodi, Governor of Deccan. Behind the battle lines, she died in her husband's arms.

Shahjahan grieved for many months. For a while he contemplated abdicating the throne and dividing the Empire among his sons. But to do that would make it impossible for him to carry out the final wish of Mumtaz Mahal, which was that over her body a memorial should be erected of such artistry and magnificence as could be equaled nowhere else in the world.

The Emperor defeated Khan Jahan Lodi and disposed and killed his followers, returned to Agra and commenced a Taj Bibi Ka Rauza Mahal, or "Royal Tomb of the Empress." Artists, masons and architects were summoned from all over the East: they came from India, from Persia, Arabia, even from China, Turkey and Italy. By the end of 1631 Shahjahan had approved plans submitted to him, and construction on the "marble poem of love" was begun.

Thousands of tons of white marble were imported from Makrana and Riwala in Jaipur; red sandstone came in by endless caravans from Fatehpur Sikri; jewels were brought from India, Persia, Burma and Tibet; and rare stone from Italy.

Twenty thousand workmen were employed in erecting the Taj, the mosques, the many subsidiary buildings. Into the project Shahjahan poured all the wealth of his imperial treasury. He spent the equivalent of twenty million gold dollars on it, and European architects today have estimated that it could not be duplicated for ten times that sum. It took seventeen years to build, and was completed in 1648.

Nothing is said of the awful burden this lavish outlay placed upon the Grand Mogul's subjects. Historians do not mention the thousands who died under the strain of lifting the huge blocks of marble into their high place beside the Jumna. We do not know this tragic counterpart to the romance of Shahjahan and Mumtaz.

The power of a man who could divert the lifeblood and sinew and gold of a whole race into the creation of a single rhapsody in stone must have been terrible to contemplate. But grant that as so, the fact of the Taj remains.

Forget the sufferings of dead, stupid men, but rejoice in this incomparable expression of an individual's loyalty to his two ideals of love and beauty that ranked with the high distance of the stars.

I do not know how to describe the Taj Mahal. I could say that it is so many feet this way and so many that; how it contains so many tons of

Snow strikes a classic adventurer's pose before the Taj Mahal.

polished Jaipur marble; that its dome is this lofty and its nave is that wide, and that the four minarets which guard it contain so and so many steps. I could tell you the length of the lotus pool that joins its patterned platform to the stout red sandstone gate, and I could apprise you of the number of walks that thread through its exotic green gardens. I could tell you which chapters of the Koran are inlaid in its apses and how long it took the ingenious calligrapher to inscribe them so that optical illusion is defeated and the rows of writing appear to be the same width at the hundred-foot top as at the eye-level bottom.

But after all that you would still know nothing of the Taj Mahal. For its values are emotional; its quality of allure is that of a purity which oddly confuses and stirs in you a sense of tall passion; something that transcends the earth and lifts you to a plane where a kind of white-winged ecstasy tears through your heart.

I have never seen anything so wonderful as the Taj Mahal. I have not seen anything anywhere with which it might be compared or contrasted. A very few times in the East I have come suddenly upon a thing of the same rapture; once at sunset when I stood upon the Altar of Heaven at Peking; once when through a clearing mist I saw the topmost shrine of Nikko; once when moonlight flooded the golden shaft of the Shwe Dagon at Rangoon. But the cool sculptured loveliness of the Taj, so full of repose and delicacy and yet massive with a tremendous strength, dwarfs all.

In the hours I spent in the gardens and strolling beside the Jumna I tried to decide what it was that gave this royal fabric an extraordinary glamour for me. Was it the upthrusting triumph of dome and minaret, the blending of arc and angle in an octagonal facade, the perfect harmony of every linear movement with a curve? Was it the strange play of light and darkness in its grottoed niches? Was it the sharp contrast of the blood-red sandstone in the mosques that flank the tomb of utter marble?

I think now that what moved me was the realization that men, small, wretched, and imperfect, did for a brief moment attain heights from which they could conceive and execute a thing so purely beautiful. How is it that, having once matched nature in an act of creating, these men slipped back into the ordinary? Why is it that this edifice was molded by a horde of invaders (whom the Indians regarded as vandals and barbarians, and whom we consider to have been less advanced than ourselves)? I should like to know why it is that men who reached such an eminence should have fallen back again to the level of our own prosaic civilizations.

The Trial of British Communists at Meerut, India

Of the several "conspiracy" trials being held in various cities of India and Burma the most prolonged and in some ways amusingly ironic is the notorious Meerut case. In it 31 men are charged with "waging war, or attempting to wage war, against the King-Emperor." The trial has now lasted two years and six months, and the prisoners, who include three Englishmen, have been in jail during that period, or a little longer. It is estimated that at least another year will elapse before a verdict is rendered.

The men were arrested in March, 1929, when the Government came to the aid of Indian textile manufacturers in ending a nine months' strike of the workers. They were accused of having organized a militant labor movement, exhorting the strikers to adopt methods of violence and terrorism, and planning a complete overthrow of the present Government, all of which comprised an effort to deprive the English King of his sovereignty in India.

At the time of this arrest police were bent upon destroying the Indian Workers' and Peasants' Party, an affiliation of the Communist Internationale which gained considerable strength during the textile and railway workers' strike. Those being tried at Meerut were the most prominent leaders of that party. All but a few of them are avowed Communists, a fact which was emphasized by the Court in its refusal to release any of the latter on bail.

The trial at Meerut appears to be an anomaly when considered in the light of the revolutionary propaganda now being disseminated throughout India. Every day hundreds of Indians attend meetings and listen to seditious speeches openly preaching revolution. Hundreds read literature advocating the liquidation of the present Government. Daily, congress leaders call upon the masses to preserve their "war mentality" and prepare for "the coming struggle with the British Imperialists." Legally, this constitutes treason aimed at the destruction of the King-Emperor's throne. Yet few arrests now take place.

Meanwhile the 31 alleged conspirators, perspiring in a temperature ranging around 110, are conducting a brilliant and interesting defense. It is unique in that it is planned to expound fully upon the Soviet system of Government, and its application to conditions in India. Bradley, Hutchinson and Spratt, the three English Communists, and their Indian associates, have arranged for each of the accused to present in great detail some special phase of communism. Thus one prisoner in his statement devoted several days to a discussion of proletariat dictatorship, another dilated upon collectivization, another upon state control of industries, another used for his defense an attack upon the capitalist system and its resultant evils in India.

The trial has thus had the curious effect of enabling newspapers all over India to publish material that under ordinary circumstances would be banned as Communist propaganda. The Communists have reached and perhaps interested a much wider group of the petty bourgeoisie, workers and peasants, than they might have done had they been allowed to carry on outside of jail.

When one reads back through the newspaper files since the trial began it is an education in the economics of Karl Marx, and their revolutionary application by Lenin, his associates, and their successors. One notes, also, that the statements made by the defense have been arranged so that a minimum of repetition occurs, each defendant covering different material. Indeed plans are already made to publish, in condensed form, the story of the Meerut trial, which will be used as the handbook of the Communist Party of India.

Some of the most trenchant criticism ever directed at British rule in India has come forth at the Meerut trial, and has been published in the Indian press. For instance, this is a selection from Philip Spratt, a Cambridge man, who has been on the stand for six weeks and whose statement already has run to more than 10,000 words:

"The substance of the matter is that the British policy, which is directed to two main ends, that is, the exploitation of the country to the maximum and the maintenance of its political control, is chiefly responsible for its (India's) backwardness.

"This policy is shown in several principal ways. These are: first, the low level of the industrial development of the country—there is no doubt that the British policy is one of conscious opposition to industrialization; second, the support of a land system and a social structure which is to a large extent feudal in form; third, the maintenance of an irresponsible absolutist Government which relies directly upon superior military force for its control; fourth, the various well-known measures of social and political character intended to safeguard British rule by keeping the population backward—such as encouragement of the caste system, preserving communalism, and rigidly limiting the spread of mass education.

"The result of this is the terrible condition in which India finds herself today. The standard of living has sunk to the lowest in the world. The Court will agree that I need quote no statistics to prove that. The great majority of the population are living in medieval ignorance, under the rule of feudal or semi-feudal landlords who exploit them mercilessly and practically control their whole lives. Slavery, as admitted by Government publications, still exists, *de facto,* on a considerable scale.

"Ninety-three percent of the population is still illiterate; the standard of culture is far below what it was a century ago; and the former active and progressive forces of Indian civilization have been carefully destroyed. Sanitary conditions are worse than in any other country on earth; the death rate is the highest of all nations." This statement, with a mass of figures later introduced to support its assertions, was published in practically every Indian paper.

Spratt and his fellow prisoners are confined in a special barracks at Meerut. They take their position philosophically and with a properly "materialistic" sense of humor. They call themselves the "Meerut Jail Soviet," hold daily meetings and keep minutes of the proceedings. They published, on a battered typewriter, a journal known as the "Indian Jail Soviet Weekly." Copies of it have been sold outside, and have fetched high sums, which were applied to expenses of the defense. One issue reached Moscow, where it was enshrined in the Soviet Museum. The prosecution objected, however, and this has now been stopped.

In the "Jail Soviet" there is one of the most complete communist libraries in India. It contains the writings of Marx and Lenin and many volumes of minutes of the Komintern. It also holds recent books on Russia by European and American commentators. Most of the library has been contributed by friends and sympathizers in India and abroad.

The trial appears to become more and more embarrassing for the Government. Europeans in India are much irritated by the vast publicity given to it, and an English newspaper in Bombay has called it "a piece of judicial idiocy." Another British paper, *The Manchester Guardian,* deplores the short-sightedness of the policy adopted by the prosecution. It is pointed out that had the prisoners been separately tried, in different courts of simple sedition, they would all have been disposed of long ago. "As it is," one journal comments, "we are treated to the spectacle of all India being tutored, from His Majesty's Court, on the essentials of Marx and the destructive theories of Bolshevism. It is bound to produce undesirable effects on the mind of idealistic and impressionable youth in India."

The Revolt of India's Women

"No, and again no, father," declared a defiant young Indian girl two years ago. "I shall not marry any man till India is free!"

"Nonsense!" stormed her stern Mahometan parent. "I will be dead by then, and so also will you be dead. You must marry the man I have chosen for you now—a marriage already three years delayed. If you do not, I will no longer be responsible for your chastity and good name. I will turn you from my house—a wretched, idle girl without filial piety!"

But Safie was obstinate and with a will strong as her father's. She kept her vow, and he kept his. With head high, she left her home, but not for the scarlet life her father predicted. She married, but not the husband her father would have bought for her.

"The bridegroom I chose" she told me months after this, when I met her in Bombay, full of pride and youth and a sense of drama, "was the cause of India." She was a slender little figure, lithe and graceful, with a pretty face lit by dark, intent eyes that had in them a secret fire whether she laughed or was grave.

"Now I have no family," she said, "except India—and I am glad." She had just been released from jail, where she was incarcerated as a satyagrahi, a participant in India's non-violent civil disobedience revolution. Among the young workers for independence she was a recognized leader of women in the revolutionary Youth League.

To do what this girl did required character greater than the American can at once appreciate. As a Mahometan daughter, her act was heretical. She had renounced the cherished traditions and elemental prejudices that for centuries have stood as immutable prison walls around the women of India. Though her political activities in the end may not count for much, her gesture of freedom from male domination is a fine and courageous thing. That has real significance. It typifies the *esprit de femme* behind the social revolution that has begun to stir the more advanced women of her country.

Her case by no means stands alone. During the dramatic struggle in India, checked last March by the Gandhi-Irwin truce, many thousands of Indian women for the first time in history broke caste and religious taboos to take part in a political offensive. They did all the things male satyagrahis could do, often much to the discomfort of their less patriotic husbands, who vainly ordered them to return to the kitchen stoves.

Some of them such as Mrs. Munshi, Kamala Nehru and Sarojini Naidu, led great armies of men in challenging British rule.

They wrote and lectured and spread seditious literature. They boycotted foreign cloth, picketed shops selling British liquor, trespassed on government property and chopped down toddy palms on government estates. They persuaded peasants to default their taxes, they led great demonstrations and they held giant mass meetings in forbidden areas. They did what was possible, without committing violence, to sabotage British prestige and authority.

All their acts were well disciplined and objective. At least 100,000 Indian women took part, and all of them obeyed their group leaders. When they joined in civil disobedience they took the vow of Ahimsa, kept it and peacefully submitted to arrest for their crimes, which they regard as done in defense of India. More than 4,000 of them actually went to jail.

This fervid response of women astonished even Mahatma Gandhi, although to him it was, and remains, merely a by-product of the central issue. He is not particularly interested in "modernizing" Indian women. In some respects he is definitely opposed to tampering with the traditional position of women in Indian society. For this reason he did not seek to win women followers nor to create a feminist movement as an integral part of his campaign. But whether he willed it or not, this last attempt to free India from British imperialism has furnished the stimulus that history will record as the turning point in the evolution of a twentieth-century woman of India.

During the campaign of civil disobedience leading Nationalists discovered this new power and assertiveness in their women and, at first surprised, then pleased, they utilized them fully. They were given positions of responsibility in that wonderfully complex and subtle organization of rebellion, the Indian National Congress. They were put in charge of groups of volunteers and in executive jobs as heads of branch Congress committees. In the schools and in other public institutions women sometimes replaced or substituted for the male mentors who had been taken to jail. Many educated women, previously repressed by male prejudice against female participation in any activity outside the home, now found openings in varied professions.

The outcome of India's epochal contest with Britain is still unknown. Whether the Indian National Congress must lead another and yet another fight for *swaraj*—self government—will not be decided until the conclusion of the Round Table Conference sessions at London. But the new sense of freedom and importance that Indian women have won during the last few years has come to stay and to expand. The husband-gods are beginning to totter on their pedestals, and the virtual enthrallment that wives of India have endured for ages appears to be nearing an end.

Educated Indian women are still comparatively few, but those who have benefited thus are determined to raise the status of the rest. Through the women's organizations which have germinated so rapidly all over the nation, women's opinion is now a potent and readily wielded instrument. They stand, as one of their Bengal leaders, Mrs. A. N. Chaudhuri, recently put it, "for independence of women in the home as well as for India in the family of nations." They are united in their demand for full social and political emancipation. With self government possibly imminent, they are determined to introduce into the constitution certain clauses that will modify the old tragic social system responsible for the degradation of Indian women. Through Katherine Mayo's somewhat perverse and pathological lenses many Westerners have observed the revolting results of that system when operating at its worst. But, in order to understand the difficult combat which faces the protagonists of India's new femininity, it is perhaps well to recall here what the conventional male attitude toward Indian women has been.

A good wife, according to accepted beliefs, is one who is literally the servant, at times the slave, of her husband. From conversations with many Indians, Islams as well as Hindus, I gather that this is still considered to be the ideal marital relationship. It is believed that a virtuous wife must be completely self-effacing, subservient, uncomplaining, meek and in every respect as docile as a well domesticated animal. Consider the code of conduct that is supposed to govern the life of a high caste Hindu woman. In these excerpts from the sacred Padma-purana it is clearly defined:

> There is no other god on earth for a woman but her husband. The most excellent of all the good works that she can do is to seek to please him by manifesting perfect obedience. Therein should lie her sole rule of life. Be her husband aged, deformed, infirm, offensive in manners; let him also be choleric, debauched, immoral, a drunkard, a gambler; let him frequent places of ill-repute, live in open sin with other women, have no affection whatsoever for his home; let him rave like a lunatic; let him live without honor; let him be blind, deaf, dumb or crippled; in a word, let his defects be what they may, a wife should always look upon him as her god, should

lavish on him all affection and care; paying no heed whatsoever to his character and giving him no cause for displeasure.

A woman is made to obey at every stage of her existence. As daughter, it is to her father and mother that she owes submission; as wife, to her husband, to her father-in-law and to her mother-in-law; as widow, to her sons. At no period of her life can she consider herself her own mistress.

If her husband laughs, she must laugh; if he be sad she must be sad; if he weep she must weep. . . . She must take heed not to remark that another man is young, handsome or well proportioned, and by the gods! let her not speak to him. Such modest demeanor will secure for her the reputation of a faithful spouse.

And well it might! No wonder Indian women are in revolt! Although thousands now scoff at this creed, they know that thousands of others are still enslaved by it and similar superstitions. Women's associations in all the provinces have agreed on an aggressive program to destroy such beliefs. At the recent All-India Women's congress, attended by more than 500 delegates selected from every major district of India, a platform of reform was unanimously adopted. It includes these resolutions:

That the custom of sanctioning polygamy must be prohibited by legislation; that all interference with the remarriage of widows must be vigorously prosecuted by law; that public opinion must be mobilized against the continuation of the purdah, the dowry and other obnoxious customs; that the recent Sarda act, which prohibits marriage of girls under the age of 14, should be strictly enforced; that legislation should be enacted granting daughters the right of equal inheritance with sons; and that women should be allowed to compete with men in the spheres of science, art, commerce, politics, etc., on a basis of full equality.

Mild and just as these demands appear, their effect on the reactionary masculinity of India is electric. Protests come from many religious societies and from various organizations, both cultural and commercial. Certain prominent Indian politicians publicly express doubt over the policy of admitting women into revolutionary activities. The Women's Congress is denounced with special vehemence for having considered a resolution favoring "divorce where that step is called for." It shocks men of the old school of orthodoxy that this was discussed, although it was defeated. Hindu husbands who have long regarded marriage as a sacrament, an indissoluble tie regardless of their own conduct toward their wives, now begin to fear that the halcyon irresponsibility of the male is doomed. They sense the approach of iniquitous alimony from the West.

But the women have got beyond bother over the outcries of the chagrined husband-jailers and the wife beaters. They feel confident now of the support of the more enlightened men of India, though at present they are admittedly in the minority. At the annual meeting of the Indian National Congress in Karachi last March the women's delegation secured from this unofficial but puissant political organization some vastly significant concessions. In the bill of fundamental rights adopted at that meeting these reforms are promised under any form of self-government established in India: Equal privileges and obligations of all citizens; free primary education for both sexes; protection of women workers, especially with regard to adequate provision for leave during the period of maternity; total prohibition of child marriage and equal opportunity for men and women to hold public office or to engage in any legitimate trade or profession.

Considering the low percentage of literacy among India's women under the present educational system, it is remarkable to find them already represented in all the professions and in public offices. Teaching has called many; there are now women professors in most of the large colleges and universities and in hundreds of rural and primary schools. In other cases women have launched educational experiments of their own, such as brilliant Mrinalini Chattopadhyaya's school in Bombay. There are many women doctors and hundreds of Western trained nurses. In one city I met a woman dentist who had been educated in America.

Many women barristers prosper in the courts of Bombay and other cities; some of them have told me they earn as much as from 5,000 to 10,000 rupees annually. In some Indian states and in seven of the nine provinces of British India, women members now sit with men in the councils of state. There are women magistrates and judges. Recently a woman was elected president of the Madras legislature. The "Dravidian"—perhaps the most influential daily paper of Madras—is edited by a spirited little Hindu lady, Mrs. Alumelum Ammal. Women may be found in the chief's chair in several other Indian journals and magazines, and at least one important publishing house is owned and managed by a woman who runs a school as well. In both the English language and the vernacular press female contributors are frequent. Many publications run regular features written by and for women, although as a class "the reporteress" scarcely exists.

Incidentally, despite its social backwardness in other respects, India does not restrict the free publication and dissemination of information on birth control and other sex subjects. Scientific sex knowledge, much of it in the form of books written by Indian medical men and women, is now abundantly available. But its benefits are confined largely to the literate classes, although there are now several agencies through which such knowledge is given to wives of workers and peasants.

Lord Irwin, former viceroy of India, recently placed solemn blame on the cinema as one of the chief factors contributing to the rapid growth of political revolution in India. The "movies" are also responsible, in a large measure, for the rebellion of women. Western social ideas, given wide currency through the silver screen, have worked at the undermining of India's medieval social structure. This is particularly true of metropolitan life in Bombay, Madras, Delhi, Calcutta and other large towns.

The American or European visitor who has carefully schooled himself by reading "Mother India," and its sequel is usually confused to discover that in most of the cities mothers and virgins (easily distinguished from each other by the way they wear their ornaments) mingle with men in the streets and bazaars and appear to enjoy considerable domestic freedom.

As was the case until recently in China and Japan, women in India were barred from the theater. Men impersonated them, but they never developed much genius in the art—a fact which probably accounts for the poor quality of the Indian theater and latterly, its decline. Thus, when "movie" directors searched for feminine players, they got no help from the stage. They next turned to the singing girls and nautch dancers. But here there were strong social objections. These professional courtesans were skilled enough in histrionics, but many Hindus disapproved of their appearance in "movies" which their wives and children could see. The "flower women" of India enjoy no such prestige here as they are given in countries farther east; they are members of a low and depressed class which includes magicians, acrobats, musicians, prostitutes, gypsies and so on. Once, in Udaipur, I watched a favorite Indian dancing girl present a petition to Her Highness the Maharani, in which she humbly begged the right to build a stone house—a privilege generally denied to her profession!

To circumscribe these difficulties young Indian directors enterprisingly appealed to the public for a new attitude toward artists of song, dance and pantomime. They succeeded in interesting several prominent families in the utility of the cinema in India for spreading education. Sons and daughters from middle class and upper class families were induced to enter the films.

Within the last three years a number of pictures have been produced with what are described as "all society" casts, which in India means "all Brahmin" castes. Among these was the life of Buddha, filmed as "The Light of Asia," which was greeted with enthusiasm when shown in America. That and subsequent pictures such as "Shiraz," "Shirin Farhad," "Swamy," "Vasantasena" and one or two others, have done much to popularize Indian-made films with the high-caste Hindus. The recent introduction of Indian talkies has served also to create interest in native music and dancing, which had fallen into disrepute in recent years and were looked upon as synonymous with carnality and vice.

Since these arts, revived in their purer and less sensuous forms, have been brought to the sound picture by young actresses like Zubeidat, Reyaka Khatoun, Gohur (who manages her own studio) and Enakshi Ramakhan, public opinion has altered. A number of schools now offer studies in the singing and dancing which in former times were a necessary part of the education of cultured Indian women.

But politics and social work attract more talented Hindu and Moslem women than anything else. I do not know why; perhaps it is because they offer greater opportunities for service to India, perhaps because they offer greater opportunities for personal expression. The women engaged in these fields form an intensely interesting group. Many of them have been educated abroad, and in the process of assimilating Western ideas they have perforce been obliged to drop some of the more stupid, unscientific beliefs foisted upon them in childhood. Some who have never been out of India but come from erudite parentage have an excellent understanding of the economic problems at the root of both the social and political evils in India.

Here I think of the Chattopadhyayas, the most clearly emancipated from old superstitions and surely the most interesting family I have known anywhere. A study of them exhibits a cross section of the social change in India during the present generation. Their place is somewhat like that of the Roosevelts in America, the Soongs in China or the Tokugawas in Japan. They differ from other romantic families in this respect; no two Chattopadhyayas have ever been known to agree on politics, religion, love—or an opinion on the Family Chattopadhyaya.

There are four daughters. One of them is India's best known woman poet, speechmaker, matchmaker, bourgeois politician, meat-eating Brahmin and delegate to the Round Table Conference. One is an atheist, a Communist, the most beautiful Indian woman I have ever met and has a vibrant singing voice which she refuses to develop because she devotes all her time to the cause of a proletarian revolution in India. Another is a modern educator, spinster, philosopher, editor and leading Theosophist. The fourth is a foremost authority on Indian art in all its tangents, but specializes in music and dancing and is also famous as a dramatist.

It is true that such families as this are a small minority of India's millions. But leadership necessarily rests with a few. The encouraging thing is that educated women see their task and are taking it up with energy and a will.

If they do nothing else, these women furnish example; and it is example that the masses require. Victimized by their own religion and archaic social structure, a system of government that has kept them in dark ignorance and illiteracy and a philosophy based on one of the most fundamentally corrupting of all superstitions—that the suffering one endures in this life is the result of sin in a previous existence—the millions of Hindu women in semi-slavery need to be awakened to the needless futility of their lives and to be shown how release is possible. For that they require exemplars; they need pattern and precedent.

Sources

Forty-two articles written by Edgar Snow are reprinted in this collection. Thirty-five of his Consolidated Press articles were originally published in "The World Today" column of the *New York Sun;* five of those thirty-five also appeared in the *China Weekly Review.* "The World Today" format quickly became a model for many of the stories Snow wrote and filed with Consolidated Press, but he filed other types of stories as well, usually sending copies to the *China Weekly Review* of those that he thought J. B. Powell might be interested in publishing. His editors at Conso Press had no objection.

In "Canton, Where the Chinese National Revolution Began, Plus Hong Kong and Macao," I chose to reprint four articles about life in Canton that were originally written for Conso Press, but apparently only published in the *China Weekly Review.* These make clear that on this portion of his journey Snow's principal interest was in Canton, the city where the modern Chinese national revolution had the longest period to prove itself. Similarly in "Colonial Burma and India," I added the last two articles, which did not appear in "The World Today" column, to indicate the serious effort Snow made to understand the social struggle going on during his substantial travels in India.

I. Formosa

"The Japan-ization of Formosa": *China Weekly Review,* November 1, 1930. Also published as "Taiwan, Better Known as Formosa, and Its Chief Seaport, Keelung, Where a Pirate Chief Once Ruled," *New York Sun,* February 5, 1931.

"Some Results of 35 Years of Japanese Rule in Formosa": *China Weekly Review,* November 15, 1930. Also published as "Taihoku, Principal Port of Formosa, and Center of Japanese Government's Campaign to Completely Japanize This Island, Which They Renamed Taiwan," *New York Sun,* February 26, 1931.

"A Thrilling Ride on the 'Kiddie-Car, Limited' in Central Formosa and a Visit to the Lake of the Moon and the Sun": *New York Sun,* February 12, 1931.

"A Visit to the Formosan Aborigines": *China Weekly Review,* November 8, 1930. Also published as "A Trip to Kaban, Largest Village of the Savage Taiyal Tribe of Headhunters in Central Formosa—Made Just Prior to Their Recent Rebellion," *New York Sun,* February 12, 1931.

"From Keelung to Hongkong—Some Ship-Mates!": written for *New York Sun* but published by *China Weekly Review,* December 13, 1930.

II. Canton, Where the Chinese National Revolution Began, Plus Hong Kong and Macao

"Canton, Metropolis of South China, Where the Feverish Rush of Occidental Cities Is Noted—Much of the Old Has Made Way for Modern Progress": *New York Sun,* April 9, 1931.

"The Island of Shameen in the Pearl River, an International Settlement Reclaimed from a Sandbar Which Now Is the Site of the Foreign Concession": *New York Sun,* May 20, 1931. Also published as "Shameen—the Foreigner's Sanctum-Sanctorum at Canton," *China Weekly Review,* August 29, 1931.

"Two Cantonese Doctors Who Made Asiatic History": *China Weekly Review,* November 29, 1930.

"Justice Is More Advanced in Canton Than Elsewhere but There Are Occasional Lapses!": *China Weekly Review,* December 6, 1930.

"How 5,200 Policemen Keep Order in Canton": *China Weekly Review,* November 29, 1930.

"The Hard Lot of Women Prisoners in Hon San-so": *China Weekly Review,* January 17, 1931.

"Hongkong, England's Own Little Corner of China, Which Refuses to Become Anglicized—a Beautiful and Mystic City by Day and by Night": *New York Sun,* June 2, 1931.

"Macao, Picturesque Port on the South China Coast, Which Was Founded by the Portuguese Four Centuries Ago, Inaugurating Sino-European Trade": *New York Sun,* March 19, 1931.

"Tang Kai Chuen in South China, Home of Ex-Premier Tang Shao-yi, a Village Which Is Clean and Where Opium Is Barred": *New York Sun,* March 12, 1931.

"The Little Brick Home of Sun Yat-sen, in the Village of Choy Hang, South China, Is Today a Revered Shrine of the Kuomintang": *New York Sun,* March 26, 1931.

III. Indo-China and Yunnanfu (Kunming)

"Haiphong, the Great New Port Built by the French in Northern Indo-China, Which May Look French, but Is Oriental": *New York Sun,* June 9, 1931.

"Hanoi, Chief City of the French 'Protectorate' in Tonkin, Annam and Laos, Where Everything Is Gay—on the Surface": *New York Sun,* June 16, 1931.

"Entering the Notorious Yunnan Province in South China and Planning a Caravan Trek across This Mysterious Bandit Ridden Region": *New York Sun,* June 23, 1931.

"The Railroad Journey to Yunnanfu Is Filled with Scenic Thrills, on a Line That Is One of the Engineering Marvels of the Orient": *New York Sun,* June 30, 1931.

"A Regiment of Defeated Chinese Soldiers, Sacrificed as a Convoy for Opium Shipments, Overruns All Classes of Railway Carriages Entering Yunnanfu": *New York Sun,* July 7, 1931.

"The Story of Yunnanfu—Ancient Chinese Legend of the Fall of the Chou Dynasty and the Rise of the T'ang Dynasty Which Acquired Yunnan": *New York Sun,* July 14, 1931.

"How Two Powerful, Rival Generals Marked Time While Their Compromise Candidate Ruled the Vast Barbaric Province of Yunnan, China": *New York Sun,* July 28, 1931.

"Life in Yunnanfu, South China, Where the Government Is Oppressive and Life Is Safer for the Foreigner Than the Natives": *New York Sun,* July 28, 1931.

IV. From Yunnan to Burma by Caravan

"Start of a Trek over the Age-Old Trail of Commerce across the Mountains of Yunnan Territory toward Tibet and Burma": *New York Sun,* August 4, 1931.

"'Step Ladder Going' on the Age-Old Caravan Trail from Yunnanfu toward Tali, China, and a Little Bandit History": *New York Sun,* August 11, 1931.

"Chinese New Year's Eve Celebration in Talifu in the High Hills of Yunnan, under 'the Eves of Roof of the World'": *New York Sun,* August 13, 1931.

"From Tali to Yungping, China, by Caravan with an Occasional Stop at Some Buddhist or Mohammedan Monastery High in the Mountains": *New York Sun,* August 25, 1931.

"A Night in a Mohammedan Mosque by Virtue of an Almost Forgotten Persian Phrase and an Opium-Addict Magistrate in Yungping": *New York Sun,* September 1, 1931.

"A Dangerous Stage on the 'Golden Road to Burma,' Where One of China's Most Turbulent Streams Must Be Crossed on Flimsy Bamboo Rafts": *New York Sun,* September 8, 1931.

"The Sulphur Springs of Remote and Inaccessible Western Yunnan, China, Where the Old Chinese Custom of Bargaining for a Wife Still Exists": *New York Sun,* September 15, 1931.

"The 'Lao-lu,' Old Road to Bhamo, Just across the Burma Border from Kanai in the Yunnan Province of China": *New York Sun,* September 22, 1931.

"A Visit in the Home of a Cultured, English Speaking Ruler of 50,000 Chinese and Shans, in Faraway Kanai, China": *New York Sun,* September 29, 1931.

"Arrival of Caravan in Burma, Land of Teak, Elephants and Glittering Pagodas, after a Brush with Kachin Bandits on the Chinese Border": *New York Sun,* October 6, 1931.

V. Colonial Burma and India

"Down the Irrawaddy River to Mandalay, Glamorous Chief City of Central Burma, Site of the Glittering Palace of Supiyalat": *New York Sun,* October 13, 1931.

"Rangoon, the Chief Port of Burma, during the Hot, Dry Spell Which Precedes the Springtime New Year's Celebration—the Shwe Dagon": *New York Sun,* October 20, 1931.

"Calcutta, India, City of Contrasting Beauty and Squalor—the Hindu Rituals on the Banks of the Sacred Ganges River": *New York Sun,* October 27, 1931.

"Beside the Ganges River: Benares, India, Where Filth and Ignorance Abound and Where the Great Faith of the Hindu in His Gods Is Demonstrated Daily": *New York Sun,* February 6, 1932.

"Seventh City of Delhi: the Modern and Prosaic British Capital of India Today with Its Beautiful Architectural Reminders of Gay, Brave Days Long Past": *New York Sun,* April 9, 1932.

"Monuments to a Ruler: Agra, Where the Taj Mahal and Other Temples Testify to the Power and Artistic Taste of a Powerful Ruler, Centuries Dead": *New York Sun,* March 19, 1932.

"The Taj Mahal—Than Which Earth Has Not Anything to Show More Fair": *New York Sun,* February 15, 1932.

"The Trial of British Communists at Meerut, India": *China Weekly Review,* September 19, 1931.

"The Revolt of India's Women": *New York Herald-Tribune Magazine,* October 25, 1931.